Common Security in Outer Space and International Law

Detlev Wolter

UNIDIR
United Nations Institute for Disarmament Research
Geneva, Switzerland

UNITED NATIONS

NOTE

The designations employed and the presentation of the material in this publication do not imply the expression of any opinion whatsoever on the part of the Secretariat of the United Nations concerning the legal status of any country, territory, city or area, or of its authorities, or concerning the delimitation of its frontiers or boundaries.

*

* *

The views expressed in this publication are the sole responsibility of the individual author. They do not necessarily reflect the views or opinions of the United Nations, UNIDIR, its staff members or sponsors, nor those of the German Foreign Ministry.

UNIDIR/2005/29

UNITED NATIONS PUBLICATION

Sales No. GV.E.06.0.3

ISBN 92-9045-177-7

The United Nations Institute for Disarmament Research (UNIDIR)—an intergovernmental organization within the United Nations—conducts research on disarmament and security. UNIDIR is based in Geneva, Switzerland, the centre for bilateral and multilateral disarmament and non-proliferation negotiations, and home of the Conference on Disarmament. The Institute explores current issues pertaining to the variety of existing and future armaments, as well as global diplomacy and local entrenched tensions and conflicts. Working with researchers, diplomats, Government officials, NGOs and other institutions since 1980, UNIDIR acts as a bridge between the research community and Governments. UNIDIR's activities are funded by contributions from Governments and donors foundations. The Institute's web site can be found at URL:

http://www.unidir.org

"Common Security" arose from the understanding that the nuclear powers could no longer win a war given their second-strike capabilities. This continues to hold true for America and Russia today. Both have recognized in the Outer Space Treaty that in the interest of mankind the arms race should not be carried into outer space. The peaceful use of outer space allows a "passive" military reconnaissance and monitoring of the globe. Technological development will allow in the near future the deployment of weapons in space. Thus, a decision draws closer whether the USA will start an arms race in outer space or whether an internationally- controlled system of global security can be established. This book makes interesting proposals to this extent.

Egon Bahr
Former Secretary of State, German Foreign Ministry

Dr Detlev Wolter's informative treatment of outer space issues makes clear that humanity is on the verge of an irreversible shift to active, destructive, military use of outer space, a global revolution in human security, which will almost certainly surpass in significance the introduction of nuclear weapons. Dr Wolter makes a convincing case for a treaty regime for common security in outer space, verified and administered by an international space organization. This carefully researched, very readable account of the current legal and political regime governing the use of outer space, its pending weaponization, and the remedy for that outcome, needs the widest possible readership. This book is an indispensable resource for coping with a central issue of human survival, the weaponization of space.

Jonathan Dean
Former US Ambassador for Arms Control

The way in which we address security in outer space might very well mirror our future on Earth. Dr Wolter in Common Security in Outer Space and International Law has effectively set forth a practical legal route to enhancing collective security. This extremely ambitious work merits the attention of anyone interested in ensuring that reason, peace, and law guide the responsible exercise of the gifts of science and technology. Not only has he rigorously identified the legal basis for sound policies, but he makes the practical case for their implementation as well. This is a book for those with their feet on the ground and vision that gazes upwards.

Jonathan Granoff
Director, Institute of Global Security

Common Security in Outer Space and International Law by Detlev Wolter is a seminal work pointing the way to how the major powers can cooperate to ensure that space is kept free of weapons. This highly informed work by a distinguished diplomat is aimed at protecting the legal principle of the peaceful use of outer space. It is a valuable analysis of existing law and a stimulating challenge to the international community to demand multilateral negotiations to prevent an arms race in outer space.

Hon. Douglas Roche, O.C.
Chairman, Middle Powers Initiative

Dr Detlev Wolter, an experienced diplomat, has written a brilliant book on one of the most urgent and yet neglected questions facing the global community in the 21st century. Dr Wolter has an outstanding ability to inform and at the same time inspire the reader with an understanding of why and how we need to put in place a new international legal regime for common security in outer space. If you think of yourself as a global citizen, this book is essential reading.

Pera Wells
Deputy Secretary-General,
World Federation of United Nations Associations (WFUNA)

CONTENTS

Page

Chapter 10
An International World Space Organization
for safeguarding the peaceful use of outer space

ABOUT THE AUTHOR

Dr Detlev Wolter studied law, political science and history at Johannes Gutenberg-University, Mainz, Germany; University of Geneva, Geneva, Switzerland; and Columbia University, New York, United States. In 1987 he entered the German Foreign Service and from 1998 to 1999 he served consecutively as Second Secretary, Political Section Embassy in Moscow, Deputy Ambassador to Zambia, and First Secretary, Political Section, Permanent Representation of Germany to the European Union. In 1999 he became Head of Unit, European Department at the German Foreign Ministry and in 2003 Political Counsellor at the Permanent Mission of Germany to the United Nations. Since 2004 he is Chairman of the Group of Interested States in Practical Disarmament and in 2005 he was Vice-President of the First Committee of the General Assembly of the United Nations. Dr Wolter has published extensively on topics in international law and international relations. The German edition of *Common Security in Outer Space and International Law* was awarded the prestigious Helmuth James von Moltke Prize by the German Society for Military Law and International Humanitarian Law in 2005.

The principles underpinning the United Nations Charter reflect widely-shared global values of tolerance, justice and fair play; of security with, not against, others; of the fundamental importance of the rule of law both within and among states; of the primacy of human dignity and of the need for states to cooperate to these noble ends.

Nothing has happened since the drafting of the United Nations Charter to render these principles any less relevant and any less vital as guideposts for the international community. Global problems require global solutions that fairly address the legitimate needs and interests of all. This is the only basis for a sustainable future. It is the basis of the United Nations Charter—*combining* to achieve *common* aims—and it is more relevant than ever, given the complex and profoundly interdependent world in which we live.

Yet, at the very moment when a strengthening of the rules-based international system is urgently needed to confront threats as diverse as climate change, profound poverty and heightened nuclear weapons proliferation, this system is under attack from without and within; including from within the very state that was the prime architect of the international system.

What is needed is bold action to enhance and buttress the duty to cooperate that is enshrined in the United Nations Charter. Multilateral cooperation is not a luxury or an act of charity or an activity we pursue only with a chosen few. It is *the* imperative for the survival of humanity. It is instructive to recall the Outer Space Treaty of 1967, which declares the use of outer space to be the province of all mankind—thus a global commons not subject to claims of national sovereignty. Space is to be used solely for "peaceful purposes" and its exploration and use shall be for the benefit of all states, requiring an *active* duty to cooperate to this end—revolutionary principles for their time representing a promise, as yet, largely unfulfilled.

This is the proactive mode and it is the basis for Detlev Wolter's brilliant book—visionary in its scope, yet detailed and pragmatic in its prescriptions. His aim is nothing short of a *pax cosmica*—an internationally agreed cooperative regime governing outer space that will not only prevent its weaponization but also pave the way for nuclear disarmament on Earth. It will also provide us with a concrete, working model of an international organization operating under United Nations aegis using an unabashedly *community*-oriented international law, based on a presumption of interdependence taking precedence over national sovereignty.

There is no time to lose. Since the dawning of the space age with the launching of the Soviet satellite Sputnik in 1957, states have held the line at so-called "passive" military uses of space such as satellite surveillance. Every year at the United Nations General Assembly the overwhelming majority of states—including four of the five permanent members of the United Nations Security Council—vote against the weaponization of space. But the increasing emphasis in a growing number of states on the use of military space systems in support of terrestrial military operations has begun to dangerously blur the line between "passive" uses and "active" military uses with destructive effect, undermining in turn the principle of peaceful uses. There is broad international support for the Conference on the Disarmament (CD) to negotiate a legal instrument banning weapons in space. But the CD agenda has been blocked since 1998, stymieing any meaningful progress towards an agreed, verifiable weapons ban.

The current US Administration, in its quest for the ultimate military high ground, seems determined to break the norm against weaponization and is actively contemplating a dramatic change in its space policy to provide for the deployment of offensive anti-satellite weapons and space-based weapons for attacking targets on Earth. Scientists and other international security experts warn that such a course would be ruinously expensive and entirely counterproductive, almost inevitably setting off a new arms race, and rendering all space assets—including commercial communications and broadcast satellites—more, not less, vulnerable.

Wolter does not flinch from the hardest question—can a practical system of cooperative security be elaborated for outer space without the support and active cooperation of *the* major space power? His answer is a provocative challenge to the rest of us—can we envisage a system of common security for outer space that is demonstrably in the interests of the United States by considering the possible cooperative deployment of a limited ground-based missile defence system as a multilateral hedge against nuclear break-out in a nuclear weapons-free world?

In the ferocious international debate that raged before the US-led invasion of Iraq in the spring of 2003, it seemed that two world views were in play—a belief shared by many, if not most, that the interactions of nations must be guided by international law and international institutions—and a contrary view, espoused most vocally by the single most powerful member of the international community, that national sovereignty and unilateral military measures are the only real guarantors of national security.

We are perilously close to the unilateralist, militarist vision of outer space eclipsing the cooperative model laid out so painstakingly by Detlev Wolter. Yet, despite the increasing militarization of space, all space-faring states continue to emphasize the importance of the peaceful scientific and commercial uses of outer space and of international cooperation to this end. The die is not yet cast. Let this book be both a call to action and a roadmap for getting on with the negotiation of a multilateral Treaty on Common Security in Outer Space.

Peggy Mason
Ottawa, Canada
Former Ambassador to the United Nations
for Disarmament Affairs (1989–1994)

PREFACE

The idea of developing the interdisciplinary concept laid out in this book dates back to my studies at Columbia Univesity in New York and to two internships at the United Nations, one in the Legal Department and the other in the Department for Disarmament Affairs, in the years 1983–1985. It was sparked by the Strategic Defence Initiative (SDI) speech of US President Ronald Reagan in March 1983, which raised for the first time the spectre of a deployment of weapons in outer space. With the end of the Cold War there seemed to be no need for or risk of such a development. Yet, the plans for the weaponization of outer space have returned with force. Today, international security is further aggravated by nuclear proliferation and the risk of nuclear terrorism. These risks and the horrific attacks of 11 September 2001 have convinced me that the international community has to establish a comprehensive order of common or cooperative security that will prevent the weaponization of outer space and pave the way for nuclear disarmament on Earth.

I hope that the present analysis will contribute to laying an interdisciplinary foundation for such an international order of common security in outer space.

I should like to acknowledge my indebtness to the many individuals and institutions who have assisted me in my research. I am particularly grateful to Professor Christian Tomuschat from the Humboldt University in Berlin, Dr Götz Neuneck from the Institute for Peace Research and Security Policy at the University of Hamburg, Dr Jürgen Scheffran, now at the University of Illinois, Dr Bernd Kubbig from the Hessian Foundation for Peace Research, Dr Randy Rydell, United Nations Department for Disarmament Affairs, Senator Douglas Roche, Jonathan Granoff from the Global Security Institute and (ret.) Ambassador Peggy Mason from the Pearson Peacekeeping Centre for their critical comments and advice. I would also like to thank many colleagues of mine from the German Foreign Ministry, in particular Nikolai von Schoepff, Heiner Horsten, Dr Rüdiger Reyels, Hans-Joachim Daerr, Heinrich Haupt and Dr Thietmar Bachmann for their encouragement, advice and useful briefings. The responsibility for the analysis, as well as the views expressed in this book is, however, entirely my own.

I would like to thank UNIDIR for publishing the book. I am particularly indebted to the Director, Patricia Lewis, for her encouragement and guidance and to Steve Tulliu and Kerry Maze for their invaluable assistance in editing the manuscript.

The book is dedicated to my 11-year-old daugther Laura-Nastassja in the hope that her generation will be spared the costs and risks of an arms race in outer space.

PART I

Introduction

The extent of the structural changes in international relations in our time requires a far more basic reorientation of our thinking in international law.

Wolfgang Friedmann
1964[1]

In the end, the root of man's security does not lie in his weaponry. It lies in his mind.

Robert McNamara
United States Secretary of Defense
1967[2]

Is safety to be found in nuclear arms or in their elimination?

Jonathan Schell
1984[3]

Outer space is an internationalized common area beyond the national jurisdiction of individual states. Security in space must therefore be the common security of all states. The objective of this analysis is to apply the concept of common security as developed by the Hamburg Institute for Peace Research and Security Policy and cooperative security as labelled by the Brookings Institution to outer space.[4] The study will explore the legal foundations for its application in outer space law, in particular the principle of cooperation and the mankind clause in Art. I, para. 1 of the Outer Space Treaty, which declares the use of outer space to be the "province of all mankind". By applying these clauses to the subject of international security in outer space, the analysis will further draw pertinent conclusions for interpreting the highly controversial notion of the "peaceful use of outer space".

As a complete demilitarization of outer space seems beyond reach, it is critical to understand the international legal foundations of common security with respect to outer space in order to preserve its status as an internationalized common area beyond national jurisdiction. The international community is now faced with a possible qualitative shift from the current military use of outer space, which is of a passive nature, towards the active military use of space, which would be of a destructive nature. In view of the controversial interpretation of the principle of the peaceful use of outer space that has taken place over the past half century, this analysis attempts to develop a comprehensive theory of the peaceful use of outer space by conducting a structural analysis of the central tenets of the Outer Space Treaty—tenets that stipulate that the use of outer space is the "province of all mankind". The development of such a comprehensive theory serves as a foundation for applying the concept of common security to outer space and for elaborating the necessary legal standards and criteria for its practical implementation.

Analysing the structural prerequisites of the "interest of mankind" in outer space in the security field is of topical importance in light of the current plans for deploying space-based weapons as part of a ballistic missile defence (BMD). A cooperative strategic transition towards common security within a multilateral framework would safeguard the security interests of the international community in outer space and underpin the principle of peaceful use of outer space. After the US renunciation of the Anti-Ballistic Missile (ABM) Treaty in December 2001, the principle of the peaceful use of outer space remains the only international legal restriction on the introduction of weapons other than weapons of mass destruction (WMD) into space. New approaches are needed to overcome the unfruitful dichotomy of interpreting "peaceful" through the minimalist understanding of "non-aggressive" or the maximalist notion of "non-military". The interpretation and application of the peaceful purpose clause have to be further developed in light of the "interest of all mankind" clause in the Outer Space Treaty and the common heritage of mankind (CHOM) principle. In this context, Wolfgang Friedman' s seminal work on the structural change of international law as reflected by the mankind clause from a law of coexistence of sovereign states to a law of participation and cooperation in an interdependent world, will serve as the basis for elaborating the legal foundations for common security in outer space.[5]

A central part of the analysis will deal with the procedural and institutional implications of applying the CHOM principle with regard to security in outer space. Although the Outer Space Treaty does not explicitly apply the CHOM principle to outer space *per se*, the arguments of this analysis will demonstrate that the Treaty does indeed contain the principal elements of the CHOM principle, and thus can be considered to be a structural element of outer space law. Based on the concept of an international legal community,[6] the application of the CHOM principle of outer space law to the security field will lay the foundation for the substantial and procedural realization of the peaceful purpose clause, and for safeguarding the interests of the international community in the peaceful use of outer space. The analysis will focus in particular on the obligations of the space powers that follow from the CHOM principle with regard to new military uses of outer space as well as on the regulatory or norm-creating competence for the establishment of an international regime to safeguard the peaceful use of outer space.

The regime for the peaceful use of outer space encompasses rules regarding the admissibility, control and verification of military activities in space. In this context, possible institutional provisions to safeguard the peaceful use of outer space through the establishment of an international satellite verification agency along the 1978 proposal by the former French President Giscard d'Estaing,[7] will be examined.

Drawing on the "Advisory Opinion on the Legality of the Threat or Use of Nuclear Weapons"[8] of the International Court of Justice (ICJ), which applies the concept of the international legal community to questions of arms control and international security,[9] the analysis develops the idea of the interest of mankind in overcoming the doctrine of mutual assured destruction (MAD) and nuclear deterrence through the nuclear-weapon powers' fulfilment of their obligation to conclude a treaty of comprehensive and complete nuclear disarmament. Since the interest of mankind is mandatory under the mankind clause of the Outer Space Treaty, a spaced-based missile defence in the nuclear field will have to respect the interest of mankind in overcoming nuclear deterrence. Once the use of the common space and thus the interest of mankind in the peaceful use of outer space are at stake, it will be imperative to develop a new strategic relationship between the nuclear-weapon powers in the interest of international security and stability, and of active non-proliferation as a central part of cooperative/common security.

Based on the numerous proposals submitted by states at the Geneva Conference on Disarmament (CD), the drafts by non-governmental organizations and the elaborate ideas in the arms control and legal literature on the prevention of an arms race in outer space, the concept of common security in outer space will include, beyond the prohibition of active military uses of a destructive nature in outer space, a comprehensive package of confidence-building measures with multilateral satellite monitoring and verification systems as well as a protective regime for peaceful space objects based on immunity rules for satellites, such as a "rules of the road" and a "code of conduct". In the concluding chapter these elements will be presented through a proposal to negotiate a multilateral Treaty on Common Security in Outer Space (CSO) as the adequate mechanism for implementing the Outer Space Treaty, to be accompanied by the establishment of an international Organization for Common Security in Outer Space (OCSO) tasked with monitoring the implementation of the CSO Treaty.

The access of man to outer space and the daily rendering of satellite images of the globe have reinforced a universalist view of mankind. In terms of legal philosophy, this could lead to a legitimization of the structural change of international law towards a legal order of mankind that would find its primary embodiment in a community-oriented space law and receive its structural characteristics from the preponderance of common security in outer space, which could also overcome the traditional antagonism between states. Future generations will be grateful to today's governments for respecting the ethical and legal obligation "not to arm a common territory which has never been armed".[10]

PART II

Limitation of military hegemony in outer space by international law

This Treaty, following the precedent of the Antarctic Treaty, concluded outside the United Nations in 1959, reserved an unspoiled area for strictly peaceful purposes to benefit all mankind.

US President Lyndon Johnson in his
"United Nations Day Proclamation"
of August 1967 with regard to the
Outer Space Treaty[11]

CHAPTER 1

GENESIS OF THE PRINCIPLE
OF THE PEACEFUL USE OF OUTER SPACE

1.1   OUTER SPACE USE PRESERVED FOR
PEACEFUL PURPOSES

1.1.1   BEGINNING OF THE SPACE AGE AND DECLARATIONS
ON THE PEACEFUL USE OF OUTER SPACE

The legal order for outer space that exists today is closely related to the international community's efforts to prevent the United States and the former Soviet Union from entering into an arms race in space.[12] From the beginning of the space age, the international community raised within the framework of the United Nations the demand that the exploration and use of outer space be oriented exclusively towards peaceful purposes in the interest, and for the benefit, of mankind as a whole. The United States and the Soviet Union, the only two states capable of sending satellites into space between 1957 and 1965, originally supported this demand.[13] Both powers introduced the principle of peaceful use in proposals aimed at developing a legal order that would limit the military use of outer space. The initial space activities of both countries corresponded to the International Council of Scientific Unions' multilateral appeal for artificial satellites to be launched into space during the International Geophysical Year of 1957-1958, which the Council had dedicated to the peaceful international exploration and use of outer space.[14]

As technology progressed in the mid-1950s, and the two powers acquired the capacity to use outer space militarily, the United States proposed in 1957 to the United Nations General Assembly in its first memorandum devoted to arms control in outer space,[15] that the United Nations should establish a multilateral control system with "international inspection and participation" as:

9

the first step toward the objective of assuring that future developments in *outer space* would be devoted *exclusively for peaceful* and scientific *purposes* [emphasis added].[16]

The United States had in fact already established a general arms control basis for the peaceful use of outer space the previous year when it had submitted its first memorandum on general and complete disarmament, including the proposed control regime for outer space, to the First Committee of the United Nations General Assembly charged with disarmament and international security matters.[17] Roger Handberg stresses that President Dwight Eisenhower's immediate reaction to the Soviet Union's success with Sputnik was to try to limit the potential military implications by working out treaty obligations on the prevention of an arms race in space and to see to it that "the United States would, if possible, project a peaceful image regarding space activities".[18]

The principle of the peaceful use of outer space was thus enshrined in the first resolution on outer space of the United Nations General Assembly of 14 November 1957.[19] This resolution, adopted from a joint proposal by Canada, France, Great Britain and the United States in August 1957, provided for the establishment of an "international system of inspection" tasked with guaranteeing that objects sent into space would be "exclusively for peaceful purposes". US President Eisenhower expressed support for the United Nations proposal in a letter to Soviet Premier Nikolai Bulganin on 13 January 1958 as follows:

> I propose that we agree that outer space should be used only for peaceful purposes. We face a decisive moment in history in relation to this matter. Both the Soviet Union and the United States are now using outer space for the testing of missiles designed for military purposes. The time to stop is now.[20]

In addition, the United States had incorporated the principle of the peaceful use of outer space and the mankind clause into its domestic law. The National Aeronautics and Space Act, adopted by the US Congress on 29 July 1958, states in its introduction that:

> The Congress hereby declares that it is the policy of the United States that activities in space should be devoted to peaceful purposes for the benefit of all mankind.[21]

The Soviet Union submitted a draft treaty to the United Nations General Assembly on 15 March 1958,[22] which, albeit linked to the dissolution of military bases abroad, provided for a complete prohibition of any military use of outer space, including for the passage of intercontinental missiles. Point 1 of the draft reads:

> A ban on the use of cosmic space for military purposes and an undertaking by States to launch rockets into cosmic space only under an agreed international programme.

The first proposals by the United States and the Soviet Union on the subject of the use of outer space were directed towards preventing an arms race in outer space and, thus, from the onset of the space age, the international community attempted to enshrine this goal in an international agreement within the framework of the United Nations.

1.1.2 LEGAL PRINCIPLES FOR OUTER SPACE

While the two space powers engaged in tedious negotiations both bilaterally and through the Geneva-based Disarmament Committee over a step-by-step plan for comprehensive and complete disarmament, which according to the Soviet Union would include the prohibition of military uses of outer space,[23] the United Nations led by the United States took the first concrete steps towards creating an international order for the peaceful use of outer space in 1958.[24] Following from a proposal by US Secretary of State John Foster Dulles to establish an ad hoc committee "to prepare for a fruitful program on international cooperation in the peaceful uses of outer space",[25] the United Nations General Assembly decided in December 1958 to set up the ad hoc Committee on the Peaceful Uses of Outer Space.[26] In its first unanimously adopted report, the Committee stressed that outer space was the common interest of mankind and that its exploration and use had to be for the benefit of all mankind.[27] In recognition of the importance of this question to the international community, the United Nations decided in the following year to change the ad hoc Committee into a permanent Committee on the Peaceful Uses of Outer Space (COPUOS) of the General Assembly.[28]

While initially fearing that under the leadership of the United States, the group of Western states would dominate COPUOS, the Soviet Union voted against the resolution for its establishment and refused to participate in its work.[29] It was, however, soon understood that the common interest in the peaceful use of outer space could only be realized if all states, or at least all of the major groupings of states, participated in the development of legal principles governing space activities. India and the United Arab Republic contributed to reaching a compromise by refusing to take their seat in COPUOS if both space powers were not participating in its work.[30] This compromise led to an increase in the Committee's membership from 18 to 24 states. Over the years, the number of members has increased several times, reaching 67 states today.[31]

The Soviet Union's demand for veto power in the Committee could only be resolved by adopting the "method of consensus"[32] for the work of the Committee and its sub-committees.[33] All resolutions prepared by the Committee were adopted by consensus by the General Assembly. The consensus method contributed decisively to the fact that all agreements and declarations on legal principles prepared in these bodies tasked with developing space law[34] would be unanimously adopted by the General Assembly, and thus generally accepted and subsequently ratified by the majority of United Nations Member States.[35]

With its resolution 1721,[36] which was prepared by COPUOS and adopted on 20 December 1961, the United Nations General Assembly recommended that Member States be guided in their exploration and use of outer space by two leading principles:

1. The application of general international law and in particular of the United Nations Charter to outer space; and
2. The prohibition of national appropriation of parts of outer space and its resources.

States are additionally required to submit to COPUOS all necessary flight information for objects launched into space in order for the Committee to establish a public space register. With resolution 1802, adopted on 14 December 1962 and entitled "International Cooperation in the Peaceful Uses of Outer Space",[37] the United Nations General Assembly reiterated that all states shall fully inform COPUOS of all space programmes, and it further tasked the Committee to elaborate comprehensive legal principles governing the peaceful use of outer space.

In the following year, the United Nations General Assembly adopted the "Declaration of Legal Principles Governing the Activities of States in the Exploration and Use of Outer Space" (known in short as the "Principles Declaration", resolution 1962 (XVIII) of 13 December 1963), which was prepared by COPUOS and put forward a general legal framework for all space activities.[38] The original intention of the "Principles Declaration", which affirmed in para. 1 that the peaceful use of outer space should be "for the benefit and in the interests of all mankind", was to have the international community endeavour to incorporate outer space into arms control regimes from an early stage.[39] Furthermore, within COPUOS, Brazil, India, Japan and Lebanon had proposed that any potential outer space treaty that would emanate from the "Principles Declaration" should include as a genuine operative paragraph an "unequivocal provision that space may be used only for peaceful purposes".[40] For the first time, the "Principles Declaration" additionally put forth the need to consider the interests of developing countries in the framework of the mankind clause.[41] Unanimously adopted by the United Nations General Assembly,[42] the Declaration contained all of the main legal principles that came to be included in the Outer Space Treaty of 1967. Paragraph 4 of the Treaty affirms that all space activities shall be conducted "in the interest of maintaining international peace and security and promoting international cooperation and understanding" and para. 6 introduces the obligation of consultation in the case of the possible harmful interference with the peaceful use of outer space:

> If a State has reason to believe that an outer space activity ... planned by it ... would cause potentially harmful interference with activities of other States in the peaceful exploration and use of outer space, it shall undertake appropriate international consultation before proceeding with any such activity or experiment.

By having initiated and approved these principles, both space powers had thus accepted that the rules governing the use of outer space are of concern to the international community as a whole and that the use of space should be exclusively for peaceful purposes and to the benefit of mankind as a whole.[43] Further, both space powers were, from the outset, primarily motivated by the desire to prevent the other side from achieving a military advantage through the use of outer space. Therefore, parallel to the elaboration of COPUOS, intense multilateral disarmament talks on outer space were first conducted in the Ten-Nation Committee on

Disarmament, which became the Eighteen-Nation Committee on Disarmament in 1962 and finally the Geneva CD in 1979.[44] The Soviet Union and the United States submitted to the Ten-Nation Committee on Disarmament on 19 March and 18 April 1962, respectively, ambitious drafts for a treaty on general and complete disarmament, which were intended to support peaceful cooperation in outer space by requiring the prior notification of all satellite and missile launches to an International Disarmament Organization.[45]

According to both drafts, the proposed organization was to have inspection teams at its disposal for on-site inspections. However, the two sides failed to agree on these measures, mainly due to Moscow's request for the simultaneous dissolution of all military bases abroad, and also due to the unresolved modalities of the on-site verification and inspection. Washington saw the Soviet demand for the dissolution of military bases abroad as an attempt by Moscow to take advantage of its temporary technological advance in the development of ballistic missiles in order to decouple the security of Western Europe from that of the United States.

1.1.3 PARTIAL DEMILITARIZATION OF OUTER SPACE

On 31 October 1958, Great Britain, the Soviet Union and the United States convened in Moscow a conference on the cessation of nuclear tests. The negotiations turned out to be particularly difficult with regard to the question of local inspections and the treatment of underground nuclear tests, which the United States viewed as hard to distinguish from natural earthquakes.[46]

In order to avoid making the urgent question of a ban on space weapons (in particular nuclear space weapons) hostage to the uncertain outcome of overly ambitious negotiations on general and complete disarmament, Canada proposed in 1962 to have the content of the US and Soviet proposals on the space question pursued separately in either COPUOS or the Eighteen-Nation Committee on Disarmament.[47] In June 1963, Mexico submitted the first concrete draft treaty in the Eighteen-Nation Committee on Disarmament on the ban of space weapons, and in particular of placing nuclear weapons and other WMD in orbit.[48] The starting point of the preambular consideration of the draft is that outer space shall be used for peaceful purposes:

... based on the understanding that for all times the peaceful use of outer space is in the general *interest of mankind* and that outer space should neither become the place or the subject of international disputes ... and that outer space and its celestial bodies belong to all mankind [emphasis added].[49]

Similar proposals for a ban on the deployment of nuclear and other WMD in outer space regularly failed as the Soviet Union continued to reject the US demand for the on-site inspections considered indispensable for the verification of such a ban. However, as over the following years both sides developed the necessary national means for verification, the United States withdrew its insistence on inspections.[50] As a result, once President John F. Kennedy and Premier Nikita Khrushchev exchanged letters in December 1962 and January 1963,[51] an agreement was finally reached, leading to the signing in August 1963 of the Treaty Banning Nuclear Weapons Tests in the Atmosphere, in Outer Space and Under Water (commonly known as the Partial Test Ban Treaty or PTBT), which prohibits, apart from underground tests, nuclear tests and explosions in outer space.[52] In light of the anticipated cumbersome and long process of ratification of the PTBT in the US Senate, the Kennedy Administration opted to seal the prohibition of nuclear weapons in outer space not with a formal treaty, but through the exchange of corresponding unilateral commitments under the umbrella of the United Nations.[53] Shortly afterwards, the United Nations General Assembly unanimously adopted resolution 1884 of 17 October 1963 under the title "General and Complete Disarmament", which welcomed the declarations of the United States and the Soviet Union and called upon all states:

(a) to refrain from placing in orbit around the Earth any objects carrying nuclear weapons or any other kinds of weapons of mass destruction, installing such weapons on celestial bodies, or stationing such weapons in outer space in any other manner.[54]

The representatives of Austria and India to COPUOS lamented, however, that neither the Eighteen-Nation Committee on Disarmament nor COPUOS was able to achieve a general ban on the deployment of weapons in orbit.[55]

In the meantime, the two superpowers again supported the codification of the principle of peaceful uses for areas beyond national jurisdiction—namely the Antarctic and the international seabed. The

Antarctic Treaty was negotiated in Washington at the invitation of US President Eisenhower in order to prevent the militarization of the Antarctic, and provided for the area's complete demilitarization.[56] Article 1, para. 1 of the Treaty prohibits:

> ... any measure of a military nature, such as the establishment of military bases and fortifications, the carrying out of military manoeuvres, as well as testing of any kind of weapon.[57]

Concerning the international seabed, the United Nations General Assembly adopted on 17 December 1970 a corresponding resolution entitled the "Declaration of Principles Governing the Sea-bed and the Ocean Floor, and the Subsoil Thereof, beyond the Limits of National Jurisdiction", which states in para. 8 that:

> ... the area shall be reserved exclusively for peaceful purposes ... One or more international agreements shall be concluded as soon as possible in order to implement effectively this principle and to constitute a step towards the exclusion of the sea-bed, the ocean floor and the subsoil thereof from the arms race.[58]

This provision led to the conclusion of the Treaty on the Prohibition of the Emplacement of Nuclear Weapons and other Weapons of Mass Destruction on the Sea-bed and the Ocean Floor and in the Subsoil Thereof in February 1971.[59] However, similar to the Outer Space Treaty, the Sea-bed Treaty lacked a legal definition of the term "peaceful", and consequently the notion remained controversial, even though the great majority of states considered it to signify a complete demilitarization.[60] In the unanimously adopted "Declaration of Principles Governing the Sea-bed and the Ocean Floor", the United Nations General Assembly expressed the belief that the principle of peaceful use entails the obligation to provide for its "effective implementation" through one or more international agreements as a step "towards the exclusion of the area from the arms race".[61]

The principle of the peaceful use of outer space in the first resolution of the United Nations General Assembly on outer space on 14 November 1957, in addition to the PTBT, and the resolution on "General and Complete Disarmament", otherwise known as the "No-Bombs-in-Orbit" resolution, thus provide the legal foundations for a multilateral framework of a (partial) demilitarization of outer space.[62] It took the two space powers more than ten years to take concrete legal steps to reinforce the partial demilitarization of space through the conclusion of the bilateral ABM Treaty.[63]

1.2   THE OUTER SPACE TREATY

The "Principles Declaration" of 1963 largely contributed to the development of the Treaty on Principles Governing the Activities of States in the Exploration and Use of Outer Space, including the Moon and Other Celestial Bodies (the Outer Space Treaty) of 27 January 1967, which was unanimously adopted by the United Nations General Assembly.[64] During the negotiations that took place in COPUOS and the First Committee of the General Assembly, both space powers announced that their primary objective was to prevent the extension of the arms race into outer space.[65] The United States[66] and the Soviet Union[67] submitted in COPUOS on 7 May and 30 May 1966, respectively, draft treaties providing for a complete demilitarization of the Moon and the other celestial bodies as well as a partial demilitarization of outer space through a ban on the deployment of nuclear and other WMD in orbit. Unchanged, these provisions were integrated into Art. IV, para. 1 and 2 of the Outer Space Treaty, thereby providing for at least the partial demilitarization of outer space. However, while the United States originally intended to limit the whole Treaty to celestial bodies, other delegations in COPUOS, including the Soviet delegation, were pushing to extend the application of the Treaty to all of outer space.[68] The United States, although its first draft had tried to limit the ban on the deployment of nuclear weapons to celestial bodies,[69] finally agreed. The US representative, Ambassador Arthur Goldberg, declared to the United Nations General Assembly that:

> ... the central issue was to ensure that outer space and celestial bodies were reserved exclusively for peaceful activities ... and that man's earthly conflicts will not be carried into outer space.[70]

The space powers were, nevertheless, careful in ensuring that no provision of the Treaty could infringe on their plans to allow for limited military uses of outer space such as permitting intercontinental ballistic missiles, albeit not deployed in orbit, to have part of their trajectory in space. Other limited uses included the so-called "support activities" for military purposes using satellites for reconnaissance, navigation and surveillance,[71] which were viewed, mainly by the United States in the framework of its strategy of nuclear deterrence, as having a stabilizing effect for international peace and security through early warning and—as endorsed in the Strategic Arms Limitation Treaty (SALT I) of 1972— surveillance as "national means of verification".[72] According to the former Austrian chairman of COPUOS, Peter Jankowitsch,[73] this was the true reason for distinguishing between the partial demilitarization of space and the full demilitarization of celestial bodies. It is of particular importance to note, however, that the military uses envisaged at the time included neither the deployment of weapons in space nor of satellites with destructive power. The possible flight of ballistic missiles through space during war represented neither a military use during peacetime nor a permanent deployment in orbit. It is therefore evident that the space powers accepted the application of the principle of peaceful use to all of outer space—as is stated in the preambular considerations 2 and 4 as well as in Articles IX and XI of the Outer Space Treaty. Consequently, as reflected in the preamble, the signatories affirmed their commitment to the peaceful use of all of outer space as a fundamental objective of the Outer Space Treaty. Accordingly, the Soviet chief delegate declared in the Legal Subcommittee of COPUOS:

> Naturally, the USSR like many other delegations is in favour of a complete prohibition of the use of outer space for military purposes.[74]

In a similar vein, one of the first directives of the National Security Council of the White House on outer space provided that:

> ... it is the purpose of the United States, as part of an armaments control system, to seek to assure that the sending of objects into outer space shall be exclusively for peaceful and scientific purposes and that under effective control the production of objects designed for travel or projection through outer space for military purposes shall be prohibited.[75]

Paul Stares concluded in his analysis of the military space programmes of the United States that these were in the early years directed at the objective "that this new medium should be used exclusively for *non-military* purposes."[76] Handberg summarizes the early US policy of space use as "Eisenhower's legacy of no weapons race in space",[77] which was continued by the succeeding administrations under Presidents Kennedy and Johnson:

Two approaches were taken. First, international agreements were reached, banning nuclear weapons from being positioned in outer space... More encompassing was the second treaty labelled the Outer Space Treaty. This treaty established the principle that the use of space was to be peaceful in nature. There were to be no military installations in space, or at least no installations fortified with weapons.

The Treaty being in the meantime ratified by nearly 100 states and considered the "Magna Carta of outer space law" or the "Constitution of space",[78] confirms the fundamental principles of the "Principles Declaration" and states in its Art. I, para. 1 in the same wording as in the preamble and in para. 1 of the Declaration that the peaceful use of outer space is "the province of all mankind". The Outer Space Treaty thus puts the common interest of all states, namely that space should be for peaceful purposes, at the centre of the legal order for space. The freedom of individual states in space is thus not only limited by the rights of other states, but also by the common interest of the international community, which can only be sought and attained by the peaceful use of the common space.[79]

It cannot be overlooked, however, that the space powers have been able to validate *de facto* their dominating position in space through several other provisions of the Treaty. For instance, Art. XII of the Outer Space Treaty provides for access "to all stations, installations, equipment and space vehicles on the moon and other celestial bodies" (for instance the right to inspection) only "on a basis of reciprocity", which automatically excludes the non-space powers from exercising this right.[80]

1.3 THE PEACEFUL USE OF OUTER SPACE AS A LEGAL ARMS CONTROL MEASURE

Already the multilateral negotiations leading to the adoption of the Outer Space Treaty prove that the two space powers have recognized their responsibility towards the international community not to extend the arms race into outer space; the principle of the peaceful use of outer space; and the principle of putting the interest of mankind above individual state interests. In addition, they have themselves introduced these principles in the negotiations of the Outer Space Treaty, and have never expressly challenged them afterwards. Instead, both states have consistently taken the view that their military activities in outer space, which until the beginning of the 1980s were limited to military actions of a non-destructive nature, should be in accordance with the principle of the peaceful use of outer space.[81] And thus, with regard to the application of the mankind clause to military uses of outer space, the two space powers have maintained that outer space activities shall serve the benefit of all mankind precisely in the arms control context.[82] The space powers themselves put the mankind clause in the context of security policy and not only—as was claimed in retrospect by some authors—in the context of the commercial use of outer space.[83] The international community, including the space powers, thus entered into the space age with the unanimous view that the use of outer space shall be exclusively for peaceful purposes.[84]

It has been argued, however, that the space powers lacked good faith when putting forward proposals for complete disarmament since they must have known that elements of their respective proposals would not be acceptable to the other side, and thus their recognition and support for the principle of the peaceful use of outer space could be interpreted as not having been seriously intended.[85] However, negotiating parties typically table seemingly unrealistic or maximalist positions knowing that they would be unacceptable to the other side, with the purpose of creating room for concessions further along the negotiation process. Legally, this does not undermine the intended seriousness of such a proposal,[86] as, according to the Vienna Convention on the Law of Treaties, only reservations made in writing have legal credibility.[87] As such, in light of the National Aeronautics and Space Act of 1958[88] and having incorporated the principle of the peaceful use of outer space into domestic law, it would be questionable to assume that such reservations or lack of good faith between the space powers existed. Further, the space powers failed to make an interpretative declaration on the occasion of the adoption of the principle of the peaceful use of outer space in the resolutions of the United Nations General Assembly and the Outer Space Treaty indicating that the principle would not preclude the development or deployment of space-based weapon systems or that it would not be applicable to outer space as a whole. On the basis of the consistency of recurrent affirmations and accepted common purpose obligations of every space activity, according to the principle of estoppel,[89] the international community is thus entitled to rely on the relevant affirmations of the space powers to keep outer space free from an arms race as having been made in earnest.

In summary, both the principle of the peaceful use of outer space and the mankind clause in the Outer Space Treaty were from the outset closely linked to the efforts of the international community to limit the military use of outer space. In particular, the mankind clause was introduced into outer space law by the two space powers and the United Nations with this very objective. Therefore, the views later expressed in the literature that the clause has no legal relevance, or that it is too vague with regard to the assessment of the admissibility of military uses, are mistaken.

However, from the beginning there was no common interpretation of the notion "peaceful" and the extent of the principle of the peaceful use of outer space. It is clear that the two space powers did not want to exclude certain military uses of satellites or the flight of ballistic missiles from the range of permissible space activities. Consequently, they accepted only a partial demilitarization of the whole of outer space and agreed that only the Moon and other celestial bodies would be completely demilitarized. Yet, it was not the intent of the space powers at the time to use this differentiation to render the military use of satellites also and the deployment of space weapons lawful.[90] The desire to limit the complete demilitarization to celestial bodies is also apparent from the negotiation protocols of Art. IV, para. 2.[91] This left the question open as to what extent the Outer Space Treaty, apart from the express ban in Art. IV concerning nuclear and other WMD, would impose further limitations on the deployment of weapons in outer space as a whole.

1.4 THE UNCLEAR BALANCE BETWEEN THE INTERESTS OF MANKIND AND THE FREEDOM OF SPACE OF INDIVIDUAL STATES

As the genesis of the Outer Space Treaty demonstrates, the *de facto* hegemony of the two space powers was not endorsed by the international community, which had, on the contrary, insisted that all states were to participate with equal rights in the use of outer space as a territory beyond national jurisdiction in the "interest of all mankind". It is only in the military field that the United States and Russia dominate space issues today. In light of the current level of civil space activities taking place internationally, it can no longer be said that there is a dominant position of a few space nations.[92]

With the mankind clause proposed by both the United States and the Soviet Union in the elaboration of the Outer Space Treaty, and promptly endorsed and further enhanced as the CHOM principle by the developing countries, the preponderance of common over individual state interest took root in outer space law, laying the basis for the far-reaching structural change of international law in the era of the United Nations. In contrast to the freedom of the high seas, which limits the sovereign freedom of individual states only through that of other states, the legal status of outer space was oriented from the beginning to the interest, particularly security interests, of mankind as a whole. The resulting centrality of the common interest implies that the hegemonic position of the space powers is legally restricted *ab initio* by the rules of international space law as they were created with the active involvement of the newly independent states. The director of the Institute and Centre of Air and Space Law of McGill University, Nicolas Matte, rightly characterizes outer space law as representing an enhanced orientation of a new structure of law that shifts the emphasis away from state sovereignty towards the interest of the international community.[93] Applying this development to the military use of outer space, the former President of the ICJ, Manfred Lachs, remarked in 1970:

> The old principle that everything not prohibited is permitted is not valid today ... This is of particular importance to outer space.[94]

While the rights of states traditionally limit the freedom of action of other states, it follows that the self-limitation of sovereignty becomes all the more relevant when accounting for the common interest obligations according to the mankind clause.[95] It does not, however, lead to the conclusion that the freedom of states does not apply to outer space as a territory beyond national jurisdiction. On the contrary, this freedom is recognized as a leading principle in Art. I, para. 2 of the Outer Space Treaty, comparable to the principle of common interest. Thus, the Outer Space Treaty has for the first time recognized the juxtaposition of the common interest and the freedom of states with the consequence that in each instance the freedom of action in space has to be harmonized with the common interest rule and that in doing so there is no longer a presumption in favour of state sovereignty.[96] Applying this to the admissibility of military uses of outer space and to the deployment of space weapons specifically, it follows that it is not sufficient to assess these factors merely in terms of an express prohibition but also in view of the positive contribution they could make to the central common interest clause of the Outer Space Treaty.[97]

In sum, instead of accepting or even endorsing the factual sovereign hegemony of individual space powers, the Outer Space Treaty establishes the interests of the international community in the form of the mankind clause as the guiding principle of the space order. This new limitation of the freedom of states in turn is the normative foundation for developing the CHOM principle as the general structural principle of the legal space order.

This validation of the common interest also explains the enthusiasm with which the international community, including the two space powers, welcomed the beginning of the space age and of the peaceful exploration of space. Not least with regard to the issue of international security and disarmament, the international community put great hopes in the principle of the peaceful use of outer space in the "interest of all mankind". The ensuing first period of *détente* led the two space powers to propose for the first time in 1963, in addition to the conclusion of the PTBT, a multilateral draft treaty on general and complete disarmament. This, in addition to Art. VI of the Nuclear Non-Proliferation Treaty (NPT) in particular, represents the recognition of the nuclear-weapon powers—as the ICJ had stated in its "Advisory Opinion on the Legality of the Threat or Use of Nuclear Weapons"—for viewing multilateral disarmament as a binding obligation towards the international community.[98] As long as an arms race in outer space has not yet begun, the positive assessment of the Outer Space Treaty by Eileen Galloway holds true. The US space lawyer links US space policy with regard to the peaceful use of outer space in the interest of mankind with the result:

> ... that we have been successful in achieving the main goal: preserving outer space for peaceful space exploration and uses and preventing the new environment from becoming the arena for orbiting weapons and international conflicts.[99]

Today, however, this success is more than at risk. The United States is about to amend its security policy to include the possible armament of space and therefore it is seemingly prepared to diverge from the principle of the peaceful use of outer space, which it had initially championed, and which became accepted by the international community as the *acquis* of outer space law.

CHAPTER 2

THE PASSIVE MILITARY USES OF OUTER SPACE

2.1 THE PRINCIPLE OF THE PEACEFUL USE OF OUTER SPACE IN PRACTICE

2.1.1 DISTINCTION BETWEEN PASSIVE AND ACTIVE MILITARY USES OF OUTER SPACE

In order to assess the international community's acceptance of current military uses of outer space, including new forms of military uses such as the deployment of space weapons, it is necessary to distinguish between military uses that are passive and non-destructive versus those that are active and destructive.[100] This distinction appears in state practice,[101] international law,[102] as well as in the international security and arms control literature.[103] The drift towards an active weaponization of space is viewed in the literature as a qualitatively new step in the military use of outer space, which could lead to the very arms race the international community has been aiming to prevent through the adoption and the annual reaffirmation of the 1982 resolution on the prevention of an arms race in outer space. Even the military strategists who view SDI and national missile defence (NMD)[104] as merely another step in the ongoing research of anti-satellite (ASAT) and anti-missile weapons, have recognized that outer space has so far been kept free from active military uses and in particular from the deployment of any kind of space weapons.[105]

In political science literature, Gerald Steinberg, of the Massachusetts Institute of Technology, made an extensive distinction between purely passive military uses and active military uses of outer space in an October 1982 publication (six months before President Reagan announced his far-reaching SDI plans). In particular, he emphasized the fundamental differences among such military uses according to their impact on international security and strategic stability. According to Steinberg:

... passive military space systems are ... not weapons themselves, but are used to enhance military systems *below*. Reconnaissance, early warning, communications, navigation and other satellites allow for effective use and coordination of aircraft, tanks, missiles, ships etc. [emphasis added][106]

This definition focuses on the character of passive military uses as not having an independent destructive capability and as being a support for military activities on Earth, not in space—this is in contrast to the active military uses of outer space whereby the destructive impacts occur in space itself. Steinberg has considered passive military uses to be stabilizing particularly with regard to early warning and verification, and active systems with destructive effect in space to be inherently destabilizing. As a result of this differentiation, the two space powers, according to Steinberg, are faced with decisions that could either lead to:

... entering an arms race they have sought to avoid to date ... [that] promises to be expensive and destabilizing

or to

... mutually advantageous limitation agreements which will allow both to develop passive military space systems without interference.[107]

On the same issue, Bhupendra Jasani has warned of the imminent weaponization of space, posing the question in 1982 of whether outer space has become the battlefield of the future.[108] In a study published in 1991, Jasani proposed a definition of space weapons on the basis of their destructive objectives:

A space weapon is a device stationed in outer space (including the Moon and other celestial bodies) or in the Earth environment designed to destroy, damage or otherwise interfere with the normal functioning of an object or being in outer space, or a device stationed in outer space designed to destroy, damage or otherwise interfere with the normal functioning of an object or being in the Earth environment. Any other device with the inherent capability to be used as defined above will be considered as a space weapon.[109]

From a legal perspective, in 1981 Ivan Vlasic has warned of how a move towards active military uses of a destructive nature in space would undermine the principle of the peaceful use of outer space.[110] With a view to international legal policy, Carl Christol has made reference to this distinction through defining "passive operations" as:

> ... the provision of communications facilities, the gathering of intelligence, the operation of early warning capabilities, the perfection of navigation, and the effective forecasting of weather conditions.[111]

Referring to Vlasic, Andrew Young has distinguished between "space militarization" as the:

> ... stabilising/passive/non-intrusive/supportive military activities conducted in space, such as communications, early warning surveillance, navigation, geodesy, meteorology, and reconnaissance

and the "weaponization of space" as the:

> ... active/potentially intrusive/independent/and thus destabilising military space activities, such as anti-satellites (ASAT) and spaced-based ballistic missile "defences".[112]

Robert Bowman has emphasized that with regard to the arms control proposals on outer space, the question is no longer about turning back the irreversible passive military uses of space but of preventing its weaponization.[113] When discussing this topic at the International Law Association, the Chairman of the Association's International Space Law Committee, Daniel Goedhuis, further emphasized that the dual-use capabilities of existing passive military uses could not be reversed and that these would have to be considered in view of future manned space stations as permissible,[114] as long as they do not have any destructive capabilities or functions.[115]

In state practice, the distinction between current passive and possible active military uses in the future became clearly apparent at the United Nations Conference on the Exploitation and Peaceful Uses of Outer Space (UNISPACE) II in 1982, where three categories of military uses of outer space were distinguished:[116]

> – So-called "support systems" such as satellites for communication, meteorology and navigation which can also be used for civil purposes.

- Military surveillance systems, such as high definition cameras, electronic intelligence systems, radars, early warning systems and nuclear tests detectors.[117]
- Space-based weapons systems, in particular anti-satellite weapons and laser and particle beams-weapons.[118]

The distinction between passive and active military uses plays a key role in the various proposals at the CD for the negotiation of an agreement on banning space weapons. In particular, some Western states take the distinction as a basis for their proposals on the prevention of an arms race in outer space as they would like to see existing passive military uses remain outside the ban. As such, in view of the complete demilitarization of space, the French delegation submitted a working paper to the CD in 1983, stating that "constraints resulting from the long-standing and by now irreversible overlapping of civilian and military uses of outer space" exist. The main objective of arms control efforts for outer space should therefore be "to prevent outer space from becoming a base for military action".[119] Specifically, Italy and Sweden referred to this distinction when presenting their respective proposals on measures to prevent an arms race in outer space.[120] The Italian representative expressly excluded passive military uses from the ambit of the Italian draft protocol for a ban on space weapons.[121] Similarly, the 1981[122] and 1983[123] Soviet proposals refer solely to active uses of a destructive nature without questioning the existing passive military uses, in contrast to previous years when the Soviet Union was still demanding a complete demilitarization of space.

The majority of the non-aligned states of the Group of 21 continue to strive for a complete ban on any military use of outer space. They recognize, however, that this is not likely in the near future, and thus equally refer to the distinction between existing passive and future active military uses by advocating interim measures for the prohibition of active military space activities, in particular of ASAT weapons and BMD systems. An example of the position of the Group of 21 is reflected in the paper China presented to the CD in 1985. While supporting the objective of a complete "demilitarization of outer space", it recommended measures as an interim solution to safeguard the de-weaponization of space with a first step being the negotiation of a complete ban on the testing and the production of space weapons of any kind.[124] Further, Venezuela,[125] Sri Lanka,[126] Peru[127] and India,[128] while considering a complete demilitarization of space to be desirable, called for an immediate ban on active space uses of a destructive nature as an urgent and necessary interim solution.

2.1.2 ACTIVE MILITARY USES OF OUTER SPACE

The definition of active military uses of a destructive nature of outer space should consist of legally relevant criteria based on objective characteristics and clear elements of differentiation in order to allow the drawing of conclusions as to the permissibility and non-permissibility of certain forms of military uses of outer space. The most important function of the definition is to provide a clear demarcation of passive military uses of a non-destructive nature by referring to an independent destructive capability in space as the deciding criterion. Various proposals made to the CD concerning the definition of space weapons could assist in determining the relevant criteria. In the Ad Hoc Committee on the Prevention of an Arms Race in Outer Space, several delegations submitted proposals, which professor N. Ronzitti has summarized in a paper addressing the terminology of space weapons:[128]

Venezuela:[130]
"Space strike weapon"' means any offensive or defensive device, including its operational components, whatever the scientific principle on which its functioning is based:
(a) capable of destroying or damaging from its place of deployment in outer space an object situated in outer space, in the air, in water or on land,
(b) capable of destroying or damaging from its place of deployment in the air, in water or on land an object situated in outer space.
The following are also space strike weapons: any offensive or defensive device, including its operational components and any system of such devices, whatever the scientific principle on which its functioning is based, that is capable of intercepting, from outer space or from land, water or the atmosphere, ballistic projectiles during their flight.

Soviet Union:[131]
The Soviet definition of active military uses of space comprises: "... to place in orbit around the Earth objects carrying weapons of any kind, install such weapons on celestial bodies, or station such weapons in outer space in any other manner ..." (Art. 1, 1981 draft treaty); " ... not to destroy, damage, disturb the normal functioning or change the flight trajectory of space objects ..." (Art. 3, 1981 draft treaty); and The draft of 1983 in addition provides "[n]ot to utilise space objects in orbit

around the Earth, on celestial bodies or stationed in outer space in any other manner as means to destroy any target on the Earth, in the atmosphere or in outer space." (Art. 2.2, 1983 draft treaty.)

Bulgaria and Hungary:[132]
"(a) Any weapon system based entirely or partially in space which is specifically designed and intended to destroy, damage or interfere with the normal functioning of, objects in space or on Earth, including its atmosphere, or
(b) any weapon system, whether land-based, sea-based or airborne, which is specifically designed and intended to destroy, damage or interfere with the normal functioning of space objects."

German Democratic Republic:[133]
"Any device or installation based entirely or partially on land, sea or in the air and/or in outer space which is specifically designed and intended to destroy, damage or interfere with the normal functioning of space objects."

China:[134]
"A space weapon means any device or installation either space-, land-, sea-, or atmosphere-based, which is designed for striking or damaging spacecraft in outer space, or disrupting the normal functioning, or changing their orbits, and any other device or installation based in space (including those based on the Moon and other celestial bodies) which is designed for attacking or striking objects in the atmosphere, or on land, or at sea, or disrupting their normal functioning."

Sri Lanka:[135]
"Any weapon or a component of a weapon or a device, either ground-based or space-based, in Earth orbit or in any other trajectory beyond Earth orbit, designed physically to damage or interfere with or attack a space object, or to attack ground or airborne targets from space is a space weapon."

Canada:[136]
"Any device specially designed or modified to inflict permanent physical damage on any other object through the projection of mass or energy."

The analysis contained in this study follows the Canadian definition. It has the advantage of precluding the risk of inadvertently including existing passive military uses by excluding any non-weapon-related components of a space-based system that are not produced with destructive objectives.[137]

Based on the Canadian proposed definition for space weapons, this study suggests the following definition for the active military use of outer space of a destructive nature as:

> … every use of a space object that was designed or modified specifically for the purpose of inflicting permanent physical damage on any other object through the projection of mass or energy.[138]

Some authors,[139] as well as the position of the United States,[140] differentiate between offensive and defensive space weapons. This, however, runs into the argument that the offensive or defensive use is a matter of the underlying strategy rather than objective capability. With a view to the question of the permissibility of military uses of outer space, such a distinction is not helpful as every weapon can be used defensively or offensively.[141]

2.1.3 CURRENT AND ENVISAGED MILITARY SPACE ACTIVITIES

2.1.3.1 Current military uses of outer space

Outer space has been used militarily since the beginning of the space age. According to the Stockholm International Peace Research Institute during the 1970s, more than 60% of all satellite launched in outer space served full or partial military purposes.[142] Today, the proportion is nearly 70%.[143] These military uses were generally known at the time of the negotiations for the Outer Space Treaty. However, although some states were already at this stage favouring a complete ban on all military uses of space by satellites with military functions or with dual-use capabilities, not a single state has formally objected to the launching of military satellites into outer space.[144] It is therefore generally accepted that the international community recognized the legality of using satellites in outer space for military purposes.[145] The original position of the Soviet Union,[146] that the use of satellites for reconnaissance purposes was illegal espionage under international law, was a temporary exception. The Soviet Union gave up its position publicly when it recognized the use of so-called "national technical means" for verification,[147] which both sides agreed to mean reconnaissance-satellites in the bilateral SALT I and ABM Treaty of 1972.

The limited ABM and ASAT systems developed in the 1960s and 1970s by both space powers in accordance with the ABM Treaty did not contain space-based components.[148] These systems included the anti-missile rockets tested and temporarily deployed (land-based) by the United States,[149] the air-based ASAT system[150] as well as the ABM system with nuclear warheads around Moscow.[151] In the 1960s both sides temporarily entertained plans to use space weapon systems in two ways: as an "orbital bombardment system", which would be deployed in orbit; and as a "fractional orbital bombardment system", which would be deployed only at the beginning of a conflict and detonated in the target area before completing a full orbit.[152] Only the latter type of system was temporarily put in service by the Soviet Union without implying a permanent deployment of weapons in space, and it was soon given up.[153]

As to be expected in an arms race, the views differ as to which side made the first step in the development of a new weapons system.[154] The Soviet Union began testing a land-based ASAT system in 1968 but declared in 1983 a unilateral moratorium on such tests.[155] Its compliance with the moratorium was, however, contested by the United States.[156] At the beginning of the 1980s, the Soviet Union was believed to possess two land-based lasers at its missile centre in Sary-Shagan that did not have space based components, but did have the capability to damage satellites in orbit.[157]

2.1.3.2 The testing and development of space weapons

The former Soviet Union and today's Russia, the United States and probably also China maintain long-standing basic research programmes for lasers and particle beams that could be developed in futuristic weapon systems. The Directive on Space Policy of the US Department of Defense of 9 July 1999 stated that the military objective of the US Armed Forces in outer space is to enable:

> … combat and combat support operations to ensure freedom of action in space for the United States and its allies … including negation of space systems and services used for purposes hostile to U.S. national security interests.[158]

As instruments of such possible future operations, two new kinds of weapon systems are primarily envisaged in addition to the upgrading of the space-based sensor satellites being tested and partially already developed.[159] As ASAT or BMD systems, they could be used against targets in space, but also, depending on the construction and specific modifications, against targets on Earth.[160]

Spaced-based lasers are considered to be possible weapons for both ASAT and BMD systems, and more recently thought of in terms of supporting conventional warfare on Earth.[161] The advantage of space-based lasers lies in the fact that they are not subject to distortions caused by gravity or by the Earth's atmosphere.[162]

There is a distinction between short- and long-wave lasers. Chemical long-wave lasers must be deployed in space due to their radiation characteristics. Short-wave lasers (excimer and free-electron lasers) need to be based on land, as they currently require large-scale energy supply systems. X-ray lasers, a particular class of short-wave lasers, have a special significance in that they are nuclear powered.[163] Directed lasers would hit enemy targets at the speed of light with energy sufficient to destroy enemy missiles and warheads or to cause satellites to become dysfunctional.

In 1981, the US Lawrence Livermore National Laboratory, under the direction of the father of the hydrogen bomb and staunch SDI supporter, Edward Teller, tested an X-ray laser with an underground nuclear explosion.[164] The US high-energy laser programme is currently pursuing the development of a powerful chemical laser in the framework of the Alpha project.[165] In addition, within the Large Optics Demonstration Program large revolving crystal mirrors are developed which should be able to direct laser beams from land or space-based laser stations onto target.[166] Several field tests undertaken for this purpose with the participation of a US spacecraft have yielded first results.[167]

A second type of directed-energy weapon is the so-called "particle beam canon". In contrast to laser weapons, the target is not destroyed from the outside (i.e., "hard-kill") but rather from the inside (i.e., "soft-kill") through high-energy atomic particle beams that overheat the insides of the target.[168]

A further type of particle beam weapons is the so-called "*radio-frequency weapons*", which would be directed against the electronic infrastructure of the adversary and would be deployed in geosynchronous orbit. Their state, however, is still too experimental for the development of a weapon system.[169] The concept of radio-frequency weapons requires the use of large-scale antennae able to direct the frequency beam onto target either in space or on Earth. Since antennas of 100 metres in diameter would be necessary for this type of weapon, an alternative variant is the use of "virtual structures" where hundreds of mini-satellites in formation would act together.[170] The chances of successfully developing such systems are viewed, however, to be small in the foreseeable future.[171] Their singular potential as weapons against the electronic platforms of the enemy makes them nevertheless an attractive option in military theory.[172]

Kinetic energy weapons (impact weapons) consist of interceptor missiles fuelled by chemical reactions or of a multitude of smaller projectiles propelled by electromagnetic canons. Their destructive effect is achieved through direct collision with the target. In the form of interceptor missiles, they must be deployed in such a way that they can reach the target in space. Classic ABM interceptor missiles have been developed for extraterrestrial launches in the framework of "Homing In Overlay Experiments" whereby attacking warheads are intercepted (homing in) during their flight above the atmosphere (overlay) and destroyed by the kinetic energy caused by the impact of the interceptor projectile. At a successful test in June 1985 a missile, for the first time, was effectively intercepted by another missile: a Minuteman-1 missile was intercepted by a modified Minuteman-1-HOE missile.[173] The enormous speed of space flight objects (7-8 km per second for a satellite in near-Earth orbit) poses a tremendous challenge for kinetic weapons.[174] In outer space kinetic energy weapons derive their destructive power from the speed of their target and the force of the resulting collision. Used against targets on Earth, the destructive impact would have to be obtained from the speed of the kinetic projectile itself. Mini projectiles can be accelerated to an extreme speed by the electromagnetic canon ("rail gun") deployed in space—up to more than 20 km per second.

A considerable disadvantage of kinetic energy weapons is that a very large number of them are most likely needed to destroy a single target. In the framework of SDI, there were plans to deploy hundreds or even thousands of self-targeting interceptor missiles in space.[175] Later, under the Global Protection Against Limited Strikes (GPALS), which succeeded SDI, work on kinetic energy weapons continued under the rubric of "brilliant pebbles", especially in view of the still considerable technological challenges presented by laser weapons.[176]

Recently the United States[177] has been reconsidering the option of equipping interceptor missiles with nuclear warheads, as the tests carried out with weapons relying on kinetc energy or conventional warheads have shown too many difficulties due to the numerous possible effective counter-measures (i.e., decoys).[178]

The use of *sensor satellites* plays an important role in the NMD plans of the former William Clinton and the current G.W. Bush Administrations. According to official US statements up until mid-2000, sensor satellites were the only space-based components of US deployment plans.[179] For this purpose the development and upgrading of existing satellites with the most modern sensor and infrared technology is planned.[180] The space-based sensor satellites would be equipped with highly sensitive infrared sensors and laser acquisition and pointing systems for early recognition, friend-foe identification and targeting.[181] They would orbit the Earth in a geostationary position and remain permanently active in order to recognize enemy intercontinental ballistic missile (ICBM) launches ideally without delay. Reaction time plays a decisive role in defending against a missile attack, in particular in the boost phase, due to the quick travel time of modern ICBMs.

2.2 AT THE THRESHOLD OF THE WEAPONIZATION OF OUTER SPACE

2.2.1 MAHAN'S HERITAGE

There is considerable temptation to establish military power in outer space including through the deployment of space weapons and the maintenance of armed space forces.[182] According to Wulf von Kries, outer space offers a truly unlimited area of operation allowing for a worldwide presence. From outer space, any point on Earth can be attacked at any time. Due to the absence of the atmosphere and very limited gravity, the manoeuvrability of weapons is multiplied.[183]

Ronald Humble emphasizes the dominance of military forces in the near-Earth orbit over their counterparts on Earth:

1 the greater immediate expenditure of work ... required of Earth-based forces to attack space-based forces; and 2 ... the inherent advantages

that the space environment affords, such as "look-down shoot-down" capabilities, unlimited interior lines of movement, superior lines of communications to similarly situated forces and greater manoeuvrability because of lesser immediate work requirements.[184]

It is not surprising that this temptation has become increasingly important in the military thinking of both space powers. Proponents of space weaponization have begun to attack the "space sanctuary" concept,[185] which seeks to keep outer space free of any active military uses of a destructive nature and was the dominant doctrine in the United States at the beginning of the space age. At the beginning of the 1980s and again more forcefully at the end of the 1990s, the US "high ground" doctrine,[186] according to which the near-Earth space should be controlled in line with the military axiom that he who controls the high ground also dominates the areas below, gained momentum.[187]

Next to eliminating international legal restrictions such as the ABM Treaty and the Outer Space Treaty in particular, the proponents of space weaponization consider overcoming the "space sanctuary illusion" as the most important step on the "road to weapons in space".[188] Based on the premise that future superiority in space will be a decisive factor for the success of military operations on Earth, the US Space Command presented a "Long-Range Plan" consisting of a comprehensive military strategy for outer space until 2020.[189] The plan, providing for the deployment of weapons in space, pursues four strategic objectives: space control; defensive counterspace; offensive counterspace; and force application. These objectives run in parallel with the Pentagon's endeavours to designate the necessary need for space weapons according to capabilities, as opposed to primarily in function of a threat analysis. In this vein, Joan John-Freese from the US Air Force University in Colorado states:

> The simple, yet compelling argument for space control capabilities, including ASATs, is that capabilities-based planning, rather than threat-based planning, dictates development of space control, including ASAT, technologies. The May 1997 Quadrennial Defense Review (QDR) implied that it was desired capabilities that would drive the future forces, based on threat, risk, and opportunities assessments.[190]

The director of the French *Fondation pour la recherche stratégique*, François Heisbourg, compares the new US military space ambitions with the British Royal Navy's endeavour to control the oceans in the 19th century.[191] The same parallel is also drawn in the US Space Command's strategy report "Vision for 2020".[192] This comparison explains the strong interest of the American proponents of a space power theory[193] in the theorist of American sea power at the end of the 19th century, Alfred T. Mahan,[194] who stressed the link between the control over the oceans and the establishment and maintenance of worldwide commercial interests of the US with the challenge "...to drive the enemy's flag from the sea ... by controlling the great common".[195] In a similar way, today's space power proponents in the US Space Command and the Pentagon see the control and military dominance of space as a guarantee of universal US commercial interests in outer space.[196] Space power is no longer viewed exclusively as a military interest, but rather is understood as a far-reaching political strategy to define "new vital interests in space".[197] In this regard, the "Vision for 2020" states:

> Space forces will emerge to protect military and commercial national interests and investments in the space medium ... the US may evolve into the guardian of space commerce.[198]

2.2.2 Soviet programmes and their potential maintenance by Russia

According to Western estimates, the Soviet Union developed the capability to deploy weapons in space early in the space age.[199] Nonetheless, the Soviet leadership continuously denied any intentions to develop, and even more so to deploy space weapons.[200] When Moscow declared a unilateral moratorium on the testing of ASAT weapons at the United Nations, aimed at strengthening its diplomatic offensive for multilateral restrictions of the US SDI plans in 1983, US estimates suggested that the Soviet Union did have such an operable system. Furthermore, it was believed that the ABM system deployed by Moscow under the ABM Treaty could also be upgraded for ASAT functions.[201] The US Department of Defense assumed in its report covering "Soviet Military Power" in 1983 that "a Soviet non-nuclear, orbital antisatellite system has been repeatedly refined and tested attacking low-altitude satellite targets under various circumstances."[202] According to this so-called "co-orbital system", conventional missiles would launch offensive, or killer satellites, into space to approach enemy satellites in orbit and then destroy them. However, the system was considered to be technologically weak, not flexible and inferior to the US air-based ASAT system.[203] Stephan Welck[204] makes the argument that Moscow stopped its testing after it announced its moratorium in mid-1983, simply because it saw no purpose in pursuing this technologically inefficient system.[205]

In the same way, according to Humble,[206] the actually deployed land-based ABM systems around Moscow were, despite several modernizations,[207] generally regarded as "modest" by technical standards. It was, however, assumed that Moscow was able to develop ABM systems of the third or fourth generation that would also include advanced space-based components.[208] Concerning BMD technology, Sayre Stevens saw the Soviet Union in 1984 as being ten years behind the United States and gave this as the main reason why Moscow wanted to preserve the ABM Treaty under all circumstances, as "the Soviet Union continues to fear the consequences of turning U.S. technology loose...".[209] On the other hand, according to Stevens, "an entirely different possibility is that a U.S. initiative might trigger a Soviet deployment response."[210]

The Soviet Union was ascribed a leading role, however, in some areas of the development of so-called "exotic technologies" such as laser or particle beam weapons. Thus, Moscow refused to agree to the original US proposal of the ABM Treaty that expressly included futuristic technologies. The refusal, however, fuelled US suspicions that the Soviet military-industrial complex would want to keep all options open in this regard.[211] Premier Mikhail Gorbachev admitted in an interview for the US television channel NBC on 2 December 1987 that the Soviet Union was conducting research in the same areas covered by the US SDI programme, but that they did not have any intention to develop or deploy a comparable system.[212] Given the emphasis of the Soviet and later of Russian space policy on manned space flight, it cannot be excluded that manned Russian space stations would be equipped with space-based laser ASAT systems. Hung Nguyen assumes that Russia could continue or even speed up the large-scale development of exotic technology and in particular for space-based ASAT and BMD systems.[213]

The various capabilities in the development of space weapons compounded by the uncertainties concerning a possible future Russian reaction to US space plans, and the considerable tradition in Soviet and now Russian research and development programmes for space weapons including futuristic technologies, could lead to large-scale Russian armament in space depending on the political environment given the lack of clear multilateral restrictions on the military use of outer space as a response to a US decision to pursue NMD.

2.2.3   THE SDI SPEECH OF US PRESIDENT RONALD REAGAN

The opinion in military circles of the necessity for the United States to achieve "space superiority" gained ground in official US space and military policy with President Reagan's SDI speech on 23 March 1983, in which he raised for the first time the development of space-based weapons as a deliberate military strategy for outer space. The new SDI plans for comprehensive missile defence were based expressly on a concept of active defence structures in space including the deployment of specific space weapons.[214] The current plans of Washington for a comprehensive space-based NMD are a continuation of these concepts. President Reagan's plan for a national defence in space against missile attacks on the US territory was driven by the hope of achieving the invulnerability of "fortress America" to overcome the dependence of the United States on MAD.[215] Guided by a deep-rooted mistrust of Soviet intentions, the Reagan Administration wanted to break free under all circumstances from this nuclear corset that was ultimately based on Soviet behaviour. As a result, great hope was put in the development of futuristic space weapons such as laser and particle beams as well as kinetic systems.[216] However, prior to a deployment in space, further logistic technologies were needed, which were also largely at an early stage of development.[217] In particular the scope of the envisaged logistical capacities for the maintenance of the space systems (which included installing nuclear reactors in space for servicing energy-intensive lasers) were a telling indicator of the extent of the weaponization of space planned within the framework of SDI.

For scientists as well as military strategists in the Pentagon, it soon became clear that even assuming rapid testing successes, SDI plans for a nationwide defence supported by futuristic weapons would not be feasible. Consequently, it appeared that it would be technically impossible to fulfil Reagan's dream "to make nuclear weapons impotent and obsolete".[218] In a spectacular joint article published in the journal *Foreign Affairs* in 1982, the prominent critics of SDI, McGeorge Bundy, George F. Kennan, Robert S. McNamara and Gerard Smith, warned that defensive systems in space would have serious disadvantages for the security of not only the space powers themselves but also for mankind as a whole:

> Sharing the gravest reservations about this undertaking [SDI], and believing that unless it is radically constrained during the next four years it will bring *vast new costs and dangers* to our country and *to mankind*, we think it urgent to offer an assessment of the nature and hazards of this initiative, to call for the closest vigilance by Congress and the public, and even to invite the victorious President to reconsider [emphasis added].[219]

The overwhelming assessment of SDI in the arms control and military-strategic literature both in the US and in Europe was negative.[220]

2.2.4 NEW DIRECTIONS OF SDI AT THE BEGINNING OF THE 1990S

A number of severe technical setbacks in the testing of SDI systems as well as the loss of personal presidential support for the programme at the end of the Reagan presidency and increasingly stringent budgetary limitations, led to a decline in the political backing and budgetary support for SDI projects in the second half of the 1980s.[221] The year 1991 represents a turning point towards a reinvigoration of the programme—albeit with a modified and particularly more limited objective. The Gulf War against Iraq in 1991 contributed decisively in two ways to this end. First, the allied military campaign "Desert Storm" was the first war to be largely determined by US military space capabilities.[222] In a manner hitherto unknown, US military satellites directed the entire ground operations. For the first time, satellite data on a large scale was directly available to ground commanders and was being used for tactical operations.[223] Furthermore, missile defence was conducted outside the laboratory in a real military operation with the successful use of Patriot missiles against Iraqi SCUDs. Both results stimulated SDI proponents to reinvigorate their plans for a functioning missile defence system. Second, following the demise of the Soviet Union, there was the argument for the necessity of ballistic missile defence against "accidental, inadvertent or unauthorized launches from the republics of the former USSR". The decisive factor for the reinvigoration of SDI, and in particular its new orientation, was the Iraqi use of missiles against coalition countries which demonstrated the eventual ability of Third World countries to develop long-range missiles that might be armed with nuclear warheads, and hence the threat of the proliferation of missile technology as such.[224] In light of the remarkable progress in ABM technology evident from the successful Patriot missile defence, President George Bush Sr. announced in his State of the

Union address of 29 January 1991 his decision, "that the SDI programme be refocused on providing protection from limited strikes." This GPALS system would continue to include space-based components, namely "brilliant pebbles" as missiles interceptors, in numbers of 700 to 1,000 deployed in near-Earth orbit at 200 to 400 km.[225] In addition, "brilliant eyes" (smaller satellites with a weight not exceeding 450 kg equipped with infrared sensors and x-ray lasers) would be deployed 700 to 1,000 km above the Earth.[226]

This limited objective demonstrated a strategic turnaround. The goal was no longer Reagan's dream of the nationwide missile defence. Rather, the new objective was the defence against a possible "Third World missile strike".[227] This limited objective did not, however, stop Republican SDI proponents to use the new "atmosphere" in favour of BMD to try to scrap the limitations of the ABM Treaty. Senator John Warner proposed the draft for a Missile Defense Act in March 1991, which provided for the immediate renunciation of the ABM Treaty in order to allow for the deployment of land- and space-based BMD components. The US Senate rejected this frontal attack on the Treaty.[228] In a compromise negotiated by the Chairman of the Senate Armed Services Committee, Democrat Sam Nunn, and adopted by Congress on 31 July 1991,[229] the President was asked to lead negotiations with Russia on a consensual amendment of the Treaty to allow the deployment of land-based BMD components as well as of space-based sensors. The annual budget allotted to the SDI programme was raised from US$ 2.9 billion in 1991 to US$ 4.5 billion in 1992.[230]

With the Democrats, who are traditionally more open to arms control in a multilateral context, coming to power and with the Clinton Administration putting a greater emphasis on a partnership with Russia after the end of the Cold War, plans for a national missile defence and the development of space weapons were temporarily put on the back burner.

2.2.5 A LIMITED NMD SYSTEM AND THE SECOND CLINTON ADMINISTRATION

Following the Gulf War and after the end of the Cold War, the new threat analysis, which identified the increasing risk of attacks with nuclear missiles by so-called "rogue states", was greatly sharpened by the first successful test of a three-stage rocket by North Korea (Taepo Dong I) on 31 August 1998. This gave added credibility in the US to the perceived risk of a possible future ballistic missile attack by North Korea.[231] It also led the Clinton Administration, which was otherwise generally critical of ballistic missile defence, to agree to BMD legislation that had been demanded by the Republican majority in Congress for years.[232] In September 1999, Congress adopted the "National Missile Defense Act" providing for the deployment of a limited BMD system. The law stipulates in particular:

> ... to deploy as soon as is technologically possible an effective National Missile Defense system capable of defending the territory of the United States against limited ballistic missile attack (whether accidental, unauthorized, or deliberate).[233]

The limited missile defence system was intended to reach its "initial operating capability" originally by 2003 and now by 2005 and be fully completed by 2011. The system rests on the principle of intercepting attacking ICBMs during their mid-course phase in outer space.[234] As such, attacking warheads from intercontinental missiles are to be hit by interceptors, namely exoatmospheric kill vehicles, above the atmosphere after they have been released from their launchers. The following system components are planned:

- *Ground-based interceptor missiles with exoatmospheric kill interceptors*, of which 100 are to be deployed by 2007 at a launch site in Alaska and an additional 100-150 at a second launch site in North Dakota beginning in 2010.
- *Space-based sensors*: A new generation of early warning satellites, namely space-based infrared systems, are to be equipped with infrared sensors which register the heat of ignited warheads. The satellites are to be equipped with "interceptor missiles with accurate mid-course guidance and target discrimination information along their entire flight trajectories".[235] Soon four such satellites should be operable in the geostationary orbit and by 2010 another twenty-four satellites in near-Earth orbit are to be added.
- *Land-based radar installations*: By the end of the last construction phase, nine early warning radar stations that follow the trajectory of attacking missiles should be operational worldwide. The five currently existing large X-band ballistic missile early warning radars in the United States (Alaska, California and Massachusetts), Great Britain (Fylingdales) and Greenland (Thule) are being upgraded for this purpose, a measure that was prohibited under the ABM Treaty. In

keeping with this timetable, the construction started in Alaska in summer 2002, which was seen as the main reason for the timing of the denunciation of the ABM Treaty (with its six month withdrawal period) by President G.W. Bush on 12 December 2001.

- *Command and control*: A missile defence battle management and command, control and communications system shall be established at the North American Aerospace Defence headquarters in Colorado to collect all data of the radar installations and of the space-based sensors.

President Clinton emphasized in his explanation of the draft bill that this did not constitute a final decision on the deployment, which would depend in part on an agreement with Russia about the necessary amendment of the ABM Treaty.[236] As further steps in the development of the space-based systems were possible without affecting the ABM Treaty, Clinton consequently decided in September 2000 to delay the limited system's deployment. According to Clinton, more time would be necessary to consult with Russia, China and the European allies. In addition, while Clinton believed that the test results at the time justified the continuation of the programme, there was not a sufficient basis for a deployment decision concerning the feasibility of the systems[237] and thus the decision on deployment would thus have to be reserved for his successor.[238] President Clinton considered a very limited system to be sufficient to defend against possible Third World aggressors, which he no longer labelled "rogue states", but rather "states of concern". This corresponded to the general scientific consensus that regional theatre missile defence (TMD) systems would be the most reasonable alternative to counter threats posed by the possible future nuclear countries with ICBM ambitions such as North Korea, Iran and Iraq. Further, TMD systems would not lead to a new arms race because such a limited system could be erected without the deployment of weapons in space.[239]

2.2.6 THE RENEWAL AND POSSIBLE EXTENSION OF THE NMD PLANS

With the election of George W. Bush as President of the United States, it is unlikely that arms control considerations will restrict the development of ambitious missile defence plans as the denunciation of the ABM Treaty on 12 December 2001 demonstrates. The Republican G.W. Bush spoke in favour of the earliest possible deployment of a comprehensive missile defence system during his election campaign, whose security positions were heavily influenced by the Heritage Foundation.[240] In a speech before the National Defense University on 1 May 2001, he set out the underlying strategic concept for overcoming nuclear terror through a new concept of deterrence based on offensive and defensive systems.[241] Defense Secretary Rumsfeld supported the far-reaching plans of the US Space Command in the Commission he chaired with the objective of laying the foundation for US dominance in outer space. BMD proponent Keith Payne correctly assumes that:

> ... the United States appears finally to be moving toward the deployment of a ballistic missile defense (BMD) system. It will consist of interceptor missiles and sensors designed to protect all fifty states from a small long-range ballistic missile attack.[242]

Thus, G.W. Bush decided as a first step to accelerate the development programme that had been delayed by Clinton, with the objective of an early deployment. The infrastructure foreseen in this programme is flexible enough to allow for a rapid extension of the limited system towards a comprehensive missile defence system. President G.W. Bush seems to keep all options open for a multi-layered defence system that would include, in addition to boost-phase and terminal defence, mid-course interception.[243] This is also recommended in the US Space Command's "Long-Range Plan",[244] which favours a comprehensive missile defence system to be operational worldwide. Steven Miller assumes that in terms of "Bush's more enthusiastic and rapid approach, aimed at the eventual deployment of *layered* defences, including sea-, air- and *space-based components* that are incompatible with the [ABM] treaty"[245] [emphasis added], NMD plans will be extended to include space-based systems. In addition to extending the development of the limited anti-missile system with exoatmospheric kill vehicles interceptors initiated under President Clinton, the G.W. Bush Administration is also speeding up the development of futuristic space weapons. In 2000, the Pentagon commissioned the development of a so-called "space-based laser readiness demonstrator". The US Air Force assumes that in the next twenty years:

> ... new technologies will allow the fielding of space-based weapons of devastating effectiveness to be used to deliver energy and mass as force projection in tactical and strategic conflict ...[246]

The technical basis for NMD, however, continues to be considered a nearly insurmountable obstacle. Given these technical obstacles, the former director of the Pentagon Operational Tests and Evaluation Department, Assistant Secretary of Defense Philip Coyle, concludes that by 2008 the Administration will, despite its far-reaching plans and the considerable increase in funding, only be able to deploy a limited, land-based system against short-range missiles.[247]

The NMD plans of the G.W. Bush Administration are thus not fuelled by concrete test successes, but rather by strategic ambitions as laid down in the final report of the Rumsfeld II Commission.[248] This report and the statements by members of the US Space Command,[249] calling themselves "star warriors",[250] as well as its "Long-Range Plan", leave no doubt of the US interest in achieving unilateral dominance of outer space.

The reinforced development of exotic technologies for ASAT and space laser weapons is buttressed by new strategic plans of the US military, in particular of the US Space Command under its former director and now head of the Joint Chiefs of Staff, General Richard B. Myers, which have become official US defence policy under President G.W. Bush. They aim at achieving "space superiority" for the US "to control outer space". The US Space Command considers the timing for such a historic opportunity to be right as the US does not expect "to face a global military peer competitor" in the next twenty years.[251] The new US military strategic concept was developed under then Chairman of the Joint Chiefs of Staff, General John Shaliskashvili, and published in 1996 as the "Joint Vision 2010".[252] It expressly articulates the objective of "full spectrum dominance" based in particular on full "space superiority". The US Space Command defines the "control of space" necessary for this purpose as:

> ... the ability to assure access to space, freedom of operations within the space medium, and an ability to deny to others the use of space, if required.[253]

The increasing emphasis of US military strategy on space-based systems and power components stems mainly from two developments.[254] The first is the intensified focus of US strategy on the use of the US technological advantage that reinforces the already strong US military dominance. A decisive militarily lead in command, control and intelligence requires full "information superiority" that relies on the use of military satellites. This in turn leads to a complete dependence of military capabilities on satellite-based functions. This introduces the second element, as from this dependence comes an increased vulnerability of all military capabilities making the protection of satellites against attacks from Earth or from space by "killer satellites", indispensable. Thus, as noted in the report of the Rumsfeld Commission,[255] the increased dependence of the military strategy on space-based information capabilities results in a nearly absolute need for protection of these space components.[256] The report states that outer space will be included in future conflicts with "virtual certainty".[257] From this hypothesis the report explicitly claims the right for the United States to deploy weapons in space for the defence of the vulnerable US space capabilities. According to the Rumsfeld Commission, the President should thus have "the option to deploy weapons in space to deter threats, and if necessary, to defend against attacks on U.S. interests".[258]

Handberg arrives at the conclusion that the plans of the US Space Command represent "an equivalent to a space arms race" and that "space control presumes a very proactive, even aggressive, posture regarding who and what is allowed to access and operate in outer space".[259] The Democratic Senator from South Dakota, Tom Daschle, expressed the negative repercussions of the US Space Command's space plans in an interview on 8 May 2001 with the *Christian Science Monitor*:

> It would be a disaster for us to put weapons into space of any kind under any circumstances. It only invites other countries to do the same thing.[260]

2.2.7 TOWARDS SOVEREIGNTY IN SPACE?

The "Long-Range Plan" of the US Space Command also contains general statements on the future legal rules governing outer space. In the context of elaborating the "policies, treaties and agreements" that are considered necessary, the report recommends shaping the "international community to accept space-based weapons to defend against threats in accordance with national policy". The authors rightly assume that currently the international community does not accept the use of outer space for space weapons. Given the status of outer space according to the Outer Space Treaty as a common area beyond national jurisdiction, and whose international legal foundation was shaped decisively by US initiatives in

COPUOS at the beginning of the space age,[261] the recommendation "to address goals for space sovereignty" and "to establish international space sovereignty policy" in a "Space Faring Nations Treaty", which is supposed to guarantee the "protection of national (commercial) space assets" must be viewed as a complete shift away from not only the original US space policy of peaceful use of outer space, but also from the existent recognition of outer space as a common area free of state sovereignty under international law.

The abolition of the sovereignty-free status of outer space would, however, only be possible with the consent of the states parties to the Outer Space Treaty or by the hardly imaginable creation of new customary international law that extends state sovereignty into outer space. However unrealistic, such changes in the international legal status of outer space would in fact be necessary if the military plans for "space superiority" or sovereignty over outer space were to proceed. Such an objective for unilateral dominance of space through the deployment of space weapons would contradict the mankind clause of the Outer Space Treaty and its obligation to use outer space in the interest of all states, and would also run counter to the prohibition of its occupation in Art. III of the Outer Space Treaty.[262]

2.2.8 THE ATTITUDES OF EUROPE, CANADA AND JAPAN

The European attitude to US missile defence plans was from the beginning, notwithstanding nuances and changes in emphasis due to the change of governments, marked by the desire to avoid a unilateral approach both inside the alliance and internationally, particularly in relation to the Soviet Union/Russia and China. A constant in all European statements has been the necessity for a cooperative approach in any NMD decision so as to exclude any potential negative side effects on international arms control and regional stability. In a speech before the North Atlantic Assembly in Stuttgart on 20 May 1985, the former German Chancellor, Helmut Kohl, underlined that a cooperative solution with the Soviet Union would be necessary in the spirit of the ABM Treaty as well as in order to achieve the desired strengthening of strategic stability.[263] The British Foreign Secretary, Sir Geoffrey Howe,[264] reported in his speech on 15 March 1985 before the Royal United Services Institute in London, that Prime Minister Margaret Thatcher and President Reagan had agreed on these cooperative principles to approach SDI decisions.[265]

Although Great Britain,[266] Germany,[267] Italy[268] and Israel[269] concluded confidential government-to-government agreements with the United States in 1985–1986 regarding the participation of their companies in the SDI programme, the participation related exclusively to the research stage. The former German Chancellor Kohl explicitly stated in the German Bundestag that this did not infer consent to possible future deployment decisions.[270]

At the Geneva-based CD, the Europeans presented a series of specific proposals on the multilateral treatment of the issue, submitting as well additional concrete draft treaties for the prohibition of space weapons including space-based BMD systems.[271] The Europeans warned against the unilateral reinterpretation of the ABM Treaty by the Reagan Administration.[272] Nevertheless, the conclusion of the bilateral government agreements on SDI was viewed in both the United States and Europe as a certain political support for the programme[273] and was, therefore, strongly criticized by US SDI opponents as well as by the social-democratic opposition in Germany.[274] Wanting to prevent BMD from jeopardizing its independent nuclear deterrent, France refused to conclude any government agreement on SDI.[275]

Both Japan[276] and Canada refused to participate in SDI as well as in the International Space Station should it be in any way linked to the SDI programme. When offered to participate in SDI on 7 September 1985, the Canadian Prime Minister Brian Mulroney declared:

> Canada has concluded that Canada's own priorities and policies do not warrant a government-to-government effort in support of SDI research.[277]

Denmark, Norway, Greece and Australia also explicitly rejected official government participation in or support of SDI.[278]

Because of a possible use of the International Space Station for SDI purposes, the Europeans insisted that there be an explicit confirmation of the principle of the peaceful use of outer space at the conclusion of the National Aeronautics and Space Administration (NASA)-European Space Agency (ESA) Agreement on 29 September 1988.[279] The negative outlook of the Europeans towards the plans of a strategic missile defence became evident in 1991 when in the framework of the limited GPALS project the

Bush Sr. Administration put forward a concrete deployment plan. Not only France, but also Great Britain and Germany rejected the offer by President Bush Sr. to agree to government participation.[280]

In the current NMD discussions of the G.W. Bush Administration, the Europeans, sharing the doubts of prominent US critics,[281] strongly re-emphasize the necessity of a cooperative approach to prevent negative international effects, and they further withhold a decision on their support as being premature.[282] German Foreign Minister Joseph Fischer laid down the following criteria for a European response to NMD:[283]

• An effective treaty-based arms control and disarmament regime must be preserved and extended, including efficient and verifiable non-proliferation;
• Russia and China must be included in a cooperative approach to prevent a global or regional arms race;
• The plans for an eventual missile defence must be linked to drastic reductions in offensive systems;
• There must be close and intensive consultations with allies and partners in Europe.

The European comments on the unilateral denunciation of the ABM Treaty by US President G.W. Bush in December 2001, which regretted or even openly criticized the denunciation, stressed again the necessity of a cooperative approach. On 13 December 2001 the spokesman of the German Foreign Ministry declared that "it remains the primary political task of the international community to strengthen the international arms control and disarmament regime".[284] The French Foreign Ministry issued a formal declaration underlining the necessity to guarantee strategic stability in a global context "beyond Russian-American bilateral relations" through "binding international rules and instruments, both bilateral and multilateral".[285]

Thus, the European, Japanese and Canadian reactions represent an essential element of state practice that calls for a multilateral, cooperative approach to the NMD issue deemed necessary to prevent decisions made concerning NMD from having a negative effect on the international arms control and non-proliferation regimes. These reactions thus reinforce the international community's interest in preventing an arms race in outer space.

2.2.9 CHINA'S MILITARY SPACE PROGRAMME AND FURTHER POTENTIAL MILITARY SPACE POWERS

China plays a decisive role in the NMD issue and in the prevention of an arms race in outer space.[286] On the one hand, China maintains its own broad programme of passive military uses and, according to Western assessments, also of the capability to develop active military uses, should the general weaponization of space not be halted. In the area of laser weapons, China has, according to a report to the US Senate, already undertaken relevant activities towards the development of ASAT systems.[287] On the other hand, Beijing sees its own nuclear strategy of "minimal deterrence" as severely affected by a NMD deployment, and claims this to be Washington's true objective.[288] The undermining of Chinese missile capabilities would also affect its position in relation to Taiwan. Beijing's military space ambitions were heightened in January 1999 when Taiwan launched, with American support, its first satellite in orbit and further by the fact that it is also considering participating in the US NMD system.[289]

Taken on its own, China's space policy is already sufficient proof that the question of a shift to active military use of space is no longer an issue between the US and Russia alone. Currently, the US is conducting more intensive talks with Beijing over NMD and the entire complex of missile defence and the military use of outer space at the CD in Geneva than it is with Moscow.

China's own space programme falls in no way behind the ambitions of the space programmes of the US and Russia. From early on, China was using its robust launch capabilities for passive military purposes in space via satellites both in near-Earth and geostationary orbit. It has the full panoply of passive military satellites in the areas of communication, remote sensing, early warning, geodesy and meteorology. Beijing is believed to have already begun a laser programme in 1986, with the support of the Soviet Union, and to have reinforced these efforts after the Gulf War and again after the war in the former Yugoslavia.[290] According to a US Senate report, China is also assumed to possess the technologies necessary for electromagnetic weapons for ASAT purposes.[291] In the late 1990s, Nathalie Hoffmann and Brian Harvey concurred that China could successfully launch a manned space flight in the course of the next ten years, and could subsequently construct its own manned space station complete with a vast array of military uses.[292]

Hoffmann considers the possibility that given Beijing's own space capabilities, China could give up its resistance to the weaponization of space depending on its perception of the international political environment. She therefore poses the question, *"dispose-t-elle de suffisamment d'atouts pour se lancer dans la course?"*.[293] The answer would probably not be a timid one for the leadership of a country "... familiar with taking big steps...".[294]

In Asia, both India and Pakistan are, at the very least, potential military space powers. Each has, at the latest with their nuclear tests in 1998, challenged China's claim to be the only official nuclear-weapon power in Asia, and are both working on programmes to develop medium-range missiles with a range of more than 3,000 km.[295] Due to the dual-use potential of communication and remote sensing satellites, since the beginning of the 1990s, India possesses military space capabilities which could be used for data collection and early warning about Pakistani or Chinese troop movements.[296]

The Indian Space Research Organization is also engaged in strategic and defence research. On 25 January 2002 and again on 10 January 2003 India successfully tested a two-stage solid fuel rocket with a range of 700-800 km, which could be used for the transport of nuclear warheads as well as for putting observation and reconnaissance satellites of a weight of up to 900 kg into orbit. There is a close link between the Indian nuclear capability and India's space and missile programme, which is aimed at the achievement of ICBM capability.[297]

Pakistan, which has missiles with ranges in excess of 1,000 km, is supported by China and Saudi Arabia in its comparable efforts to achieve ICBM capability. It possesses two-stage space rockets that are capable of putting lighter satellites into near-Earth orbit. It is further engaged in the development of remote sensing and communication satellite technologies.[298]

Israel, Saudi-Arabia, Iran (and formerly Iraq) possess medium-range missiles with a range of over 1,000 km. Israel possesses two-stage space rockets, called Jericho III and Shavet, as well as a space launch site at the military base Palmachim south of Tel-Aviv,[299] while Iraq under Saddam Hussein had developed before the Gulf War a three-stage space rocket named Al-Abed.

Like the United States and Russia, the Western European states and Japan have the most developed space capabilities. However, they continue to adhere strictly to the policy laid down in the ESA Statute and Japanese space legislation,[300] namely to use outer space exclusively for peaceful purposes and allowing only for passive military uses. Their exclusively peaceful space policy would be the first victim of a trend towards a weaponization of space.

This survey of the current and potential military space users demonstrates that even the military domain is no longer *de facto* reserved for the actions of the two space powers. The repercussions of the drift towards active military uses of space for international security, stability, arms control and disarmament could be universal. The danger of several other states participating in such an active militarization of space multiplies the urgency for finding a multilateral solution to the issue. H. Kuskuvelis assumes that the two leading space powers want to restore their hegemonic duopoly through the development of futuristic space weapons.[301] However, given the potential of other states, this lead would be possible only temporarily.

2.3   CONCLUSIONS

The current military uses of outer space by satellites are of a passive nature and there are presently no weapons deployed in outer space.[302] The existing ABM systems are land-based and are only capable of so-called "terminal defence", that is of attacking warheads upon their re-entry into the atmosphere. The ASAT systems developed until the early 1980s were land-based, and are now thought to be inactive.[303] By contrast, the envisaged future deployment of laser and particle beams, as well as of kinetic weapons in outer space, either in an ASAT or BMD mode, would constitute an active military use of a destructive nature of outer space.

The distinction between passive and active military space use represents a clear and definable threshold up to which point the international community was, and continues to be, willing to accept military uses of outer space. As such, at the beginning of the 1980s when active and destructive military uses in the common space became a possibility, the international community immediately voiced serious reservations and upheld its claim that an arms race in outer space must be prevented. At that time, only exclusively non-destructive uses of outer space existed.[304] That some of the non-aligned states additionally wanted to prohibit passive military uses of space through satellites, because they viewed these as capable of extending the arms race into outer space, indicates how strong the objections of the international community were to any military use of the common space.[305] Therefore, it is inadmissible to claim that the current tolerance of the merely passive military uses of outer space implies that the international community would be prepared to accept active military uses of a destructive nature. This holds true also for the acceptance of current testing programmes, given that the reaction of other states is not clear-cut even though these tests have not yet been made with the announced intent to lead to actual deployment of space-based systems.[306]

Nevertheless, the tests undertaken successfully under Clinton's limited "mid-course NMD" were linked to a concrete timetable leading to a deployment in the foreseeable future.[307] The plans also provided for the deployment of space-based components in the form of interceptors of so-called "brilliant pebbles" and of sensor satellites. However, the Clinton Administration reaffirmed that the tests would be undertaken in conformity with the ABM Treaty, which was stricter than the Outer Space Treaty over the deployment of space-based systems. As is evident today, these tests were not close to yielding mature systems, and therefore the international community rightly assumed there was no imminent threat of transgressing the threshold of active military uses of a destructive nature in outer space.

As for current or envisaged tests of the (as of now officially limited) NMD system planned by the G.W. Bush Administration, these are carried out in parallel with continuing deployment. However, the Bush Administration has yet to state precisely whether the eventual system will include space-based destructive components. Rather, the US delegation still declared to the CD in August 2000 that NMD would not include space-based components, with the exception of sensor satellites for early warning.[308] Although the differing statements of the current US Administration no longer exclude the possibility of a future deployment of destructive space-based components, it must be noted that the international community's acceptance of the tests does not mean that it has acquiesced to active military uses of outer space in the future. This is evidenced by how the international community has reacted to the unilateral denunciation of the ABM Treaty. United Nations Secretary-General Kofi Annan expressed on 14 December 2001 his deep concerns that the annulment of this Treaty may provoke an arms race, especially in the missile area, and further undermine disarmament and non-proliferation regimes. He called as well upon all states to explore new binding and irreversible initiatives to avert such unwelcome effects.[309] Although the currently limited BMD system does not, to date, include interceptors in space, the possibility is no longer excluded and could come at any time with the extension of the system. The space-based components are currently restricted to sensors, which alone cannot be regarded as an active military use of a destructive nature. In the overall architecture, however, one can speak of a destructive system at the point where, even though the interceptors would still be based on land, the deployment of sensors and the interception of the attacking warhead would take place in space. Thus, in a "layered NMD" system with "mid-course defence" a space deployment of sensors would have to be qualified as an active military use of outer space in as much the interception would take place in outer space.

Overall, while the threshold of active military uses of outer space has not yet been transgressed, such a qualitatively new step is possible in the near future when taking into overall consideration the US development programmes of space weapons, the former Soviet and now Russian research and development programmes of space weapons technologies, and the military space capabilities of China and several other potential military space powers. As "history and logic suggest technology will broaden, not end, the arms race",[310] it is urgent to check these technological developments of space weapons through the setting up of a multilateral regime to guarantee the peaceful use of outer space.

CHAPTER 3

MULTILATERAL NEGOTIATIONS
TO PREVENT AN ARMS RACE IN OUTER SPACE

The international community not only objects to active military uses of outer space of a destructive nature but it also puts forward a claim against the space powers to prevent the extension of the arms race into outer space.[311] The military use of outer space and its repercussions for international security are a multilateral concern to be viewed in light of the common interest clause of Art. 1 of the Outer Space Treaty. The substantive as well as procedural linking of the multilateral disarmament topics dealt with at the CD further demonstrates the impact active military uses of outer space would have on the entire nuclear arms control and non-proliferation process. The close link between the common interest clause, the prohibition to interfere with international security according to Art. III of the Outer Space Treaty, and the reaffirmation of the disarmament obligation of the nuclear-weapon powers by the "Advisory Opinion on the Legality of the Threat or Use of Nuclear Weapons" of the ICJ, underline the necessity to corroborate the structural and procedural ways to secure the peaceful use of outer space in the interest of mankind as a whole.

3.1 MULTILATERAL NEGOTIATIONS
AT THE UNITED NATIONS

3.1.1 SPECIAL SESSION ON DISARMAMENT, THE CD AND THE COMMITTEE ON THE PEACEFUL USE OF OUTER SPACE

Following the sobering results of the first United Nations Disarmament Decade 1969-1978, at its 10th Special Session in 1978 (the first to be devoted to disarmament questions) the United Nations General Assembly referred explicitly to the danger of an arms race in outer space, and called upon all states to undertake multilateral negotiations on the prevention of an arms race in space in accordance with the Outer Space Treaty.[312] At the same time, by adopting comprehensive action programmes and institutional provisions, it attempted to introduce concrete steps to improve the multilateral arms control process. It decided to set up a multilateral negotiation forum called the Committee on Disarmament, consisting of the five nuclear-weapon states and initially 35 additional states.[313] In 1984, this was transformed into the Conference on Disarmament with a current membership of 66 states.[314] The CD remains the "single multilateral disarmament negotiating forum" of the international community.[315]

One year after the adoption of the Outer Space Treaty, Italy was the first country to propose a Special Protocol on the prevention of an arms race in outer space. Italy additionally requested in the preparatory committee for the Tenth Special Session on 1 February 1978, "further measures to prevent the extension of the arms race into outer space",[316] and submitted to the CD on 26 March 1979 a memorandum and a draft additional protocol to the Outer Space Treaty, which provided for the prohibition of all measures "of a military or hostile nature" in outer space.[317]

In COPUOS the deployment of weapons in space was also viewed with great concern. During the Committee's opening session in 1978, the Chairman, Austrian Ambassador Peter Jankowitsch, called upon members to make a substantial contribution to prevent the extension of military uses of outer space.[318] He repeated this appeal a year later by calling for the start of negotiations over "meaningful space arms control agreements".[319] In 1980 several states proposed that COPUOS deal with the question of the increasing militarization of outer space, and that the mandate of the Committee be enlarged accordingly.[320] After the first and only bilateral US-Soviet negotiations on a ban on ASAT weapons in outer space had been interrupted without any result,[321] Italy and Sweden favoured, "the early examination of measures to prevent an arms race in outer space".[322] Italy presented a new draft of an additional protocol to the Outer Space Treaty that aimed, in the words of the Italian Director of the International Institute of Space Law, Pompeo Magno, "to eliminate any omissions and doubts as to the interpretation [of the Outer Space Treaty] that the military use of space is not as yet internationally prohibited."[323] Several non-aligned states thought the time had come to develop a legal ban on the deployment of space weapons of any kind.[324] However, the United States rejected any discussion of the armament issue in COPUOS arguing that these issues ought to be treated exclusively within the disarmament fora.[325] In this light, in 1981 the Swedish Ambassador to the CD, explicitly referring to the

CHOM status of outer space, called upon the CD to put the issue of the maintenance of the peaceful uses of outer space on its agenda.[326]

3.1.2 PREVENTION OF AN ARMS RACE IN OUTER SPACE AND UNISPACE II

The 1980s began with a complete stoppage of bilateral US-Soviet arms control negotiations. The Soviet Union therefore called upon the United Nations in August 1981 to put the question of an international agreement on banning space weapons on the agenda of the General Assembly.[327] As a reaction to the demand, Italy on behalf of the Western states introduced for the first time a draft resolution entitled "Prevention of an Arms Race in Outer Space".[328] In view of the fact that both of the main space powers were beginning the development of space-based anti-satellite weapons, the draft resolution called upon the Disarmament Committee "to consider as a matter of priority the question of negotiating effective and verifiable agreements aimed at preventing an arms race in outer space", and in particular a verifiable agreement "to prohibit anti-satellite systems".[329] The Western initiators of the draft explicitly considered ASAT weapons as having "destabilizing effects on international peace and security".

The draft resolution submitted by Mongolia on behalf of the Socialist Group proposed to conduct these negotiations on the basis of the Soviet draft treaty.[330] The United Nations General Assembly adopted both resolutions without a negative vote and with only one abstention.[331] In clearer terms than ever before, the General Assembly, calling upon all states "... to prevent an arms race in outer space ... and to prevent outer space from becoming an area of military confrontation ...", expressed in these resolutions its position that such a use of outer space would be "contrary to the spirit of the [Outer Space] Treaty..." [emphasis added].[332]

In the following year, UNISPACE II, originally devoted exclusively to the issue of scientific exploration of space, expressed deep concern over the extension of the arms race into outer space in its final document.[333] Although the question was not on the agenda of the conference, the great majority of the more than 100 participating states demanded that the issue be dealt with. In the words of the Director of the Office for Outer Space Affairs of the United Nations and Secretary of the Conference, Nandasiri Jasentuliyana, the developing countries were no longer willing to leave the question of the militarization and weaponization of space to the two super powers alone.[334] Controversial discussions ensued as to how precisely an international legal ban on certain military measures, and particularly a ban on the deployment of weapons in space, should be drafted. United Nations Secretary-General Perez de Cuellar expressed the concern of the great majority of states and of the international community as a whole about the extension of the arms race into outer space.[335]

Following an extensive deliberation over the distinction between passive and active military uses of outer space, the non-aligned states additionally called for an explicit condemnation of active military uses of outer space, referring expressly to the status of outer space as CHOM.[336] In their view, this status required prohibiting the extension of the arms race to outer space, which would be a threat to all mankind.[337] In the final resolution, UNISPACE II unanimously agreed on a general appeal to all states on the "prevention of an arms race and hostilities in outer space", and called upon both the CD and COPUOS to consider this issue as a matter of priority.[338] In view of Soviet ASAT tests and US SDI preparations conducted in the course of 1982 and 1983, nearly all states grew increasingly concerned about the spread of the arms race into space. In 1983, the issue was also raised in COPUOS.[339] Several delegations (Mexico, Venezuela, Nigeria, and the Philippines, among others) proposed under Brazil's leadership that COPUOS take a primary interest in the issue.[340] The Soviet Union, with the support of the Socialist Group, made efforts to negotiate a treaty on a weapons ban in COPUOS. As a basis for the Committee's competence, as well as for the content of such an agreement, the Soviet delegation invoked the Outer Space Treaty that had been negotiated in this same body. In addition, it expressed the concern that at the CD "the subject would take a back seat to other urgent and perennial questions that have long been under consideration there."[341] The United States and the Western Group, however, strictly opposed addressing this issue in COPUOS and referred it to the CD in Geneva.[342]

3.2   MILITARY USES OF SPACE AND THE CD

3.2.1   MANDATE AND METHODS OF WORK OF THE CD

The CD was a result of the first Special Session on Disarmament of the United Nations General Assembly held in 1978.[343] While enjoying greater independence than other committees established by the General Assembly, it reports to the General Assembly and must take its recommendations into account. Structurally, the CD follows the traditional groupings of states at the United Nations, with the group of Western states, including three nuclear-weapon states—the United States, France and Great Britain, playing a special role. The non-aligned states forming the Group of 21 include the nuclear-weapon state China and two de facto nuclear powers, Pakistan and India. Egypt, Sri Lanka and Mexico are particularly active players within the Group of 21. The group of Socialist countries became virtually obsolete following the demise of the Soviet Union and the Warsaw Pact. The Chemical Weapons Convention (CWC), the Comprehensive Test Ban Treaty (CTBT) and the Convention on the Prohibition of the Development, Production and Stockpiling of Bacteriological and Toxin Weapons (BTWC) stand out as the most important successes of the CD.

The substantive work of the CD is done mainly in ad hoc committees on priority issues.[344] Before setting up an ad hoc committee, the Chairman can also nominate special coordinators to gauge the preparedness of the members and the possible mandate for establishing an ad hoc committee on specific subjects. The agenda and the mandate of the ad hoc committees are renewed annually, which raises the risk of blockage given that all-important questions are decided by consensus. The major agenda issues in the past years have been the general and complete nuclear disarmament; the beginning of negotiations on a prohibition of the production of fissile material, the so-called Fissile Material Cut-off Treaty (FMCT), or "Cut-off Treaty"; security guarantees for non-nuclear-weapon states; and since 1982 discussions on the prevention of an arms race in outer space (PAROS).[345] The main priority for most Western states is the FMCT; for China, Russia, and France it is PAROS; and for the Group of 21 it is nuclear disarmament, PAROS and security guarantees. China and Pakistan in particular object strongly to a FMCT unless it includes existing nuclear stockpiles.

The main problem with the approach of the CD since 1990 has been the need to agree annually to a "comprehensive and balanced work programme", which, due to continuing obstructive linkage among the issues, has resulted in a total blockage of negotiations on the substance.

3.2.2 AD HOC COMMITTEE OF THE CD ON PAROS, 1985-1994

3.2.2.1 Background

Since 1981, the United Nations General Assembly annually reaffirms in a separate resolution on the agenda topic "Prevention of an Arms Race in Outer Space",[346] its call to undertake in the framework of the United Nations the necessary steps for the prevention of an arms race in outer space. These resolutions are not simply vague political appeals, but rather represent concrete claims of the international community addressed in particular to the space powers, to immediately start the necessary negotiations to conclude one or more agreements on the issue. To legitimize this claim, the General Assembly refers to the mankind clause and the principle of the peaceful use of outer space in Art. I, para. 1 of the Outer Space Treaty. The resolution "reaffirms the will *of all States* that outer space shall be used exclusively for peaceful purposes" and declares the General Assembly to be "gravely concerned at the danger posed *to all mankind* by an arms race in outer space" [my emphasis].[347] To implement the recommendations of UNISPACE II, and emphasizing the "express wishes of the overwhelming majority of the members of the Committee on Disarmament", the United Nations General Assembly urged in resolution 37/83 of 9 December 1982 that a special multilateral working group of the CD on PAROS be set up "without delay".[348] Resolution 37/99 D introduced by the Western states calls for the examination of such negotiations.

At the CD, China,[349] with the support of several Western states,[350] proposed in 1983 the setting up of an ad hoc committee with a concrete negotiating mandate. France submitted a draft treaty with the title "Prevention of an Arms Race in Outer Space", complemented in 1984 by a working paper.[351] In 1983 and 1984 the appeal by the General Assembly became more pressing thus expressing the growing concern of the international community about the still lacking consensus of such a working group.[352] Referring explicitly to the CHOM status of outer space, India, Egypt[353] and Brazil,[354] as well as a number of other Latin American states,[355] condemned the plans of an active military use of outer space as a "flagrant violation" of the Outer Space Treaty and called for the urgent negotiating of an agreement to ban space weapons.

In 1984, India, as Chairman of the Group of 77 in COPUOS and later also at the CD, called for a moratorium on the testing of space weapons.[356] In the same year the United Nations General Assembly also called upon COPUOS to address the issue as a matter of priority.[357] The Western states voted against the proposal, and for the first time in its more than 20 years of existence, COPUOS adopted a report without consensus.[358] At the end of 1984, the Committee returned to the principle of consensus in the adoption and transmission of its final report to the General Assembly, finding a compromise on a less specific phrase, "that the Committee should consider ways and means for maintaining outer space for peaceful purposes".[359] Also in 1984, the General Assembly made an explicit link between the arms issue in outer space and general and complete disarmament. It stated without a single vote against (one abstention) that the disarmament obligation in Art. VI of the NPT applies also to outer space.[360] This demonstrates the view of the international community that a weaponization of outer space should be prevented since by its very nature any deployment of weapons in space would contravene the disarmament obligation.

An agreement on the establishment at the CD of an ad hoc working group on arms control in outer space was, however, only possible after the United States and the Soviet Union compromised at the beginning of 1985 to start negotiations on the whole range of nuclear arms control issues. This compromise was due, on the one hand, to the coming to power of Premier Gorbachev in the Soviet Union and his interest in détente, and on the other hand, to the strong resistance in the US Congress against President Reagan's SDI plans. In 1984, the US Congress adopted the "Tsongas Amendment to the Defense Authorization Bill",[361] which refused the President the right to test ASAT weapons against objects in outer space until the Administration could testify that it had conducted serious negotiations on a verifiable prohibition on anti-satellite weapons. In addition, the US Senate Foreign Relations Committee required the President:

> ... to seek, on an urgent basis, a comprehensive verifiable treaty prohibiting the testing, production, deployment and use of any space-based or space-directed weapon system.[362]

Even after the long-awaited US agreement to set up an Ad Hoc Committee on PAROS at the CD, three years after the announcement of SDI, negotiations on the issue of arms in space did not begin. The United

States was only ready to accept a non-committal mandate for the working group to conduct "talks" about possible questions for future negotiations.[363]

3.2.2.2 The attitude of the Europeans

Among the Europeans, France soon reacted to the two powers' intentions to develop space-based defence systems, and made several proposals at the CD on the prevention of an arms race in space, stressing particularly a ban on new space-based weapons.[364] The former legal adviser of the French Foreign Ministry, Gilbert Guillaume, explicitly called the questions of arms control in outer space a matter "of concern to the entire international community".[365] In view of the concern over the negative repercussions of the SDI plans for international security,[366] and underlining the "inadequacy of [existing] international instruments", the French government proposed the following four main elements:

1. A strict prohibition of all kinds of ASAT systems;
2. Prohibition of the testing and the deployment of land-, air- or space-based directed-energy weapon systems;
3. Strengthening of the registration obligation under the Convention on the Registration of Objects Launched into Outer Space (in short known as the Registration Convention) of 1974;
4. A general obligation to respect the immunity of certain satellites.

France put a special emphasis on verification that should be conducted preferably through the international satellite control agency that France had proposed in 1978. Military uses of outer space should be restricted to passive uses, which would, through reconnaissance and early warning satellites, be used for verification and in the interest of maintaining international stability and security.

Even though these proposals were clearly motivated to safeguard French strategic interests to prevent a possible degradation of its own nuclear capabilities through missile defence systems in outer space, its legal justification was explicitly based on the interest of the international community in the prevention of a new arms race in outer space.[367] France was, in the words of then Prime Minister Laurent Fabius, interested in the achievement of "Star Peace" as opposed to "Star Wars".[368] In the same sense, the Italian and Swedish proposals of 1979 and 1982 were aimed at prohibiting measures "of a military or hostile nature" in the whole of outer space.[369]

These draft treaty initiatives, which were supported by other Western European states,[370] show that the participation of some European countries in the SDI programme was not aimed at a deployment of space weapons. Rather, their objective was, as was explicitly emphasized by Germany and Great Britain,[371] to gain some influence over the programme through technological participation to prevent possible antagonism with the Soviet Union that could lead to a subsequent arms race in space. In this regard, resolution 36/97 C of 9 December 1981, introduced by the Western European states, stressed that:

> ... further effective measures to prevent an arms race in outer space should be adopted by the international community.[372]

3.2.2.3 Development of the Soviet position and the current Russian attitude

Like the United States, the Soviet Union had, in the 1970s, refrained from any multilateral effort to prohibit the development or future deployment of space weapons. Rather, without admitting this publicly, it began its own development of space weapons, particularly ASAT weapons. At the beginning of the 1980s the Soviet Union shifted its policy,[373] proposing in the framework of the United Nations a multilateral treaty banning space weapons. It submitted for the first time in 1981 a draft for such ,[374] which it expanded in 1983, in reaction to the US announcement of the far-reaching SDI plans. The draft included provisions prohibiting the testing of space-based systems.[375] In parallel, it declared Soviet readiness, as long as the United States would do the same, to renounce unilaterally any deployment of ASAT weapons.[376] In the following year, it added to this a draft resolution "Use of Outer Space Exclusively for Peaceful Purposes for the Benefit of Mankind" and proposed to declare the prohibition of an extension of the arms race into outer space a "mandatory norm of state policy" and "a generally recognised international obligation".[377] During an interview with an American journalist in June 1984, Premier Konstantin Chernenko declared that such a moratorium on the deployment of ASAT weapons in outer space could be verified effectively with national means of the parties.[378] A further step undertaken by the Soviet Union to strengthen the multilateral approach to the prevention of an arms race in outer space was the proposal, submitted by Foreign Minister Eduard Schevardnadze in 1985 to the United Nations General Assembly, to set up an International Space Authority for the purpose of implementing and verifying the arms control regulations of such an agreement.[379]

This shift in the official Soviet position with regard to arms control in outer space also led to a change of position in the Soviet international law literature. In the 1970s, the original Soviet space law theory, according to which the principle of the peaceful use of outer space did not permit military activity, evolved with the growing military use of reconnaissance satellites, finally declaring such uses as admissible.[380] With the shift towards emphasizing the need for a multilateral arms control process at the beginning of the 1980s the prevailing view became once again that military uses of outer space are legally restricted.[381] Several authors referred to the mankind clause to argue that from the legal principles of the Outer Space Treaty stemmed a ban on the deployment of new weapons systems, and in addition with regard to other military uses, the obligation to preserve a "complete exclusion of space from the sphere of military activities".[382] However, while Soviet authors claimed that the Soviet Union was adhering without fault since 1958 to a ban on military uses of outer space,[383] this runs counter to the comprehensive military space programmes actually pursued by Moscow, which at least over some time did include the development of space weapons.

In August 1993 the Duma adopted the "Law of the Russian Federation on Space Activities",[384] which corresponds to the international obligations to prevent an arms race in outer space, partly even going further than existing international rules.[385] Since an amendment on 4 October 1996, the national law includes among the principal objectives the "maintenance of international security" on the basis of "the generally accepted principles and norms of international law", also allowing for private commercial space activities in order to enhance closer cooperation with the United States in the peaceful use of outer space.[386]

3.2.2.4 Ad Hoc Committee on PAROS, 1985-1994

The work of the Ad Hoc Committee on PAROS in the CD was from its inception marked by a rift between the great majority of members to start concrete negotiations on a ban on space weapons on the one hand, and the refusal of the United States to enter into such negotiations on the other.

Thus, the work was soon bogged down by intermittent procedural questions about the content of a mandate for possible negotiations. To overcome the procedural standstill, a number of Western states such as Canada, France, Germany and Italy put forward proposals intended to advance the questions of definition with regard to a future agreement on space weapons, and to enact confidence-building measures, which should at a later stage lead to a consensus on a ban on space weapons.[387] These proposals contained concrete elements of a cooperative security order in outer space, which included not only a ban on space weapons, but also "rules of the road" and immunity rules for civil space satellites.[388]

It was felt overwhelmingly necessary to negotiate a new agreement that would solidify the principle of the peaceful use of outer space with regard to new technological developments in military space uses. In what remains its last report to date, the Ad Hoc Committee sets out its position on whether or not the existing legal regime is sufficient to prevent an arms race in outer space, as follows:

> Reaffirms its recognition, as stated in the report of the Ad Hoc Committee on the Prevention of an Arms Race in Outer Space, that the legal regime applicable to outer space by itself does not guarantee the prevention of an arms race in outer space, that this legal regime plays a significant role in the prevention of an arms race in that environment, that there is a need to consolidate and reinforce that regime and enhance its effectiveness, and that it is important to comply strictly with existing agreements, both bilateral and multilateral.[389]

By contrast, the United States believed that taken together the United Nations Charter, the existing treaties on outer space, the relevant bilateral and multilateral arms control provisions, customary international law and national law are all complementary in a manner such that:

> ... they provided an equitable, practical, balanced and extensive legal system for ensuring the use of outer space for peaceful purposes. ... there was no arms race in outer space, nor was there any indication of significant on-going development by any State with respect to arms in space. Therefore, in their view there was no need for new legally-binding instruments, or a need to revise existing agreements in this respect.[390]

As a result, over the ten years of its existence, the Ad Hoc Committee was not able to agree on a negotiating mandate for confidence-building measures in outer space, and less so to a ban on space weapons. According to the United States, substantive work was to remain purely exploratory. This view could, however, hardly be maintained after ten years of discussions in the Ad Hoc Committee, especially after the "Friend of the Chair" dealing with the outer space issue had already submitted a draft resolution on confidence-building measures,[391] which underlined rather advanced work in the Committee on the subject.

After ten years in existence, the Ad Hoc Committee on PAROS could no longer be extended because the adoption of the agenda item on PAROS, which was renewed annually, failed due to the linkages made by various sides with other topics. In 1995 at the insistence of the United States, the Western Group made a connection between the re-establishment of the Ad Hoc Committee on PAROS and the establishment of an ad hoc committee on other topics, such as transparency in conventional armaments. The link thus concerned a topic without any direct relation to the space issue. Paragraph 18 of the final report of the CD to the United Nations General Assembly, which provided for the re-establishment of the Ad Hoc Committee on PAROS, thus remained in brackets. It read as follows:

> It was agreed that substantive work on all these issues should continue at the next session of the Conference. Therefore, it was recommended that at the beginning of the 1995 session, the Conference on Disarmament re-establish the Ad Hoc Committee on Prevention of an Arms Race in Outer Space with an appropriate mandate, taking into account the work undertaken since 1985.[392]

The report clearly reflects the position of the great majority of members that it is not only urgent to start negotiations on the prevention of an arms race in outer space, but that also sufficient preparatory work had already been done to do so. Nevertheless, as a result of these linkages, no substantial multilateral talks on the question of security in outer space have taken place at the CD since 1995.

3.2.3 COMPLETE STANDSTILL AT THE CD SINCE 1998

3.2.3.1 Since 1998 only procedural negotiations

In the mid-1990s, the subject of space was almost completely neglected at the CD. However, Egypt reaffirmed the demand of the Group of 21 at the plenary meeting on 23 January 1997 for a complete ban on military uses of outer space.[393] Yet, in the following six months the Chairman's efforts to find a compromise for the re-establishment of the Ad Hoc Committee on PAROS failed, due again to the United States, which declared the existing mandate of the Committee to be out of date.[394]

While in 1998 the efforts to set up the Ad Hoc Committee on PAROS were again intensified, the dominant topic at the CD became, however, the proposal put forward by President Clinton to start negotiations on a FMCT for the production of fissile material.[395] This approach, which was of paramount importance for the non-proliferation of nuclear weapons, was rejected by China and the nuclear threshold countries, in particular India and Pakistan, which later linked it to their claim for a strict timetable for nuclear disarmament, a claim that was unacceptable to the nuclear-weapon powers. At the beginning of the plenary session, the Canadian Ambassador to the CD, Mark Moher,[396] proposed the immediate start of negotiations on PAROS, and presented a working paper on a possible mandate. Australia and Russia strongly supported the Canadian proposal,[397] referring to the position of the United Nations General Assembly on the need to renew the mandate on non-weaponization. India and Brazil strongly urged the re-establishment of the Ad Hoc Committee on PAROS with the primary task of negotiating a ban on anti-satellite weapons and an agreement on "rules of the road" for satellites.[398] However, an agreement proved to be impossible yet again. Even the compromise proposal by the Swedish Chairman of the CD to appoint as a first step a special coordinator to undertake informal consultations instead of setting up the PAROS Committee, failed because of the objection raised by the United States.

A number of Western European states, among them Germany, regretted that no agreement could be found on the proposal for a negotiating mandate on PAROS despite the years of discussions that had taken place.[399] China and the United States also undertook, without success, bilateral talks on FMCT on the one hand, and PAROS on the other.

France made another attempt to find a compromise on how to proceed,[400] recommending three priorities for the CD sessions in 1998: FMCT, anti-personnel landmines and PAROS. Again, neither the establishment of an Ad Hoc Committee nor the nomination of a special coordinator could be agreed upon. The negotiations were overshadowed by the Indian nuclear tests at the beginning of May 1998. At the beginning of the second session in 1998, Egyptian Ambassador M. Zahran reiterated the call of the Group of 21 to set up a PAROS Committee.[401] The Group of 21 distributed the final declaration of the "Ministerial Meeting of the Co-ordinating Bureau of the Non-Aligned Movement" of 19 and 20 October 1998 in Columbia, where the non-aligned states, referring explicitly to the ICJ's "Advisory Opinion on the Legality of the Threat or Use of Nuclear Weapons" called on the nuclear-weapon powers to implement their nuclear disarmament obligations. The Group of 21 also confirmed their call to start negotiations on an agreement banning the deployment of weapons in space ("non-weaponization").

Egypt and Iran wanted to deal additionally with other forms of military uses of outer space.[402] Calling the space issue a "priority", France, China and Russia also demanded that the Ad Hoc Committee on PAROS be re-established.[403] China criticized the development of missile defence systems, which would serve only to achieve "absolute strategic superiority and absolute security" for one or a few states.[404] In August 1998, the United States and Russia reported the results of the Moscow summit,[405] where a memorandum about information exchange on early warning of ballistic missile and space rocket launches had been agreed. The United States declared that this memorandum also provided the possibility of creating such an information regime on a multilateral level.[406] Yet, at the CD the US reservations to a negotiating mandate on PAROS grew even stronger, while all other states, including the nuclear-weapon states Russia, France and China, argued in favour of the immediate re-establishment of the Ad Hoc Committee.

In 1999, it was again not possible to agree on a work programme for the CD, leading a large number of delegations to fear the complete impasse of the CD on all topics.[407] Canada submitted a proposal on 4 February 1999 for the re-establishment of the Ad Hoc Committee on PAROS "with the mandate to negotiate a convention for the non-weaponisation of outer space".[408] Increasingly, the United States and China became the main antagonists at the CD. The United States rejected the re-establishment of the Ad Hoc Committee, but declared nevertheless to be confident that it could find a compromise with China on the nomination of a special coordinator on the issue of armaments in space. India and Pakistan, while affirming their readiness to begin FMCT negotiations immediately, did not, however, show eagerness to clear the way. The five nuclear-weapon states, while continuing to resist a true multilateralization of the nuclear disarmament process at the CD, no longer excluded a mandate to discuss the issue. On 26 March 1999, the Chinese President spoke before the CD reaffirming the Chinese call to commence negotiations immediately on the prevention of an arms race in outer space,[409] and for that purpose, submitted a new proposal to re-establish the Ad Hoc Committee on PAROS.[410] In a joint Russian-Chinese statement on the ABM Treaty dated 14 April 1999,[411] Russia and China declared that the US decision on the development of a missile defence system would have negative repercussions for international stability, and could not only fuel a new arms race but also threaten the entire system of international arms control. Russia and China emphasized that this statement was the expression of their common position,[412] and that the preservation of the ABM Treaty was not only a matter for the state parties, but rather a concern of the whole international community. China additionally underlined that a renunciation of the Treaty would have negative effects on the entire work of the CD.[413] In the same session, Pakistan declared the NMD plans to be highly destabilizing.[414] It claimed that the threat by new forms of WMD expressed in the new strategic concept of NATO as a motive of nuclear deterrence was exaggerated, in order to legitimize nuclear weapons. Such a legitimization would contradict the negative security guarantees undertaken by the nuclear-weapon states; the non-nuclear-weapon states inside NATO would, through their participation in NATO's nuclear strategy, base their own security on nuclear weapons as well, while at the same time condemning the nuclear tests undertaken by Pakistan, which would amount to a double standard. In the meantime, the bombardment of the Chinese embassy in Belgrade burdened the negotiations at the CD, making a compromise on its work programme even more difficult. Malaysia submitted on behalf of the Group of 21 a proposal on a programme of work and a "Draft Decision and Mandate for the Establishment of an Ad Hoc Committee on Disarmament",[415] which underlined the urgency of commencing substantive work on the space issue, and of fully respecting the ABM Treaty.

The United States, France and Great Britain submitted a joint proposal on 19 May 1999 for a CD work programme involving "enhanced Troika-consultations" to establish ad hoc committees on FMCT and negative nuclear security arrangements.[416] This proposal contained a new element inasmuch as the committee on FMCT was to remain in place until a treaty was concluded and was thus not to be subjected to an annual renewal as was the case for other ad hoc committees. On agenda item 3 concerning PAROS, it was only proposed to nominate a special coordinator "to seek the views of its Members on the most appropriate way to deal with the questions related to the item". France declared on this point in the plenary meeting that it would have preferred the re-establishment of the Ad Hoc Committee on PAROS.[417]

On 8 June 1999, after extensive informal talks, the Algerian CD Chairman, Mohamed Dembri, submitted a proposal for an Ad Hoc Committee on PAROS under TOP 3.[418] The proposal was acceptable to all delegations, except the United States. The second part of the first session in 1999 ended again without any agreement on a work programme. Canada, Belgium and the Netherlands expressed their concern over the standstill at the CD, and proposed a thematic organization to replace the no longer adequate group structure.[419]

At the beginning of the first session in 2000, China submitted a comprehensive working paper with substantial proposals for an agreement on the prevention of an arms race in outer space.[420] At the same time, it reaffirmed its connection between agreeing to begin negotiations on FMCT and the start of negotiations on space weapons, with the highest priority given to a ban on space weapons and anti-missile systems in particular. In referring to the joint Russian-Chinese declaration of 10 December 1999,[421] the Chinese Ambassador to the CD called for the "common security for all states" instead of "the absolute security enjoyed by a single state at the expense of all others" with regard to the military use of outer space.[422]

After tedious exploratory talks, the new Australian CD Chairman declared on 10 February 2000 that his efforts to reach a consensus on a work programme had failed,[423] suggesting instead the nomination of special coordinators on the basis of the procedural decision of 1990 (CD/1036) on the controversial issues of nuclear disarmament and outer space. Germany declared its concern over the continuing standstill at the CD,[424] while Russia reiterated its interest in giving the highest priority to PAROS.[425]

China claimed that space-based surveillance and interceptor capabilities, an integral part of the development of the NMD and TMD systems, would constitute typical space weapon systems and that until the agreement of a new treaty on the express prohibition of such systems is reached, the development, testing and deployment of space weapons and anti-missile systems should be renounced.[426] Russia supported the Chinese demand to start CD negotiations on banning such systems and their components in outer space, declaring the prevention of an arms race in outer space to be a universal norm that existed independently of the bilateral ABM Treaty.[427]

On 8 March 2000 the US Principal Assistant Deputy Secretary, Frank Miller, made a statement at the CD that the United States would continue to support the long-term objective of a complete elimination of nuclear weapons.[428] A first step and a litmus test would be the agreement to start negotiations on FMCT. After the implementation of further US-Russian nuclear arms reductions, the bilateral and multilateral approaches could eventually converge. Miller distanced himself from the statement of the US Space Command regarding US space plans, as they did not reflect the official US position [of the then Clinton Administration], which was to preserve in principle the ABM Treaty and seek only those modifications required for the admission of a limited NMD system. During the same CD session, Canada, New Zealand and Mexico demanded the renunciation of "linkages" and the negotiation of single issues separately on their own merits.[429] New Zealand additionally circulated a resolution of the New Zealand Parliament of 23 February 2000,[430] calling for the implementation of the conclusions of the "Advisory Opinion on the Legality of the Threat or Use of Nuclear Weapons" of the ICJ.

The efforts to find a compromise on a mandate for an Ad Hoc Committee on PAROS pursued by the new Belgian Chairman in June 2000, and building on the "Dembri proposal" on outer space (while avoiding the notion of "weaponization", which would be unacceptable to the United States) also failed. The United States explained on 31 August 2000 that its NMD would be a purely terrestrial system, using observation satellites only for early warning.[431] The United States declared its readiness to have an exchange of views on the topic, but refused to enter into negotiations at that stage. On 5 September 2000 the US representative referred to President Clinton's decision to preserve the ABM Treaty for the time being, which would leave China without further excuses for its refusal to begin FMCT negotiations.[432] China reacted with the statement that the decision of

President Clinton represented only a delay in deployment, while NMD development and testing continued.[433] Therefore, China would maintain its linkage between FMCT and space weapons negotiations. In the plenary session of September Russia, China and the United States reaffirmed their respective uncompromising and opposing positions on NMD.[434] Russia declared that it would continue to refuse to negotiate an amendment to the ABM Treaty to allow an NMD system, which would run counter to the very objective of the Treaty. Russia also emphasized that the CD should strive for a legally binding international regime, which should prohibit the deployment of "strike weapons" in outer space.

On 29 June 2000 the Chairman of the CD submitted a proposal for a new work programme that included elements on PAROS.[435] On 24 August 2000 the new Chairman, the Brazilian Ambassador Celso Amorim, made a new proposal for a work programme,[436] which, in a manner of compromise, provided for the establishment of ad hoc committees on these controversial topics, but with a clear outline on the precise negotiating mandate. However, the various linkages prevented yet again an agreement on the work programme, thus leaving the Conference in two succeeding years without any actual negotiations. Instead, the respective Chairmen attempted to obtain the agreement of the main representatives of the different state groups on the Amorim proposal. Regrettably, however, no results have been achieved.

At the beginning of 2001, the policy review of the G.W. Bush Administration precluded yet again any progress at the CD. On 15 February 2001 the Chinese Ambassador, referring explicitly to the CHOM status of outer space, demanded urgently to start negotiations on the prevention of an arms race in outer space, and criticized the weapon tests undertaken by the United States in outer space.[437] However, US Ambassador Robert Grey responded that there was no need for such negotiations.[438] The Canadian Chairman, Ambassador Chris Westdal,[439] had to admit another failure in his attempts to reach a breakthrough. As the European Union President, Sweden made a statement on behalf of the European Union in support of the Amorim proposal on a work programme including PAROS.[440] New Zealand and South Africa, speaking on behalf of the Group of 21, urged to pursue all multilateral efforts and to re-engage in real work.[441] The Spanish representative warned that the Conference risked being "marginalized" with serious consequences for the whole multilateral disarmament process. The Russian representative declared that "the speedy elaboration of an international legal regime prohibiting the deployment in outer space of weapons other than weapons of mass destruction, should become one of the principal undertakings of the international community".[442] On 30 May 2001 Russia submitted a draft proposal for the opening of negotiations on nuclear disarmament and PAROS.[443] On 7 June 2001 China tabled a new working paper about a future treaty on the prevention of the "weaponization" of outer space.[444] It contained mainly treaty formalities, while referring to previous Chinese proposals with regard to the issues of the precise definition of space weapons and weapon components and their delineation from other military uses of outer space. China again called for the prevention of an arms race in outer space and warned of the consequences of the denunciation of the ABM Treaty for international security.[445] Ireland and Algeria argued in favour of a prohibition on the deployment of weapons in space at the plenary session of 28 June 2001.[446]

Again, throughout its entire session in 2001 the CD failed to enter into any substantive deliberations. The need for a general review of the working methods of the CD became inevitable. Ireland spoke out in favour of a "responsible multilateralism" with the need to alter the limiting procedural rules dating back to the Cold War, such as the group structure, the membership and the lack of non-governmental organizations' involvement in the work of the Conference.[447] On 22 June 2001, the CD resolved to nominate three special coordinators with the objective to review the negotiation structures and methods in reference to the following topics: the agenda; enlargement of membership; and working methods. Unfortunately the room for manoeuvring in procedural questions is for the time being particularly narrow and thus hopes that this could be a first step towards overcoming the complete stalemate at the CD are bound to be disappointed. There is opposition to altering the consensus principle and even to streamlining the agenda. On 27 June 2002 China and Russia introduced a joint working paper on PAROS, which would ban the deployment of weapons in space, though testing of space weapons and missile defence interceptors would be allowed.[448]

In 2003, 2004 and 2005, despite unrelenting efforts, the CD again failed to achieve any progress to restart substantial work. The Russian Federation did announce at the 2004 session of the United Nations General Assembly's First Committee (on Disarmament and International Security) that it would not be the first to place any weapons in outer space. But this unilateral move has so far not elicited any comparable initiative by other spacefaring powers. Given this record, without a fundamentally new approach to the multilateral negotiations on the preservation of the peaceful use of outer space, it seems hardly possible to make progress towards an agreement on a treaty that safeguards the interest of mankind against the transgression towards active military uses of space.

3.2.3.2 Legal assessment of the standstill at the CD

The statements of the delegations to the CD leave little doubt that with the exception of the United States, all states take the position that concrete multilateral negotiations on the prevention of an arms race in outer space should start without delay. For the overwhelming majority this represents an urgent task. A large number of CD members, in particular China and Russia, have additionally underlined the position that until the conclusion of such an agreement, according to the ABM Treaty and a general rule of international law, no tests or deployments of weapon systems or components are allowed. In doing so China was referring explicitly to the status of outer space as CHOM, as other states had done in the 1980s.[449]

The complete standstill of multilateral negotiations at the CD raises, in light of the statements of the ICJ in its "Advisory Opinion on the Legality of the Threat or Use of Nuclear Weapons", the issue of the legality of the behaviour leading to this state of affairs in view of the severely detrimental effect on the interests of the international community.[450] The ICJ views the obligation in Art. VI of the NPT, to conduct negotiations on general and complete disarmament under strict and effective international control, as "an obligation that goes beyond that of a mere obligation of conduct".[451] Rather, the nuclear-weapon powers have in addition the obligation, "to achieve a precise result—nuclear disarmament in all its aspects—by adopting a particular course of conduct, namely, the pursuit of negotiations on the matter in good faith".[452] This general *dictum* for nuclear disarmament must apply a *fortiori* to the prevention of an arms race in the common space. Complete nuclear disarmament requires the elimination of nuclear weapons together with a regime of non-proliferation. The United Nations General Assembly in its resolution of 12 December 1984 rightly declared Art. VI of the NPT to be applicable to outer space.[453] However, the great majority of states[454] as well as the overwhelming position in the arms control literature assumes[455] that the deployment of weapon systems in outer space would have serious destabilizing effects, and, hence, would fuel both the global and regional nuclear arms race on Earth.

Thus, the US refusal to enter into substantive talks, let alone multilateral negotiations on the prevention of an arms race in outer space, to the discontent of the overwhelming majority of the international community, not only represents a disregard of Art. VI of the NPT, but in fact is producing the opposite effect given the close link between an arms race in outer space and the spiralling of an offensive arms race on Earth. The refusal even to agree to a mandate on "discussions" of the military use of outer space also contravenes the enhanced community obligations under the mankind clause of the Outer Space Treaty. In addition, the mankind clause and the status of outer space as common space are violated by the unilateral deployment of weapons in outer space, when this deployment is viewed by the great majority of the other states, either subjectively and even more so objectively, as detrimental to their security interests. Such a use could not be considered to be "in the interest of all mankind".[456] Given the lack of an agreement to start negotiations on this issue, in its annual resolutions the United Nations General Assembly links its urgent call for the nuclear-weapon powers to forgo any unilateral activities contravening the prevention of an arms race in outer space with the concrete demand to respect all bilateral and multilateral arms control agreements.[457] This makes clear that the General Assembly assumes that under the existing outer space and arms control treaties there is already a duty towards the international community not to engage in unilateral arms deployments in space.

3.2.4 A NEW MULTILATERAL EFFORT

In September 2000 Russia announced at the Millennium Summit in New York that it would convene a conference under the aegis of the United Nations on the peaceful development of outer space in Moscow in April 2001 on the occasion of the 40th anniversary of the first man in space. At the conference, Russian President Vladimir Putin declared: "We must by joint efforts preserve peaceful space. And to do it for ourselves and future generations."[458] Russia again tabled its proposal to negotiate at the CD on space weapons, including the necessary verification and institutional mechanisms.[459] The Moscow Conference was supposed both to discuss steps to prevent an arms race in outer space on the basis of the Russian draft proposals for a prohibition of space weapons, as well as discuss ways of deepening the peaceful cooperation in outer space. Heads of national space agencies as well as representatives from foreign ministries were invited. However, specific results could not be achieved due to the lack of US willingness to enter into substantive space arms talks.[460]

3.2.5 BREAKING THE LINKAGES?

The US-Russian Treaty on Strategic Offensive Reductions signed on 24 May 2002 between President G.W. Bush and President Putin to reduce the number of nuclear warheads to one third of the current stockpiles and over a "Joint Declaration on the New Strategic Partnership", could have been an indication that five years after the "historic"[461] ICJ "Advisory Opinion on the Legality of the Threat or Use of Nuclear Weapons" the leading nuclear-weapon powers would be ready to fulfil their moral and international legal obligation to finally pursue a genuine reduction of nuclear weapons. This would have required, however, that the agreement would lead to the real destruction of warheads and would be complemented by an additional agreement on launchers, which is yet to be achieved. Yet the hope that this bilateral step would help overcome the standstill of multilateral arms control negotiations at the CD was disappointed. Hence, according to Richard Falk, judging from the history of the arms race unfortunately it is still true that the Advisory Opinion would not decisively alter the behaviour of the nuclear-weapon powers.[462] In addition, a compromise between the US and Russia on the space issue has been further complicated by the unilateral denunciation of the ABM Treaty. It remains to be seen whether or not the establishment of the high-level group on nuclear strategy and space issues that was decided at the US-Russian summit, will bear any fruits on the space issue.

It would be an important task of the CD to see to it that in such a compromise the security interests of the international community are fully respected. Yet, for the time being negotiations at the CD, and in particular on a mandate on PAROS, remain completely blocked. Strenuous attempts to break the standstill, made by the Finnish, French and German chairpersons in 2002 remained unsuccessful. The complete standstill is in the final analysis also detrimental to the security interests of the United States and Western Europe given that the Group of 21, in particular China and Pakistan, continue to draw a linkage between the start of negotiations on the prevention of an arms race in outer space and the beginning of negotiations on FMCT. This objection has the direct result that the nuclear non-proliferation regime is also at an impasse, in particular with regard to the nuclear threshold countries, among them precisely those countries from which the greatest risk of a new ballistic-nuclear threat is supposed to emanate.

The complete standstill of the multilateral negotiations in Geneva demonstrates the extent to which the international security interests are damaged by the persistent refusal to enter into negotiations on the prevention of an arms race in outer space or at least to discuss the eventual results of bilateral arms control negotiations in the appropriate multilateral fora.

3.3   MULTILATERAL NEGOTIATIONS ON THE PREVENTION OF AN ARMS RACE IN OUTER SPACE AND THE POSITION OF THE US

Since 1981, the annual resolutions of the United Nations General Assembly regarding outer space and the prevention of an arms race in outer space have repeatedly requested the nuclear-weapon powers to:

- Actively participate in the prevention of an arms race in outer space "with a view to reaching agreement" as well as to restart or speed up parallel bilateral arms control negotiations concerning outer space;
- Refrain from any contrary activities; and
- Constantly keep the international community informed about the progress of the bilateral efforts in the framework of the CD.

In addition, the General Assembly has referred to the incompatibility of unilateral measures with international cooperation in the peaceful use of outer space. In particular, given that "... the legal regime applicable to outer space does not in and of itself guarantee the prevention of an arms race in outer space ...", the General Assembly emphasized the urgent need, "to consolidate and reinforce ... that legal regime and enhance its effectiveness...".[463]

These strong and repeated calls illustrate the international community's position that the space powers are obliged not only to refrain from any activity that could lead to an arms race in outer space, but also to participate actively in the elaboration of appropriate multilateral agreements to prevent such an arms race.[464] The central elements of the resolutions are of a normative character inasmuch as they explicitly refer to the provisions of the Outer Space Treaty, in particular of the mankind clause in Art. I as well as to the obligation to use outer space in the interest of the preservation and strengthening of world peace and international security, as well as of international cooperation and understanding of Art. III of the Treaty.[465] The United States has until today not voted in favour of these resolutions, and has attached an "explanation of vote" to its abstentions.[466] While this declaration emphasizes that the United States does not see any urgent need for measures to prevent an arms race in outer space, it does contain a recognition of the principle of the peaceful use of outer space as well as an implicit recognition of the necessity that, according to Art. III of the Outer Space Treaty, military uses of outer space have to serve world peace and international security. In view of the status of the principle of peaceful use of outer space, in its distinction between passive non-destructive uses and active military uses of outer space with a destructive effect, as customary international law, it is important to note that all military uses of outer space that the United States mentioned in the declaration are of an exclusively passive nature of non-destructive effect. This attitude is also the basis of the resolution adopted by the US Congress in 1983 and reaffirmed several times since then, which provides in its preamble, that "an international agreement to prohibit the introduction of weapons of any kind into space is needed in order to avoid the financial, social and human costs that could result from such an arms race".[467] In Section 1, the resolution instructs the President to negotiate an agreement on a comprehensive prohibition of space weapons including the testing of such weapons.

Thus, the central elements of the General Assembly's annual resolutions and the distinction of the military uses can be regarded as generally accepted, even though different positions persist between the overwhelming majority of the international community and the United States over specific applications. Although due to the legal status of resolutions of the United Nations General Assembly as recommendations that are not legally binding (Art. 10 of the United Nations Charter) eo ipso, legal standards of the peaceful use and the prevention of an arms race of outer space can be developed on the basis of those resolutions combined with other legally relevant activities of the states and the international community.

In this assessment of relevant state practice, one has also to include the positions of states at the CD. All states that have submitted specific treaty proposals on the prohibition of space weapons to the CD are, in addition to pointing to the mankind clause and the principle of the peaceful use of outer space, also making clear that they consider an implementation agreement of such a prohibition to be indispensable.[468] The negotiations at the CD illustrate that the non-space powers do not accept the imminent move towards active military uses of space, but rather favour concluding an agreement on the prevention of an arms race in outer space.[469] At the same time, a number of states make clear that they consider a unilateral transgression of this threshold to be in violation of international law.[470] As a latest example, Sri Lanka declared at the General Assembly on 19 October 2004 that "the annual presentation of the PAROS resolution in the First Committee and the almost universal endorsement of its principles ... has had the salutary effect of according to these objectives the status of customary law."[471]

3.4   STRENGTHENING PEACEFUL COOPERATION IN THE USE OF OUTER SPACE AND UNISPACE III

After the Cold War ended, COPUOS intensified its efforts to put substance into the principle of the peaceful use of outer space; to advance international cooperation in outer space in the field of new space technologies; and to broaden the scope for multilateral programmes such as the use of satellite remote sensing for environmental monitoring purposes and for the benefit of developing countries, including through the voluntary transfer of technology.[472] This was also the main objective of UNISPACE III in June 1999 in Vienna. The Conference was premised on the assumption that in view of the geopolitical shift from confrontation to cooperation, "collective efforts should be made to achieve common objectives of humankind" and to prevent outer space from becoming the arena of national rivalries or conflict.[473]

Thus, the international community pursued its efforts to safeguard the use of outer space for exclusively peaceful purposes in the 1990s more than before through a dual approach. One was the constant and increasing insistence on fulfilling the obligation to negotiate the prevention of an arms race in outer space at the CD, and the other sought to take advantage of the end of the Cold War to enhance international cooperation in space and develop the multilateral mechanisms for this cooperation. For this reason and with a view to pursuing a fruitful distribution of work, a controversial debate over the arms issue was avoided in COPUOS and in UNISPACE III, in contrast to the way this issue was treated during the 1980s. The international community intends to counter the increasing militarization and the threat of arms deployments in space by enlarging cooperation in the civil exploitation and use of outer space in the interest of all states.

3.5 LEGAL CONSEQUENCES OF THE OBJECTION OF THE INTERNATIONAL COMMUNITY TO THE DEPLOYMENT OF SPACE-BASED WEAPONS

The various reactions of the international community, mainly at the CD and the United Nations General Assembly, leave no doubt that the international community does not recognize an "exclusive regulatory competence of the major space powers" over the military use of outer space.[474] The overwhelming majority of United Nations Members have, over a long period of time, manifested their legal position over the inadmissibility of active military uses of outer space in a sufficiently clear and consistent manner. In view of the obligation to mankind on state activities in outer space that is recognized by the space powers, states have the duty to seek prior consent from the international community before engaging in new forms of space use. Thus, the situation with regard to the use of outer space differs from the cases in the jurisdiction of the ICJ,[475] where the lack of formal protests against unilateral actions either entails recognition in the form of "acquiescence" or has, according to the legal principle of *estoppel*, the consequence that the silent state is bound to accept that the other state could assume acceptance in good faith. Because of the special mankind obligation of all uses of the common space and of the unambiguous call of the international community that the space powers refrain from activities that could lead to an arms race in outer space, the eventual lack of formal protests with regard to space weapons tests cannot be construed as an implicit acceptance of the future deployment of active military systems in outer space. Since 1981 the majority of states manifest their legal position in the annual resolutions of the General Assembly that the nuclear-weapon powers are legally obliged to enter into multilateral negotiations on the prevention of an arms race in outer space. "Acquiescence" would require that the states remain completely passive with regard to the emerging plans for active military applications in space. In this regard, the declarations of the great majority of states at the CD and the General Assembly on the prevention of an arms race in outer space prove the contrary. In this light, it cannot be expected from the numerous smaller states that express their principled position on the inadmissibility of armaments in outer space in the annual resolutions of the United Nations

General Assembly, to lodge additional formal protests at each announcement of a test of system components in outer space. A formal protest would be necessary, however, if the testing itself already constituted an illegal act in terms of explicitly leading to a later deployment of the system in outer space. As such, the space powers have so far not made such explicit announcements with regard to the testing of destructive space weapons components.[476]

For these reasons, the strong call of the non-aligned states to put an end to the standstill of negotiations on the prevention of an arms race in outer space is to be viewed as a legal act for safeguarding their rights with regard to planned future active military uses of space. A genuine protest under international law is not required so long as there are only plans and tests for future deployment. In addition, with express reference to the Outer Space Treaty as a legal basis to refrain from any action that could lead to an arms race in outer space, the international community makes its legal position clear that such measures cannot be considered lawful.

CHAPTER 4

CONCLUSIONS

The reactions of the international community since 1978 over the testing and development of space-based weapons manifest the legal claim of the international community, based on the Outer Space Treaty, that the space powers are obliged to participate in the elaboration of an international order to prevent an arms race in outer space. This demand, abundantly justified in peace research and security and arms control literature,[477] can be based in international law on the common status of outer space and the common purpose principle that outer space has to be used in the interest of mankind, inasmuch as it allows to derive a specific legal obligation owed to the international community to prevent an arms race in outer space. The community status of outer space in connection with the rise of the mankind clause in the Outer Space Treaty of 1967, accompanied by an increasing legal understanding of the international community,[478] serves as the starting point for actualizing the principle of the peaceful use of outer space and the obligation to prevent an arms race in outer space, thereby leading to a legal obligation to achieve an agreement on the non-weaponization of outer space. Such an obligation was recognized by the ICJ in its "Advisory Opinion on the Legality of the Threat or Use of Nuclear Weapons" with regard to the common interest in nuclear disarmament, derived from the concrete treaty obligation in Art. VI of the NPT.[479]

PART III

Structural change of international law, the common heritage of mankind principle and common security in outer space

Outer space is the province of all mankind. So says the Outer Space Treaty (1967), adopting the principle that there are areas where common interests must be served and given priority.

J. E. S. Fawcett
1984[480]

The potential for conflict accompanied mankind's advance into outer space. In the cold war atmosphere of the 1950s, unbridled East-West competition threatened to transform a vacuum yet into another arena for the clash of arms, ideology, and national interest. This spectre helped impel nations to seek a common vision of their future relations in a newly accessible environment.

Philip D. O'Neill, Jr
1984[481]

CHAPTER 5

THE CHOM PRINCIPLE IN OUTER SPACE LAW AND ITS REPERCUSSIONS FOR SECURITY IN OUTER SPACE

5.1   GENESIS OF THE CHOM PRINCIPLE IN OUTER SPACE LAW

Even before the first space activities began, the need to create an international regime covering the common interests of mankind in outer space was developed in international law.[482] Thus, in 1952 Oscar Schachter declared outer space to be a:

> ... *common property of all mankind* over which no nation would be permitted to exercise domination". This would "dramatically emphasize *the common heritage of humanity* and ... might serve, perhaps significantly, to strengthen the sense of international community which is so vital to the development of a peaceful and secure world order [emphasis added].[483]

Schachter underlined the need to develop common principles for outer space that would overcome purely national interests for the sake of international security. Based on early European space law literature, Alfredo Cocca, the Argentine space lawyer and later Ambassador to the United Nations, came to the conclusion in his work *Teoria del Derecho Interplanetario* of 1957 that in the framework of a law of mankind (*derecho público de la humanidad*) the international community as a whole would exercise sovereignty over outer space.[484] A year later, at the first colloquium of the newly founded International Institute of Space Law of the International Astronautical Federation, Cocca developed this point by proposing that the Moon should be used by the "international community of nations" and that for this purpose "regulations for the utilization of the Moon for *peaceful purposes*" [emphasis added] should be adopted.[485] In so doing, Cocca was also aiming at the "emergence of mankind as a new subject created by Space Law".[486]

The United Nations General Assembly was heavily influenced by these early community-oriented thoughts regarding the status of outer space. In its most far-reaching and unanimously adopted "Principles Declaration" of 1963, the General Assembly expressed the objective of creating the foundations for the legal order of outer space, and proclaimed as well that outer space should be "used exclusively for peaceful purposes for the benefit and in the interests of all mankind" (para. 1).[487] In this early development of space law, the notion of the "interest of mankind" was from its very inception closely linked to the context of international security, which is exemplified by the General Assembly's emphasis of the "peaceful use" of outer space.[488] The mankind clause was laid down in the "Principles Declaration" and in the Outer Space Treaty adopted on 27 January 1967, which at the same time sealed the internationalization of the common space as an area beyond national jurisdiction.[489] In the same year, Cocca introduced the CHOM principle as a fundamental legal principle governing the status of outer space at the United Nations.[490]

Through the inclusion of the mankind clause, the "Principles Declaration" and the Outer Space Treaty transmit the five core elements of the CHOM principle not only to celestial bodies but also to outer space as a whole:[491]

1. Use in the interest of mankind and of all countries irrespective of their degree of economic or scientific development (mankind clause, Art. I, para. 1 of the Outer Space Treaty; "Principles Declaration", para. 1);
2. Prohibition of national appropriation or occupation (exclusion of sovereignty, Art. II of the Outer Space Treaty; "Principles Declaration", para. 3);
3. Exploration and use exclusively for peaceful purposes (legal principle of the peaceful use, preambular para. 2 and 4 and Art. IV, para. 2, Articles IX and XI of the Outer Space Treaty; "Principles Declaration" preamble and para. 6);
4. Preservation of the common heritage for future generations (principle of environmental protection, Art. IX of the Outer Space Treaty; "Principles Declaration", para. 6);
5. Promotion of international cooperation (Articles IX–XIII of the Outer Space Treaty; "Principles Declaration", preamble and para. 3).

According to Rüdiger Wolfrum,[492] the United States began developing the notion of the "interest of mankind" originally with a clear security-related objective.[493] In addition, it should cover the necessity of cooperation in the exploration and use of outer space, and address a just distribution of the benefits thereof.[494] Wolfrum sees this as the true birth of the notion of CHOM, since it clearly marks the conceptual transition away from the traditional international law of coexistence to a new law of cooperation.[495]

With regard to the future exploitation of the resources on celestial bodies, Argentina presented in 1970 to the Legal Subcommittee of COPUOS a draft for a Moon Treaty covering all celestial bodies, where it proposed having the CHOM principle govern the status of the Moon and all celestial bodies.[496] While the Soviet Union and Bulgaria initially rejected the principle,[497] the United States submitted in 1972 a compromise proposal, which explicitly supported the CHOM principle.[498] In the end, a compromise text prepared by Austria was accepted.[499] The text provided for the application of the CHOM principle in the wording as adopted in Art. 11 of the Moon Treaty.[500] Nevertheless, in the same way as during the negotiations of Chapter IX of the Law of the Sea Convention about the international regime of exploitation of the resources of the seabed and subsoil, the corresponding stipulations in the new Moon Treaty, although more strongly shaped in the interest of the space powers, remained controversial, as evidenced by the fact that most industrialized and developing countries have yet to ratify the Treaty.

The fact that states remain hesitant about ratifying the Moon Treaty due to the open question of the modalities for the future regime of resource exploitation, however, does not justify questioning the validity of the CHOM principle in general. On the contrary, the concept of common heritage, constituting in its essence a sort of a "community presumption in form of a general clause in international law",[501] allows precisely for various ways of fulfilling the common purpose clause in the framework of an international regime of exploitation. Just as the "province of all mankind" clause in Art. I, para. 1 of the Outer Space Treaty is described as a "unifying concept" giving the Treaty "greater cohesion"[502] and tying the structural elements of the Outer Space Treaty together, so the CHOM principle within the Moon Treaty is a key structuring feature that links its main constituent elements in a unifying system.[503] In this vein, most authors already view the regime established by the Outer Space Treaty operational for the whole of outer space,[504] rather than for only the Moon and other celestial bodies. After nine years of negotiations, the compromise on the

Moon Treaty was, despite the open questions on the exploitation regime, an important step in the codification of the CHOM principle in outer space law.

With regard to the principle of the peaceful use of outer space, the Moon Treaty strengthens the stipulation of Art. IV of the Outer Space Treaty, extending the explicit prohibition of the deployment of nuclear weapons and other WMD also to include the orbit around the Moon.[505] The Moon Treaty also reaffirms and specifies the other structural elements that are already embodied in the Outer Space Treaty through the "province of all mankind" clause for the exploration and use of the Moon and other celestial bodies, and thus it consolidates the structural order of the mankind principle in outer space law. Hence, it confirms, as already foreshadowed in the Outer Space Treaty, the structural order of outer space as CHOM, and specifies the CHOM principle with regard to the economic use by explicitly providing for the establishment of an international regime to guarantee the just distribution of its benefits.

5.2   SECURITY ELEMENTS OF THE CHOM PRINCIPLE IN OUTER SPACE LAW

5.2.1 PEACEFUL USE

The principle of the peaceful use of outer space is generally regarded as a constitutive element of the CHOM principle.[506] Further, from the very beginning it has been closely linked to the introduction of the CHOM principle for areas beyond national jurisdiction. With regard to internationalized common areas it was generally held that the enhanced community purpose as expressed in the mankind clause could not be furthered successfully without restricting the area to exclusively peaceful use. This was laid down for the first time in the Antarctic Treaty of 1 December 1959.[507] In fact, the principle of peaceful use formed the starting point of the common purpose clause in outer space law,[508] in particular of the "province of all mankind" clause in Art. I, para. 1 of the Outer Space Treaty.

The use for peaceful purposes is a prerequisite for the fulfilment of the "interest of all mankind", a non-peaceful use could not be considered to be "for the benefit of all mankind and in the interest of all states". In this vein,

Arvid Pardo has introduced the CHOM principle for the deep seabed emphasizing the necessity of its demilitarization and for the idea of a distribution of the benefits of the exploitation of resources.[509] Closely linked to the peaceful purpose principle is Art. III of the Outer Space Treaty, which provides with explicit reference to the United Nations Charter that all activities in outer space should serve "the interest of maintaining world peace and international security as well as the enhancement of international cooperation and understanding". Thus, the Outer Space Treaty puts the use of outer space directly in the framework of the United Nations Charter in the field of common security.[510] The duty to pursue these objectives in the use of outer space stems directly from the enhanced community purpose according to the mankind clause and hence the CHOM principle.

The dissenting opinion of Kernel Baslar,[511] who does not see the principle of the peaceful use as a constituent element of the CHOM principle, rests on his view of it as a "functional" principle, and hence not only applicable to territories. According to Baslar, if one were to relate the CHOM principle to the fish swarms of the high seas, for instance, the direct application of the principle of the peaceful use would indeed be contradictory. However, it would still be possible to apply the peaceful use principle to the area where the fish swarms were exploited since its non-peaceful use would, in the end, hinder their exploitation in the interest of all countries. Less convincing is Baslar's argument that the security-related element of the CHOM principle would be far less important than the "North-South" one, and that it could be omitted with the end of the Cold War.[512] The standstill in the multilateral disarmament negotiations, the continuing proliferation of WMD, and the severe damage to global security that would ensue by the weaponization of space attest, nevertheless, to the contrary. It is relevant to note, however, that Baslar's functional concept does not lead to a divergent outcome concerning the territorial application of the CHOM principle. Baslar recognizes that the necessity for a peaceful use is in fact taken into consideration, if not as a separate element, then at least as it is contained in the framework of the fourth key element of the CHOM principle concerning the obligation towards a "reasonable use" of the area concerned.

Some authors draw from the fact that since there is no consensus in state practice or in the literature on the significance of "peaceful" as the exclusion of any military activity in outer space, the CHOM principle could not be applied to outer space *per se*. As such, it is consequently argued that the usage of the mankind clause is devoid of legal significance.[513] The only partially demilitarized status of outer space would be in contradiction to the claim of the general interest clause in the CHOM principle, which would necessitate purely civil uses. Such a conclusion, however, fails to consider that the application of the CHOM principle to outer space would have for its part repercussions for the interpretation of the principle of the peaceful use of outer space. Thus, the question of whether "military" or only "non-military" uses are admissible has to be assessed according to the mankind clause, which guides the interpretation of the principle of peaceful use. As a result, the benefit for mankind as a whole of the envisaged space use has to be established prior to use. If such a general benefit can be shown beyond doubt even for a particular form of military use, as for instance for reconnaissance satellites used to control the implementation of disarmament agreements, then one can consider even this certain type of military use to be in accordance with the CHOM principle. In short, the fact that outer space is only partially demilitarized does not automatically exclude the peaceful use component of the CHOM principle. As the CHOM principle is applied to all of outer space, it follows that complete demilitarization has to be viewed as an objective for the future order of outer space, and in turn, concrete guidelines and standards can be derived from the CHOM principle.

5.2.2 PRINCIPLES OF COOPERATION, CONSULTATION AND INFORMATION

The principle of cooperation is laid down in several Articles of the Outer Space Treaty as well as the Moon Treaty, and is specified for certain specific areas (Art. I, para. 3; Articles IX, X and XII of the Outer Space Treaty). Rudolf Dolzer speaks of a "structure of cooperation" in the Outer Space Treaty.[514] Article IX of the Outer Space Treaty further provides that states should render mutual assistance in the exploration and use of outer space. This reflects the concept of an obligation of assistance, yet realized in the form of reciprocity. The Outer Space Treaty thus contains an element of active cooperation, thus assuming an obligation to effective implementation.

These general principles and stipulations of cooperation in the two main space treaties are complemented by specific cooperation duties laid down in the specialized space agreements and the resolutions on remote sensing and direct satellite broadcasting, which were adopted by the United Nations in order to implement the Outer Space Treaty. For instance, specific obligations on consultation were provided for direct satellite broadcasting.

According to the general view,[515] outer space law contains stronger cooperation duties than general international law, thus also going beyond the content of the General Assembly's "Declaration on Principles of International Law concerning Friendly Relations and Cooperation among States". This is a concrete result of the mankind clause in the Outer Space Treaty, which lays the basis for, according to Wolfrum,[516] the departure of outer space law "from the traditional *structure of public international law*" [emphasis added] towards giving primary importance to the obligations of cooperation and mutual assistance among states in the use of the common space. According to Carl Christol, the cooperation principle in the Outer Space Treaty cannot be viewed as merely a general appeal for cooperation, but rather "innovative in that it added new *operative requirements for cooperation* ..."[517] [emphasis added]. Walter de Vries emphasizes that the Outer Space Treaty is itself a result of the implementation of the cooperation principle in the United Nations Charter, and that given the enormous costs involved international cooperation in the exploitation and use of the common space represents the only possibility to ensure that all countries partake in the benefits of the use of outer space.[518] The cooperation principle is premised on two ideas that are both closely related to the concept of the mankind clause. On the one hand, most space activities are of high benefit for all mankind. On the other hand, these activities can only be carried out effectively and with least amount of cost through the framework of cooperation of the international community.[519]

Yet, the legal significance of the stipulations for space cooperation is controversial. Some deny its compulsory effect due to the often unspecified character of the stipulations.[520] This disregards, however, the fact that the provisions on cooperation are a direct corollary of the mankind clause of the Outer Space Treaty, thus providing the necessary substantive as well as procedural content. Formally, they are an integral part of the operative provisions in the Agreement, and hence share its legally binding nature.[521] In this context, the International Law Association emphasized that "international co-operation in space is not merely an aspiration or ideal, but rather a legal obligation of a general nature."[522] Unilateral actions that run counter to enhanced cooperation for the benefit of all countries would violate the Treaty.[523] While one may derive an obligation of states parties to take the necessary steps for implementation, given the general nature of the Treaty's provisions for enhanced cooperation, states have a broad discretion over the precise steps of implementation. Thus, the cooperation principle in the Outer Space Treaty is itself not sufficiently concrete to embody the level of community commitment intended by the mankind clause.[524] From the cooperation principle, the director of the International Institute for Space Law, Nandasiri Jasentuliyana,[525] derives the Treaty's objective to create, through specialized agreements, a comprehensive legal framework for an "institutionalized international co-operation" in space. With regard to the CHOM principle, Thomas Franck speaks of a consolidation of the cooperation obligations into a principle of "common heritage equity".[526]

In sum, outer space law has anticipated the structural change of general international law by assigning early on a primary importance to the principle of cooperation, and by additionally specifying it in certain areas. Alfred Verdross and Bruno Simma emphasize that with the enhanced cooperation principle, world orders containing cooperative structures can be achieved.[527] Also with regard to general international law, it is now increasingly recognized that the general cooperation principle has to be complemented by concrete stipulations, and in particular by a necessary "organizational structure", without which the general cooperation principle remains without an operative effect.[528] In the same way as the environmental protection principle in outer space law, cooperation under the Outer Space Treaty needs *de lege ferenda* to be reinforced by a comprehensive space order containing the institutional foundations for cooperation in space activities that would benefit all countries.

5.2.3 COMMON INTEREST AND THE MANKIND CLAUSE

At the core of the CHOM principle is the community clause. It is incorporated in the documents of outer space law as a specific mankind clause ("use in the interest of mankind as a whole"), and is found in all principal resolutions of the United Nations General Assembly in regard to outer space as well as in the main space treaties (Art. I, para. 1 and preambular considerations 1 and 2 of the Outer Space Treaty and Art. 1 of the Moon Treaty).[529] However, some authors raise doubts as to the legally binding character of the clause, given its allegedly vague content.[530] This view is based on the argument that the mankind clause in the Outer Space

Treaty lacks substantive and institutional content.[531] It is argued that only with regard to scientific exploration does there exist a duty in Art. XI of the Outer Space Treaty—being limited to the extent possible—to share the results with the international public. Therefore, the general clause would fail to put effective and binding limits on the principle of the freedom of action of sovereign states as enshrined in Art. II of the Outer Space Treaty. The dominant view, however, rightly rejects this argument as it fails to consider that the mankind clause has, in conjunction with the prohibition of national appropriation of the common space, a status shaping function with regard to outer space being an internationalized common area beyond national jurisdiction.[532] Thus, already the mankind clause is not merely a political goal, but rather a central legal principle of the Outer Space Treaty.[533] At its 54th conference, the International Law Association concluded that while the Outer Space Treaty does not oblige states "to carry out their activities exclusively to the benefit of all countries",[534] the mankind clause enables the common interest to be considered as being a binding limitation on the freedom of states in space that has to be respected at least next to the pursuit of national interests, despite the lack of concrete mechanisms. Furthermore, the clause is directly and concretely expressed in the Outer Space Treaty in further stipulations and principles and thus the Treaty itself reinforces its relevance.[535] Thus, Art. I, para. 1 of the Outer Space Treaty contains in its essence "all the fundamental principles governing the uses of the space environment".[536] An intermediate view contends that the mankind clause is to be applied as a "principle of finality" in the sense of a general guideline for the interpretation and application of all other stipulations of the Outer Space Treaty.[537]

In the first place, the systematic legal interpretation militates in favour of a binding effect of the mankind clause. The specific common purpose clause in outer space law receives its material substance directly from the Outer Space Treaty, even though some of these principles themselves require elaboration.[538] This, however, can be achieved through a systematic, teleological interpretation of the objectives of the Outer Space Treaty as laid down in the preamble by respecting the status of outer space as an internationalized common space beyond national jurisdiction, and by applying the CHOM principle. In particular, the Treaty principles of the peaceful use (Art. I, para. 1); the obligation to promote world peace and international security (Art. III); the cooperation principle (Art. I, para. 3 and Art. XI); the due account of the interests of other states (Art. IX); the principle of environmental protection in the interest of present and future generations (Art. IX, para. 2); and the principle of a just distribution of economic benefits (Art. I, para. 1) are all oriented towards furthering common interest. Mutually reinforcing each other, they form the concrete legal content of the mankind clause.

The creation of the legal order for outer space began from the concept of an internationalization oriented at the common interest of the international community,[539] and included for the first time the full participation of developing countries in the elaboration of a new area of international law, resulting in the first incorporation of a general clause on the need to share the benefits of the common space among all states. Already in 1967, the Outer Space Treaty thus expresses a material understanding of the principle of state equality as part of the general interest clause "in the interest of all countries irrespective of the degree of economic or scientific development", and the implied duty for assistance of the developing countries to participate in future space activities.

Secondly, the genesis of the clause confirms its binding character. The notion of "interest of all mankind" is mentioned for the first time in United Nations General Assembly resolution 1148 (XII) of 14 November 1957 and again in resolution 1721 (XVI) of 20 December 1961, and reaffirmed explicitly as a principle of space law in the "Principles Declaration" of 1963.[540] In the negotiations on the Outer Space Treaty the countries from the south[541] and the Socialist countries[542] expressly rejected the proposal to remove the mankind clause from the operative part of the Treaty in Art. I to the preamble. Hence, the legally binding nature rather than the purely political significance of this central clause was an explicit subject of the negotiations. Thus, during the discussions on the draft treaty, the British delegate[543] declared in the Legal Subcommittee of COPUOS that the Subcommittee intended to create a legally binding obligation for the use of outer space in the interest and to the benefit of all mankind. Further, by signing and ratifying the Outer Space Treaty, the two space powers recognized the legal significance of the mankind clause, and its effect to establish a duty for cooperation, the sharing of benefits and the pursuit of common security in outer space. In the hearing before the US Senate Foreign Relations Committee on the Outer Space Treaty, then Senator and later US Vice-President Albert Gore declared on Art. I:

> If Article I were a preamble that would be one thing. But it isn't, it is an article, and a treaty obligation, and I think it brings us into an obligation

to make the use of outer space available to all countries, to treat our use of that for the benefit and in the interests of all countries. Indeed that is exactly what it says.[511]

The chief US delegate at the negotiations of the Outer Space Treaty, Ambassador Arthur Goldberg, confirmed this in the same hearing, while at the same time emphasizing that the clause was not a "self-executing norm" but rather needed to be implemented by specialized treaties.[545] He also made clear that the United States did not view the clause as prejudging the form in which cooperation would take place. The US Senate Foreign Relations Committee linked its approval of the ratification of the Outer Space Treaty to an "understanding" that:

> ... nothing in Article I, paragraph 1 of the treaty diminishes or alters the right of the United States to determine *how* it shares the benefits and results of its space activities [emphasis added].[546]

Hence, the controversy was not over the question of "whether" an obligation to cooperate in the interest of mankind existed but rather on "how" it should be implemented. In the same vein, the Soviet chief delegate in COPUOS, Juri Kolosov,[547] also recognized that the Outer Space Treaty had to be implemented by specialized treaties, in particular with regard to the principle of cooperation laid down in Art. I, para. 3. In his evaluation of these national statements, M.G. Marcoff rightly underlines that the qualification of a norm of international law as "non-self-executing" concerns its effectiveness, but not its legally binding character.[548] The legally binding nature of the mankind clause in Art. I, para. 1 of the Outer Space Treaty is thus corroborated by the statements in the US Senate on the occasion of the ratification of the Treaty, as well as by the statement of the Soviet delegate, Kolosov.[549]

Thirdly, the objection that the mankind clause is too vague to be legally binding underestimates the formative effect the stipulation has on the legal structure with regard to both the Outer Space Treaty and the CHOM principle. This "common interest" provision, which is central to the CHOM principle, stems from the fact that all space activities have a universal impact,[550] and thus concern *eo ipso* the interests of the international community as a whole. From this an inherent justification also accrues for the clause's influence as a legal principle that permeates the entire space order. The crux of the views that reject the legal validity of the "community and general clauses" lies in their restrictive approach to interpreting the clauses on the basis of classic public international law, while in fact completely leaving aside the important structural change of modern international law. This automatically leads to contradictions, and cannot be a valid justification for denying the legally binding nature of the general clauses. It is actually by filling the content of the enhanced common purpose and the mankind clause of the Outer Space Treaty with the structural elements of the CHOM principle that such contradictions can be overcome.

5.2.4 CONCLUSIONS

The status of outer space as the common heritage of mankind, in connection with the principle of the peaceful use of outer space and the principle of cooperation in outer space law, entails special community obligations that give rise to legal standards for cooperative or common security. While the Outer Space Treaty does not in itself explicitly oblige states to conduct specific negotiations on the prevention of an arms race in outer space, the mankind clause and the principle of the common heritage of mankind contain the obligation to safeguard the peaceful use of outer space through the establishment of an adequate international regime. The CHOM status of outer space sets out relevant criteria for elaborating the necessary legal standards to implement the mankind principle and for establishing the material, procedural and institutional prerequisites thereof. If the plans to build BMD meant that a state would carry out armament measures solely on its own territory, then without an explicit disarmament obligation comparable to Art. VI of the NPT with regard to nuclear weapons, it would probably be excessive to derive from the common interest clause specific prohibitions on behalf of the international community on other kinds of weapons. However, BMD entails the planned use of an acknowledged common area beyond national jurisdiction, which the Outer Space Treaty declares to be the "province of mankind". The explicit reference to the CHOM principle in the current negotiations at the CD in connection with the claim of the international community for the immediate start of multilateral negotiations on the prevention of an arms race in outer space,[551] indicate that also in state practice the *opinio juris* is developing that states have a legal obligation towards the international community to refrain from any measures that could cause an arms race in outer space.

CHAPTER 6

CHOM AS A STRUCTURAL PRINCIPLE OF OUTER SPACE LAW

6.1 STRUCTURAL CHANGE OF INTERNATIONAL LAW

In his ground-breaking work on the structural change of international law, the director for International Legal Research of Columbia University, Wolfgang Friedmann,[552] extensively analyses the influence of the changing international relations since the end of the Second World War. Friedmann considers international law to have shifted from a law of coexistence to a law of cooperation.

The German international lawyer Alfred Bleckmann has likewise developed a specific notion of the structure of international law, defining it as that "which in a comparison with the modern national legal orders would stand out as the *specificity* of public international law".[553] In 1978 and again in 1982 he refers mainly to the traditional structures of classic international law, defining them as follows: decentralization; lack of a central power; relatively minor relevance of international legal community interests; freedom of state action; and the strong adaptation of international law to the *de facto* behaviour of states.[554] This list might be adequate for a wide range of classic international law. However, it leaves out fundamental changes in the international system and law, in particular with regard to the rise of new branches such as the law of cooperation, the law of development, and the new sector regimes for common areas beyond national jurisdiction. The features of modern international law are more varied and differ by sector.[555] In fact, it is possible to discern almost countervailing structural tendencies in these new branches. The rise of different structural characteristics in various fields of international law is not a contradiction, but rather a confirmation that the international legal order is in the middle of a deep transformation, where some sectors have been transformed more rapidly than others.[556] Albert Bleckmann also recognizes that "the historic public international law will have gradually to be adapted to the new structures imposing themselves on the international legal order".[557] He also discerns an increasing orientation of the international legal norms towards the community interests of the international community, even though considered at the time to be still very weak.[558] Later, Bleckmann views the new structural elements of the law of cooperation to have become dominant, and, due to the increasing interdependence of states, to have led to individual states "identifying themselves ever strongly with the interests of other states", and thus "also in public international law, common interests of the international legal community have developed".[559]

In 1973 Eberhard Menzel analysed the "fundamental political-social structures" of the modern world, in order to establish the "legal structure of international law".[560] He views the purpose of drawing on these fundamental structures in using them as criteria to "evaluate the concordance of the international legal order and the general political-social realities of the era".[561] This would allow the international lawyer to assure himself even in times of "epochal change ... of the capacity of international law to adapt to these changes".[562]

René-Jean Dupuy, in his work on the international community, considers the structural change of international law and its increasing orientation towards community purposes to be a decisive factor in the progression from a "*droit de la société relationnelle*" towards a "*droit de la société institutionnelle*".[563] In the same vein, Georges Abi-Saab[564] attaches primary importance to the "Declaration on Principles of International Law concerning Friendly Relations and Cooperation among States" in the "*transformation des structures juridiques*". While considering the principle of the sovereign equality of states a "*principe structurel*"[565] of classic international law, he sees in the principles highlighted by the Declaration of a positive duty to cooperate ("*justice distributive*") and of permeating state sovereignty by the right to self-determination the structural transformation principles of the new international law. Its main structural principle, according to Abi-Saab, can be defined as "*un intérêt juridique de la communauté en tant que telle, consacrant une valeur qu'elle considère comme supérieure aux intérêts individuels de ses membres*".[566] In the jurisdiction of the ICJ as well,[567] the structural change of international law plays an increasing and particular role in the context of the recognition by the Court of obligations owed to the international community as a whole. After an extensive analysis of the Court's *erga omnes* jurisdiction, Andreas

Paulus concludes that it opens the prospect of "law breaking free from the classic bilateral structure".[568] The interrelationship between the change of the international system and its repercussions for the structure of international law is also the subject of legal sociology.[569] Structural questions and their influence on the interpretation and implementation of norms are also analysed in other branches of international law[570] such as international environmental law, international private law[571] and in recent works on the history of international law.[572] Taken from a globalization perspective, Klaus Dicke has recently developed Friedmann's analysis of the structural change of international law, and concluded that as an "international legal conceptual consequence" it would give rise to a "Law of Mankind".[573]

With a view to questions of the preservation of world peace, Ulrich Scheuner emphasized the significance of the changing structural order of the international state community.[574] Scheuner noted as one of the major "structural questions of the international state community" that the international community, being increasingly pushed towards an enhanced homogeneity and interdependence, is calling for new fundamental principles of cooperation to achieve its potential in an organized and rational process for far-sighted solutions to the challenges facing all mankind, and in particular with regard to the preservation of peace.

A similar approach is pursued by Horst Fischer,[575] who has developed the main elements for a foundation of the concept of common security in international law. Since the CHOM principle contains a constitutive security component, Fischer's work is a useful basis for analysing the structural significance of the CHOM principle for the question of the peaceful use of outer space.[576]

6.2 CHOM AS A STRUCTURAL PRINCIPLE OF INTERNATIONAL SPACE LAW

6.2.1 FOUNDATIONS

The structural change of international law is of particular importance for common spaces beyond national jurisdiction. Peter-Michael Sontag notes the possibility that with regard to the limitations of state freedom in outer space "changes in the structure of the international community have led to a shift in the value assumption, so that previously exclusive interests of the states are now superposed by community interests".[577] In his lecture before the Academy for International Law in 1969, Friedmann interpreted his concept of the structural change of international law in view of the newly developing sector orders for the "global commons" of Antarctica, the high seas and outer space.[578] Wilhelm Kewenig was the first to have outlined the structural effects specifically with regard to the CHOM principle.[579] Following his approach, several authors have emphasized the structural foundations and implications of new international legal norms,[580] in particular explicitly of the mankind clause in the Outer Space Treaty and of the CHOM principle, with regard to the new legal branches like outer space law and the law of the sea. Harry Almond states with regard to the Outer Space Treaty:

> In addition to providing a constitutive basis to the legal regime of outer space, the treaty provides a generalized normative *structure* to which states must conform in their daily activities in outer space [emphasis added].[581]

Frans G. von der Dunk points to the special structural character of the legal order of outer space as a "truly internationalised res communis".[582] Wolfgang Durner's dissertation on international environmental law has recourse to structural approaches with regard to common spaces beyond national jurisdiction and universal environmental goods.[583]

Like earlier for Friedmann,[584] Dupuy[585] and Bleckmann,[586] the formation and validation of community interests are also for Abi-Saab[587] and Dicke[588] the decisive elements of transformation in international law. The community interest is at the same time the central element of the CHOM principle and of the mankind clause of the Outer Space Treaty. From this, the CHOM principle can be qualified as the structural principle of the new international law, as it was laid down in the early law of outer space. The CHOM principle could thus also be the appropriate structural principle for the development of an international legal order envisaged as a "Law of Mankind".

6.2.2 STRUCTURAL CHANGE OF THE INTERNATIONAL SYSTEM AND PUBLIC INTERNATIONAL LAW

Given the lack of an international legislator, the capacity to absorb fundamental social changes is essential for the decentralized international system and hence the international law that governs it. More than any national order, the international system must be capable of adapting its structures with the technological, economic and political changes of the state system.[589] The interrelationship between order and change analysed by Edmund Burke in his philosophy of states in the 18th century, stating that a society loses its capacity to survive without the ability to adapt to change, applies also to the international system.[590] On the international plane, this implies that the maintenance of universal order and the very survival of mankind depend on the ability of the international system to absorb change. It is hence a logical development that with the rise of global risks and challenges with repercussions for mankind, the international community and consequently the international legal order respond to the development of enhanced universal common interests, since its very survival is at stake. Inasmuch as this has to take place in the form of self-regulatory structural changes, given the deficiency of central institutions and legislative procedures, the analysis of these structural changes takes on a particular significance in making the conditions for the stability of the system and its legal order apparent. From this, the fundamental changes in international relations described in the political and international legal literature can be characterized as the rise of a universal world community, where the unprecedented increase in state interdependence leads to the legal recognition of community interests.[591] Philip Allot attributes to this process the objective "to enable international society as a structure-system of human well-being".[592] The genesis of this world community as a "one world society" in the "global village" and in the "common global civilization of science and technology"[593] has become an ordinary reality as a result of global communication, daily images from all corners of the globe and recent satellite images of the Earth with a resolution of a few metres. However, this transition to a world community portrayed daily in the media has not yet fully been transposed into the structures of the international order.

A necessary corollary of this epoch-making process of change of the international system is the need for a corresponding structural change of international law, which Friedmann[594] has analysed in general and Scheuner[595] in particular, for the development of the welfare aspect in international law as a constituent element of the maintenance of peace in a broad sense. Friedmann emphasizes two major tendencies of the structural change of international law. One is a horizontal change by the entry of a great number of new subjects of international law as a result of decolonization. The second is a vertical change by the extension of the domains governed by international law, which increasingly covers economic, financial and social questions that can no longer be ruled exclusively on a domestic plane in the globalized world economy.[596] In his Hague lecture in 1969, Friedmann emphasized the global consequences of these structural changes more clearly. The interdependence and universal repercussions arising from these changes have led to the fact that states are no longer indifferent to the interests of other states; rather they identify increasingly with community interests. In addition to the necessity to create the institutional structure for the implementation of public international law, Friedmann emphasizes four global challenges that have shaped the transformation of the law of coexistence into a law of cooperation:[597]

- *"the threat to mankind's resources"*
  The increasing danger of destroying and polluting the environment due to the demographic explosion, over-exploitation of resources and unrestricted industrialization. This necessitates the urgent elaboration of a law of cooperation "for a co-ordinated effort of the nations to control, preserve and develop the resources of the earth for the common benefit".
- *"the impact of democratization"*
  The decolonization, and in particular the independence of a large number of former colonies since the end of the Second World War that increased the number of states to be covered under international law by more than a hundred. This led to a democratization of the international system and at the same time to a greater heterogeneity in comparison to the former homogeneous world of the *jus publicum Europaeum*. However, as the new states were increasingly participating in the norm-creating process,[598] universal values of the world community were recognized to a growing degree, which was enhanced by the demise of the East-West divide.[599] This process left its imprint on the changing structure of international law.[600] Thus, the genesis of the CHOM principle since 1957, when the mankind clause was introduced for the first time in the United Nations resolution on outer space, coincided with the height of the decolonization process.[601] At the same time, mankind developed for the first time the

technological capabilities for the exploration and use of outer space and the deep seabed. The exploration of outer space opened on the one hand the chance for the peoples of the world to grow together in an international community of law and security, but on the other hand ran the risk of a world hegemony of one or a small number of states with space capabilities.[602]

- *"the concern with international economic development"*
  This led to the demand for social justice and development assistance at the international level, hence the rise of the idea of international welfare. Its application to the international plane was a logical corollary of the growing interdependence with the individual states no longer being capable of fulfilling their welfare tasks in autarky.[603]
- *"the concern with survival and the futility of war"*
  The atomic bomb poses more clearly than ever the alternative between an organized international community, which would put international authority in charge of matters of war and peace, or an anarchic world of independent states that have the unilateral power to destroy mankind. This makes the institutionalized condemnation of war as a means of policy indispensable, as well as the recognition of community interests in a global community of common destiny.[604]

Friedmann's assumptions make clear that the need to cooperate and to pursue community interests has become even stronger, due in particular to the rapid development of interdependence and globalization. The structural change described by Friedmann, expressed in international law with the rise of *ius cogens, erga omnes* obligations and international crimes of state, led to a "community-oriented public international law",[605] which justifies the prognosis that "the international legal order will be redefined increasingly from the idea of an international community".[606] Paulus analyses in his concluding chapter the link between the structure of the state community and the development of a community-oriented international law.[607] Due to the institutional weakness of international law, he sees the main task to be the creation of a substitute function for the enforcement of community interests, so that these can be effective even in the remaining structures of bilateralism. He views as the essence of present international law the realization of community interests in bringing about a compromise between the structures of the society of states and the upcoming community of states.

The CHOM principle and the legal order for common spaces represent the deep structural change of international law, which expresses the rise of community interests. The characteristics of this structural change in international law are: the transformation of state sovereignty;[608] the development of the international community as a "legal international community"[609] as expressed in the increasing reference to the notion of mankind in international legal documents;[610] the enhanced contribution of the new states to the development of international law;[611] the rise of the international obligation to solidarity;[612] and the development of a broad notion of positive peace by recognizing the duty to preserve peace.[613]

Comparing the structural changes of international relations and of international law with the central elements of the CHOM principle in outer space law, one comes to the conclusion that the CHOM principle's five main elements reflect the major undercurrents of the changing international system. The prohibition of national appropriation and the principle of the peaceful use of the common spaces correspond with the rise of the common goals of the global community in the security field, which, by its internationalization, excludes a priori hegemony over the greatest space beyond national jurisdiction by a single state.

The enhanced common interest obligation according to the mankind clause and the principle of "equitable sharing" with particular consideration to developing countries, follow directly from applying the welfare standard to the international domain. The principle of the preservation of the common heritage for future generations reflects the rise of global interest in protecting the environment. And lastly, the enhanced principle of cooperation of states in order to meet the general community interest corresponds to the structural transformation of the law of coexistence to a law of cooperation. Hence, the CHOM principle was introduced neither without preparation nor was its content incompatible with the changing structure of international law and outer space law in particular. Rather it reflected, at the time of its introduction, the rising new structural elements of international law. Especially, in its application to internationalized territories beyond national jurisdiction and in particular to outer space, as well as in relation to mankind's interest in nuclear disarmament and international security, the principle embodies the change of international law towards a law of an "international order" in the pursuit of the community interest.[614] As such, the CHOM principle further reflects the need for an international regime for the "global commons", such as the development of a "community-oriented" law of the international community.[615]

6.2.3 STRUCTURAL CHANGE OF INTERNATIONAL LAW AND THE GENESIS OF THE CHOM PRINCIPLE IN OUTER SPACE LAW

6.2.3.1 The rise of community interests

The change from a law of coexistence to a law of cooperation and coordination is accompanied by the enhancement of community interests of the international society. The far-reaching structural change of the international system has also led to a diminution of the basic structural principles of classical international law such as the principles of sovereignty and equality of states. In particular, with the rise of global challenges there is an increasing recognition of community interests at the international level, which has led to a new perspective on the principle of state sovereignty.[616] Dicke speaks of the "sovereignty-centered concept of international law" having come to its limits.[617] This, however, according to the overwhelming majority of literature does not question the principle of state sovereignty in a fundamental way, nor does it deny its character as a constitutive basic principle of international law.[618] Due to the inescapable interdependence of states,[619] the classic understanding of state sovereignty being limited to safeguarding the freedom of action of states in their own territory has become an anachronism. This diminution of state sovereignty, however, does not mean that the state has lost its relevance for the development and implementation of international law. Even accepting the proposition that international law is undergoing a third structural change with the rise of transnational actors like global, transnational companies or non-governmental organizations,[620] the sovereign state continues to remain of primary importance with regard to the fulfilment of the community interests. Because of the shift from a law of coexistence to a law of cooperation, the main concern is no longer the "coexistence between equally rival sovereignties",[621] but the attainment of common interests of mankind by states that bear a responsibility for the common interest of the international community.[622] Likewise, state sovereignty is transformed to become the basis for the development of the "international community as an international legal concept" or of a "community-oriented international law".[623] According to Christian Tomuschat and Bruno Simma the substance of community interests lie in the following central areas:[624]

1. Preservation of peace and security, which can only be achieved cooperatively;[625]
2. Solidarity as a necessary element of peace.[626] Only by recognizing the "global welfare" aspect can mankind be understood as a community;
3. Preservation of the environment for present and future generations;
4. The CHOM principle as the foundation of regimes for the "global commons" ensuring the common interest;[627]
5. Universal human rights.

The recognition of common interest obligation is also found in the jurisdiction of the ICJ, in particular in the context of *erga omnes* norms.[628] While Art. 53 of the Vienna Convention on the Law of Treaties speaks of the "international community of States", other references in international legal documents, such as in Article 33 of the draft articles on the "Responsibility of States for Wrongful Acts", adopted during the fifty-third session of the International Law Commission in 2001,[629] make clear that the notion of the international community is not meant to be a mere juxtaposition of the individual states, but rather to be understood as also encompassing the interests of mankind.[630] The ICJ has indicated the need to take other interests into account in its "Advisory Opinion on the Legality of the Threat or Use of Nuclear Weapons", emphasizing the "overriding consideration of humanity" as being at the heart of humanitarian international law, and stating the "growing awareness of the need to liberate the community of States and *the international public* from the dangers resulting from the existence of nuclear weapons" [emphasis added].[631] In addition, there is a growing number of international legal references to "mankind" in multilateral treaties, ranging from the preamble of the United Nations Charter, which declares wars as the "scourge of mankind", the Antarctic Treaty ("interests of science and mankind") and the NPT ("devastation that would be visited upon all mankind by nuclear war") to the mankind clause in the Outer Space Treaty, the Moon Treaty and in the Convention on the Law of the Sea and in bilateral treaties such as the Intermediate-Range Nuclear Forces (INF) Treaty ("conscious that nuclear war would have devastating consequences for all mankind"). The notion of mankind, which simply means the sum of all human beings,[632] is not identical with the notion of the international community. However, the two are closely linked inasmuch as measures that are proven to have detrimental effects for mankind cannot be considered to be in the common interest of the international community. In the end, in all of these instances there is a need to recognize international legal community interests that concern the whole of mankind.

6.2.3.2 Effect of the structural change of international law on outer space law and security in outer space

The impact decolonization has had on international law demonstrated early on the clear structural changes in the legal orders for areas beyond national jurisdiction, over which the new subjects of international law could effectively exercise influence.[633] This was the case in particular for outer space law, which developed nearly in parallel to the decolonization process. Friedmann thus underlined that outer space law was most strongly influenced by the structural change of international law,[634] which was to a large degree affected by the new majority of developing countries. According to classic international law, the principle of formal equality of states would have left the space powers a free hand to extend their sovereign freedom to outer space in a way that the majority of states without space capabilities, albeit formally treated on an equal footing, would be *de facto* kept aside from benefiting from the common space for a long time to come. Instead, very much in the vein of the new orientation towards community interests, the use of outer space is stipulated in the preambular considerations 2 and 3 and in Art. I, para. 1 of the Outer Space Treaty to serve the interest of all countries and mankind as a whole. This is rightly viewed as an expression of the "general philosophy of the treaty",[635] aiming to ensure that the freedom of space also comprises the potential freedom of the developing countries and other future space powers.[636]

In the same way as the introduction of the general prohibition of the use of force according to Art. 2, para. 4 of the United Nations Charter put the weaker states on the same footing as the powerful states in legal (yet not factual) terms,[637] the sovereignty and freedom of action in outer space has not been reserved to the powers with actual capabilities for the use of space. Rather, the drafters of the Outer Space Treaty have instead given precedence to the legal equality of all states in obliging them to pursue the common interest of all countries in the use of the common space. The freedom of action of individual states in space, which under the structure of the classic law of coexistence would grant states full freedom in their activities limited only by the other states' *a priori* unlimited freedom of action, is according to the new structure of the international law of cooperation instead additionally restricted by the predominance of the common interest as embodied in the mankind clause. Furthermore, with the obligation to cooperate in the pursuit of the common interest, the Treaty is also based on a material understanding of equality of states, which makes outer space law a first example of the developing international welfare concept, including a duty to international solidarity. In particular through the specific emphasis on the preservation of outer space and celestial bodies for future generations, the Treaty also enhances the development of an international environmental law, including the idea of inter-generational solidarity.[638] Christol underlined the significance of the increasing interdependence of states with regard to the new outer space law, and particularly security in the common space:

> In meeting the varied challenges of the space age man has been able to combine the forces of the social complex which favor world interdependence and social organization with his concept of values and his international organizations ... Peaceful and shared use, rather than ownership or exclusive control, has become the dominant theme of the New Law.[639]

The structural change in the legal order of outer space is evident particularly in the consistent provision of the principle of cooperation for all areas of use of the common space. Goedhuis relates the principle of cooperation directly to the structural changes in the system of international relations.[640] The positive compromise since 1994 on the question of the "space benefits" is in turn a reflection of these structural international changes.[641] The major developing countries, such as India, China and to a lesser degree Brazil, have themselves become space powers in the 1990s. The end of the East-West antagonism opens also a chance for overcoming the North-South divide. Thus, the fulfilment of the cooperative objectives in the mankind clause in the Outer Space Treaty and the CHOM principle become for the first time potentially achievable.

Stephan Hobe concludes his monograph on the legal order of the economic use of outer space with an assessment of the degree to which this order reflects the features of the new cooperative law. Hobe underlines that indeed the regime of economic space uses is characterized by new structures of an international administration *in nuce* premised on the concept of equity, and on the "normative guideline" of the common interest clause in Art. I of the Outer Space Treaty, which results in a "limitation of the freedom of states and, hence, in a new understanding of sovereignty."[642] This lends a leading role to outer space law in enhancing the transformation of international law from governing a society of states towards a legal order of a genuine state community.[643]

This development would, however, require that the controversial issue of military uses of the common space be resolved. In this respect, the structural change of international law implies a far stronger role for the principle of cooperation with regard to security in outer space. In questions of peace and security, the Outer Space Treaty is premised on the fundamental condition of the international community, according to which the nuclear threat to mankind signifies that "security can no longer be guaranteed by the individual states; security becomes *international security*" [emphasis in the original].[644] Hence, in accordance with the unfolding structural change, encompassing economic security interests in the mankind clause and the CHOM principle, the Outer Space Treaty incorporates a broad notion of security, including economic justice, to be achieved through the sharing of the benefits of space activities. This establishes both a substantive legal and structural concordance between common security and the community status of outer space. Without a structured implementation of the Outer Space Treaty's fundamental principles on the preservation of peace and security in outer space, the mankind clause risks becoming what Mircea Mateesco-Matte deplored as an "*euphémisme juridique*".[645]

Kay Hailbronner has shown that the "de-emphasis" of state sovereignty and the materialization of the principle of state equality have, in conjunction with the enhanced principle of cooperation, decisively shaped the new law of outer space.[646] The exclusion of state sovereignty over outer space would have caused a regulatory and power vacuum in the structure of the legal space order.[647] The Outer Space Treaty has filled this vacuum by providing a new structure based on the community status of the common space, which is reflected in the adaptation of all space activities according to the mankind clause of the CHOM principle for the common benefit and in the obligation of all states to work together in accordance with the enhanced cooperation principle. And thus, the Treaty establishes the basis for the realization of the interests of mankind.

Pardo justifies his proposal for introducing the CHOM principle by the necessity to change the structure of state relations.[648] In this sense, the mankind clause and the CHOM principle in outer space law embody the main components of the new international law. With its five major elements, the CHOM principle ideally contributes to the horizontal task, ascribed to the concept of international welfare and security in a broad sense, to enhance international development, environmental protection and maintenance of world peace. Antonio Cassese has described this process in the final chapter of his 1986 work on public international law, which is devoted to the CHOM principle, as follows:

> The introduction of the concept of the common heritage of mankind no doubt represents a great advance in the world community. In particular ... it marks the passage from the traditional postulate of sovereignty to that of co-operation. In other words, the expression 'common heritage of mankind' succinctly expresses—with all its merits and limitations—the 'new model' of world community that has gradually emerged since 1945. Although it has not yet displayed all its potential, the concept has already changed legal habits and institutions and introduced momentous new notions as regards the right to appropriate certain resources, their peaceful use and joint exploitation, and the need to promote scientific research and protect the environment. These are lasting and by now undisputed achievements, which accrue to the benefit of all mankind, both of the rich and the poor.[649]

In view of this concordance of the CHOM principle with the main features of the new law of outer space, the principle can be qualified, according to an expression of Eibe Riedel, as a "new material structural principle of international law".[650] Riedel defines the CHOM principle as a "right of mankind" and compares it to the right to development, inasmuch as it can be qualified as a legal standard combining the applicable customary and treaty rules in different sectors, and representing as such a general principle of international law. This qualification by Riedel is fully corroborated by the preceding analysis, which has shown that the process of the internationalization of common spaces and the validation of community interests are focused within the CHOM principle. The principle's five elements reflect the enfolding structure of the new law of cooperation. In contrast to certain allegations, the CHOM principle can no longer be viewed as a concept in essence alien to international law and outer space law.[651] Rather, it represents the adequate principle of the evolving new structural order for common areas beyond national jurisdiction, having its legal basis both in customary and treaty norms of the new law of the sea and of outer space. It thus reflects far more than the mere aspirations of the international community for a more just and peaceful world, as it reflects the inherent change of the international community to a world society, and consequently of international law towards cooperation for the benefit of all mankind, having paradigmatic repercussions for the concept and implementation of international security in the areas governed by the CHOM principle.

6.2.3.3 The CHOM principle and the peaceful use of outer space

The CHOM principle is of great importance for the interpretation and application of the peaceful purpose standard, as it provides the over-arching context, the rationale, and the guiding orientation for its synchronization with the mankind clause. As early as 1965 Wilfred Jenks defined the "principle of the common interest of mankind in space" as an important legal principle enshrined in the United Nations General Assembly's "Principles Declaration" of 1963, containing the same main elements as were later attributed by the Outer Space Treaty to the common purpose principle of the "province of all mankind" clause and subsequently by the Moon Treaty to the CHOM principle.[652] He drew two principal conclusions from it. Firstly, the principle implies a predisposition in favour of the interdependence of states instead of a presumption in favour of state sovereignty. According to the objective of the mankind clause this means that states have to contribute actively to the attainment of the common good for the entire international community. Secondly, referring to the growing interdependence of states as a fundamental premise of international law, the principle reflects a change in the norm-creating process, according to which it is part of a rapidly growing community-oriented law of the global community, in contrast to particular international legal rules requiring the specific consent of the states.[653] Jenks bases the main argument for this conclusion on the recognition of the growing interdependence of states as the new fundamental condition of modern international law.[654]

Bleckmann underlines a third corollary of the qualification of the CHOM principle in outer space law as its function in determining the underlying structural order that will render an authoritative interpretation, application and specification of its main constitutive elements with regard to new issues and uses of outer space.[655] This corresponds to Jenks' statement that:

> ... the principle of the common interest of mankind in space is, like the general welfare clause of the Constitution of the United States, a continuing source of authority for new applications of the fundamental concept as further problems come into focus and call for solution on the basis of law.[656]

Another consequence of the CHOM principle is that in all questions of interpretation, the objective of specific legal rules and institutions for its implementation has to be fitted into the structural order governed by the CHOM principle. Thus, the principle is a binding guideline for interpretation as well as for filling the eventual *lacunae* through specification and norm-creating *de lege ferenda*, and for the balancing of community and individual state interests. Even for general international law, a number of writers have epoused a tendency to view the classic presumption in favour of the freedom of states as restricted by the increasing interdependence of states in the international community and by a predominance of vital community interests.[657] For internationalized common spaces beyond national jurisdiction, this tendency has become consolidated in a new paradigm that grants the international community the role of trustee over the common interest of CHOM. The enhanced community interest expressed by the mankind clause has led to a presumption opposite to the classic *Lotus* principle by restricting the freedom of states as laid down in Art. I of the Outer Space Treaty and by obliging a state to secure the consent—be it tacit or explicit—of the international community prior to undertaking new forms of space activity. It follows that with regard to the uses of outer space in any field an international regime with clear and transparent rules and competencies to ensure respect for the common interest has to be established. This necessity increases to the extent that unilateral or bilateral measures threaten the fulfilment of the common purpose of space activities to be carried out in the interest of all states. In the security field, these conclusions are corroborated by the effectiveness of the security element of the CHOM principle, which in turn is a reflection of the structural change of international law in general and the law governing the maintenance of world peace and international security in particular. The common interest of the mankind clause leads to a paradigmatic shift towards common security, with the implication that states are no longer allowed to pursue national security exclusively in their own interest when it is at the cost of international or common security of all states.

CHAPTER 7

STRUCTURAL CHANGE OF INTERNATIONAL LAW AND COMMON SECURITY IN OUTER SPACE

7.1 COMMON SECURITY IN OUTER SPACE AND PUBLIC INTERNATIONAL LAW

In questions of security and peace, the principle of collective security laid down in the United Nations Charter is the most direct expression of the representation of the international community as a community of law and security. However, the atomic age has made it necessary to recognize the need of mankind for common security against the threat of the atomic bomb. This need follows from the experience that in the age of MAD, not even the most powerful state can achieve security in "splendid isolation".[658] In recognizing that all states are threatened by the potential of nuclear war, the ICJ has underlined that the "attitude" and "concern" of the international community have to be taken into account beyond state practice with regard to nuclear weapons,[659] and in particular in view of the obligation of the nuclear-weapon states for general and complete disarmament according to Art. VI of the NPT. Thus, in the context of security and disarmament, the structural change of international law has led to the advancement of an international community based on the common security interests of mankind, which in turn becomes a relevant factor when assessing the legality of all activities by single states in the context of global security.[660]

Recognizing that in the atomic era peace and security can only be guaranteed cooperatively, and that war as the continuation of politics by other means has been replaced by the absolute "futility of war",[661] Eric Stein in 1971 came to the conclusion that the maintenance of common security would necessitate by definition a cooperative element:

> Thus, the two superpowers gradually came to recognise a co-operative aspect to their adversary relations: common interest not in terms of

similarities between their value systems but in terms of "being in the same boat".[662]

As a consequence, this recognition leads to the elaboration of the concept of common or cooperative security, of which Helmut Schmidt's speech before the First United Nations Special Session on Disarmament in 1978 marked the starting point by introducing the notion of "security partnership".[663] The concept met international recognition with the Palme Commission's report of 1982 titled "Common Security", which states that "Security in the nuclear age is common security."[664] The report was welcomed in the same year through resolution 37/99 of the United Nations General Assembly,[665] which emphasized the central role of the United Nations "in furthering common security", and mandated the Disarmament Commission to examine the recommendations with a view to their efficient implementation.

Given the capability of mutually assured destruction, security can no longer be achieved against, but rather with the opponent. In this sense, common security is already a reality. The challenge is "to buttress the de facto existing common security by reliable international legal norms through agreements on security partnership".[666] Janne Nolan rightly states:

Cooperative security is the corresponding principle for international security in the post-Cold War era. In the face of the changing character of security threats, it [cooperative security] is the new strategic imperative.[667]

In the same sense, German Foreign Minister Fischer, in his annual speech before the General Assembly of the United Nations on 14 September 2002, in view of the experience of September 11, under the *leitmotiv* of the need to establish a "system of global cooperative security", declared this to be a "central political task of the 21st century".[668] He also referred to the indispensable foundation of such a system in international law: "Cooperative global security will be measured by the international legal framework set up to render it compulsory."

In a study for the Hamburg Institute for Peace Research and Security Policy, Horst Fischer demonstrated that the concept of common security could be legally based on a structural change of the law of peace maintenance.[669] In the same way as the CHOM principle, the concept of common security is mainly based upon the international legal principle of cooperation. In addition, its structural elements can also be derived from the international norms concerning the status of internationalized territories beyond national jurisdiction.[670] These elements are the reinforced duties of cooperation, consultation, information, coordination and an enhanced orientation towards institutionalization and confidence building as well as such typical elements of arms control as the use of international treaties and the function of unilateral measures. A further essential international legal corollary of common security is the duty to negotiate arms control and disarmament,[671] referred to in the corresponding provisions of Art. VI of the NPT and in the "Agreed Statement D" of the bilateral ABM Treaty. All these elements are found in the Outer Space Treaty, and play an important role in the elaboration of the principle of the peaceful use of outer space as manifested in the CHOM principle.[672]

Comparatively the CHOM status of outer space rests in its security element of the peaceful use of outer space on the same international legal elements as the concept of common security. This parallelism reaffirms the obligation under the general interest clause to prevent unilateral military activities in outer space harmful to the general interest, and the presumption in favour of a corresponding obligation to negotiate rules to prevent an arms race in space. Achieving common security in outer space is not only a direct result of the general interest obligation of the mankind clause, but also of the physical conditions of outer space, from where every point on Earth can be attacked. According to the US political scientist Daniel Deudney, the use of outer space offers the possibility to either establish a "planet-wide hegemony" of the strongest or the "opportunity for an alternative security order".[673]

Also from the angle of political science, the necessity for a cooperative security order in outer space operates through the "elaboration of an adequate security structure" in order to "realize new cooperative regimes" on a multilateral basis.[674] This should now be easier to achieve as the East-West confrontation has been overcome by the "demise of bilateral confrontational structures" of the two big powers.

A further parallel between the concept of common security and the security element of the CHOM principle is the fact that both are based on a broad notion of security that also encompasses the economic dimension.[675] The concept of common security, being an expression of the notion of security in a broad sense, corresponds to the development of global economic interdependence. As Egon Bahr states, "With common security economic interdependence becomes such that it generates additional peace preserving and stabilizing common interests".[676] Thus, the obligation to use outer space exclusively for peaceful purposes also implies the obligation to cooperate already at the exploration stage of outer space. If this were to be fully achieved, it would represent a highly efficient element of cooperative security in view of widespread "dual-use" capabilities of space technologies. The authors of the ground-breaking work on cooperative security edited by the Brookings Institution, which corresponds to the concept of common security, describe the parallelism of the normative and institutional mechanisms for the global economy and international security in the following perspective:

> Thus there are many conceptual parallels between the principles and institutional requirements for the emerging rules of the game for international trade and investment and the proposals ... for a new international security system. ... The conceptual complementarities in principles and purpose are already evident. The need for new enforcement mechanisms for both economic and security regimes has also been mentioned. Given the essential harmony between the purposes of the two, it might seem reasonable to suggest that both would gain in stature and authority by being set up as the economic and military sides of a single new international framework, into which some existing international institutions with related functions might be absorbed ...[677]

The development of common security repeats the same process in the security field that the international economy underwent through globalization, where investments in research can no longer be understood as a "national public good", but rather as an "international public good".[678] Cooperative security in outer space, which starts with joint exploration efforts, benefits the joint economic use of the common space in the interest of mankind as a whole. Common economic activities for the benefit of mankind support, in turn, the pursuance of common security, reinforcing each other for the benefit of all states "independent of their scientific or economic development" (Art. I, para. 1 of the Outer Space Treaty).

In a remarkably far-sighted view, Jenks perceived in 1969 the political and military effects of the upcoming use of outer space as a chance to make them the basis for common security:

Virtually all of the probable space services have important political and military aspects. The intelligence potential of observation and detection satellites may be left to contribute with other space and missile systems to perpetuating and accentuating world tension and insecurity or may become the foundation of a *mutual security system* hitherto inconceivable ...[679] [emphasis added].

7.2 STRUCTURAL ELEMENTS OF COMMON SECURITY

The main elements of common security may be listed according to Dieter Lutz and Egon Bahr[680] as well as to the notion of cooperative security of the Brookings Institution[681] in five categories:

1. *Cooperative denuclearization*
The defensive reorientation of military-strategic forces allows for the drastic reduction and even abolishment of nuclear weapons:

> ... such a regime would thus put strong constraints on nuclear weapons and seek to severely devalue nuclear forces as a currency of statecraft or a tool of power projection ... A key objective guiding the recomposition of remaining nuclear forces would be to eliminate any perception of vulnerability to nuclear attack among all states, thereby also helping to discourage further production or deployment of nuclear weapons globally. Constraints on the nuclear arsenals of the established nuclear powers are a necessary, if not sufficient, condition to help persuade other states that nuclear weapons have little compelling utility. As a corollary the regime would seek the elimination of all weapons of mass destruction.[682]

Thus, the concept contributes to the fulfilment of the nuclear-weapon powers' disarmament obligation according to Art. VI of the NPT, as reaffirmed by the ICJ.

2. *Structural non-provocation and defensive configurations*
Structural non-provocation implies that military forces are to be organized and equipped in a way that they do not permit a successful military attack. Cooperative denuclearization is strengthened in a mutually reinforcing way by establishing force postures structurally incapable of supporting a nuclear attack.

The important first step is to acknowledge that the national deployment of military capability must be governed by a strict principle of nonprovocation and be reflected in force postures accordingly.[683]

This requires separating conventional and nuclear theatre weapons, and establishing equal conventional options, such as a broad balance of conventional forces.[684]

3. *Internationalization of the response to an aggression*

While the restructuring of the military capabilities towards an exclusively defensive configuration, buttressed by arms control regulations, would offer a maximum degree of international security, it could not be excluded, however, that in circumventing the agreed rules a particular state would secretly develop an offensive capability. Therefore, it remains necessary to maintain as part of a reassurance system the right to self-defence in the framework of a collective security system.[685] Common security would, in addition, create the necessary conditions in security policy for the actual implementation of the United Nations Charter provision for the establishment of a multilateral defence force, leaving individual self-defence as *ultima ratio*.[686]

4. *Restraints on military investment and proliferation*

The reduction of the perceived threat after the Cold War, the recognition that military power is no longer a determining factor in international relations, and increasing budgetary limitations have all contributed to a reduction in the military capabilities of the former military blocs that comes closer to a standard of common security. This is a prompt to formalize these standards and control their implementation.[687]

5. *Transparency and confidence-building measures*

A central part of common security, which has to be understood as a process, is transparency and confidence-building measures. They are defined as:

> ... actions undertaken by States Parties that produce transparency by reducing or eliminating misperceptions of our concerns about potential threatening capabilities and activities.[688]

They were introduced mainly in the area of conventional armaments in Europe by the Conventional Forces in Europe (CFE) Treaty, but are increasingly found in universal arms control regimes such as the United Nations Register of Conventional Arms and the non-proliferation regimes for biological and chemical weapons as well as ballistic missile technology. These precedents could be the basis for developing a treaty on common security in outer space.[689] In the nuclear domain, confidence-building measures are mainly encountered in the INF and Strategic Arms Reduction Treaty (START) agreements. Prime elements are the prior notification and inspection of potentially threatening activities. The concept of common security provides for a multilateralization and possible institutionalization of such confidence-building measures.

As with the CHOM principle, the efficiency of common security largely depends on the realization of underlying structural components.

The success of the cooperative security regime will depend centrally on the strength of the structure of norms that the regime establishes.[690]

Thus, common security in outer space requires the establishment of an international order to safeguard the peaceful use of the common space. This also follows from the structural evolution of international law, in which the setting up and maintenance of cooperative regimes to solve complex, global problems has become the kernel of a "new sovereignty".[691] One of the main functions of international treaties is to now lay the foundation for such cooperative multilateral regimes. International treaties stand "at the centre of cooperative regimes by which states and their citizens seek to regulate major common problems".[692] The negotiation of a multilateral treaty on common security in outer space would adequately address the security and legal challenges posed by the threat of an extension of the arms race into outer space.

7.3   COMMON SECURITY AND THE GREAT POWERS

The concept of common security has increasingly influenced the security relations of the two great powers since the end of the Cold War. With regard to the possible use of defensive systems in outer space, the United States had already recognized in 1985 that this could only be achieved through taking a cooperative approach. Thus, in the context of the SDI debate, in January 1985 the US Secretary of State George Shultz adhered explicitly to the objective of equal security for both sides, originally a Soviet concept.[693] The declared aim of the Reagan Administration for the start of the 1985 bilateral Defence and Space Talks in Geneva was:

> ... a co-operative transition to a more stable deterrence which relies increasingly on non-nuclear defences against strategic ballistic missiles, should they prove feasible.[694]

The main basis for the security cooperation, which started concretely after the Cold War, became the Cooperative Threat Reduction (CTR) programme initiated by US senators Sam Nunn and Richard Lugar.[695] The programme provided far-reaching cooperation, including financial support for the reduction of Soviet/Russian nuclear capabilities.[696] The cooperative security policy also found its way into bilateral summit declarations. At a summit meeting on 2 September 1998 US President William Clinton and Russian President Boris Yeltsin adopted a "Joint Statement on Common Security Challenges at the Threshold of the Twenty-First Century",[697] in which they committed themselves to further common security in the interest of international security. For this purpose, they set up an expert group on missile and space technology. In a "Joint Statement on the Principles of Strategic Stability" of 5 June 2000 US President Clinton and Russian President Putin reaffirmed "mutual cooperation and mutual respect of each other's security interest", explicitly with regard to nuclear security and non-proliferation.[698] The recognition of mutual security interests is the foundation of common security.

In addition to the general recognition of common security in summit declarations, the United States and Russia have also initiated concrete measures of cooperative security with regard to outer space. Since 1992 both countries have been working on a joint Russian-American Observation Satellite, which is supposed to be used for both civil purposes of weather and environmental forecasting as well as for early warning and verification.[699] At a summit meeting on 5 June 2000 the two Presidents agreed on further concrete cooperative security measures with regard to outer space with the conclusion of a memorandum over the setting up of a Joint Data Exchange Center (JDEC) for the purpose of data exchange on early warning and for notification of missile launches.[700]

Probably the potentially most far-reaching expression of the new security cooperation of the former antagonists was the offer of former US President Bush Sr. to develop the new and more limited (relative to SDI) project of GPALS jointly with Russia, and with the acceptance of this offer by President Yeltsin in January 1992, who declared the readiness of Russia "to work out and subsequently to create and jointly operate a Global Protection System".[701] Before the Security Council of the United Nations, Yeltsin declared:

> I think the time has come to consider creating a global defence system for the world community. It could be based on a reorientation of the U.S. Strategic Defense Initiative to make use of high technologies developed in Russia's defense complex.[702]

The G.W. Bush Administration has followed much the same approach,[703] even though its denunciation of the ABM Treaty and the funding reductions of the CTR programme raised some doubts in this regard.[704] With the signing of the "Joint Declaration on the New Strategic Partnership" at the US-Russian Summit of 24 May 2002,[705] the G.W. Bush Administration clearly builds on the cooperative policy of the two previous US administrations, and could even develop it further in the direction of common security in the nuclear-strategic domain. The objective of common security is also the basis of the new institutional cooperation of the North Atlantic Treaty Organization (NATO) and Russia in the new NATO-Russia Council, founded on 27 May 2002 in Rome. President G.W. Bush stated before the German Bundestag on 23 May 2002 that "The Council gives us an opportunity to build *common security* against common threats" [emphasis added].[706]

Russia had previously assigned a special role to international cooperation within its space activities by amending its national space legislation in October 1996. Based on the notion of security in a broad sense and in view of its own interest to integrate into the world economy Russia agreed the:

> ... development and extension of international cooperation of the Russian Federation in the interest of further integration of the Russian Federation in the system of global economic relations and of securing international security.[707]

The policy of cooperative security pursued by the two great powers since 1990 has led to a considerable improvement in mutual confidence and security for both sides, according to Ashton Carter and William Perry, who elaborated the concept of "preventive defence" based on a cooperative security structure.[708] These successes, however, are not consolidated to a sufficient degree to prevent new strains on the strategic relationship such as a unilateral approach to the missile defence.

China emphasizes the principle of common security, which it prefers to refer to as "equal security", also in the context of military uses of outer space and of missile defence.[709] In this sense, Chinese President Jiang Zemin called for "a new security concept" centred on "... mutual trust, mutual benefit, equality and cooperation" before the CD in Geneva on 26 March 1999. On the basis of a broad notion of security, President Jiang emphasized that:

> Mutually beneficial cooperation and common prosperity constitute the economic guarantee for world peace ... If the great majority of developing countries cannot have security, then the entire world will never be tranquil.[710]

7.4   COMMON SECURITY, NUCLEAR STRATEGY AND MISSILE DEFENCE IN OUTER SPACE

The strategic objective of common security is to replace the deterrence strategy of MAD by "mutual assured security".[711] Thus, it matches President Reagan's goals pursued under SDI, and the goals that are currently linked to the introduction of strategic defence systems in the framework of a "strategic transition".[712] A US national defence against ballistic missile attacks could render nuclear weapons obsolete, thereby causing nuclear offensive weapons to become superfluous. The main difference, however, is that the concept of common security wants to achieve this by cooperation and structural change, whereas the proponents of a space-based missile defence view that this could be the result of technological developments in the form of new defensive systems in outer space. Yet, the scientific consensus is quite clear that there cannot be absolute security by technical means.[713]

Overcoming deterrence through a new relationship between offensive and defensive systems, however, is only possible in a cooperative environment.[714] The recognition by the nuclear-weapon powers of the necessity to cooperate in order to achieve equal security lies at the heart of the concept of common security. Its application would be possible without new armaments in outer space or on Earth.[715]

The concept would constitute an ideal basis for a cooperative nuclear strategic transition that would allow the fulfilment of the nuclear disarmament obligations according to Art. VI of the NPT, and that would free mankind of the scourge of nuclear terror. Common security opens the perspective for genuine disarmament by establishing on all sides non-provocative structures through defensive configurations. In the words of Lutz:

> Common security requires the replacement of the deterrence strategy by a strategy of prevention renouncing any measures of preemption and retaliation (in particular with weapons of mass destruction). [716]

Deterrence and common security are not compatible. The goal of a structurally non-provocative defence configuration requires a consensual approach. Reagan's vision to render nuclear weapons obsolete can be attained only as a cooperative solution, leading either to a joint deployment of an "international missile defence" under international control or in a consensual renunciation of space-based missile defence systems.

Since the decision of the United States to deploy a missile defence is presumed to be nearly certain, and since such a system would have recourse to the military use of outer space at least by sensor satellites, the interest of mankind under international space law would take priority over national or bilateral interests, thus opening the chance for the international community to legally insist on structurally non-provocative defensive configurations and to overcome nuclear deterrence by requiring compliance with the principle of cooperation. Only under such a cooperative approach could missile defence be kept in conformity with the nuclear disarmament obligations under Art. VI of the NPT that also applies to outer space.[717] By reorienting security policy towards defensive force configurations, common security would allow for a lower level of armaments necessary to establish security.[718] Overcoming deterrence through a cooperative transition towards a new strategic relationship of defensive-offensive systems requires a drastic reduction in warheads and launchers. In this respect, the US-Russian Treaty on Strategic Offensive Reductions of 24 May 2002 can be considered only a first step in the pursuit of genuine disarmament, as it lacks any obligation to destroy the dismantled nuclear warheads and to reduce launchers as well. In particular, common security requires the multilateralization of all the questions of active military uses of outer space linked to missile defence to safeguard the security interests of the international community. The above-mentioned US-Russian "Joint Declaration on the New Strategic Relationship" opens the door for the two great powers to find a compromise on the missile defence question by closely cooperating in any development of tactical and strategic defensive systems.[719] In turn, this opportunity could lead to an adequate multilateral agreement on common security in outer space.

A strategic transition towards cooperation is also a prerequisite of an active policy of non-proliferation. Developing a multilateral Treaty on Common Security in Outer Space could facilitate the cooperative transition from MAD to CTR,[720] by allowing the nuclear-weapon powers to adopt and formalize mutual "strategic reassurance measures". Banning Garrett, who considers such measures as particularly urgent with regard to a possible missile defence decision, offers the following definition:

> Strategic mistrust in the post-Cold War era creates the need for measures to reduce suspicions between and among states about their long-term political, military, and economic objectives—that is, their strategic intentions. Broadly speaking, strategic reassurance measures are steps that one nation takes to address the concerns of other nations that are suspicious of its broad, long-run intentions.[721]

A cooperative approach towards NMD requires first of all seeking a consensus with Russia and China as only through involving the big nuclear-weapon powers in the cooperative approach can a multilateral non-proliferation regime successfully be maintained.[722] Europe, a central actor in the non-proliferation regime through the Missile Technology Control Regime (MTCR), should play a more active and independent role by pursuing an active non-proliferation policy and by declaring the near and Middle Eastern region with the main proliferation risks a "Southern sphere of responsibility".[723]

The proponents of NMD unexpectedly supported the criticism of nuclear deterrence from the peace research field with their demand for a strategic transition making nuclear weapons obsolete.[724] Overcoming MAD seems today to be inevitable. The President of the Henry L. Stimson Center, Micheal Krepon, proposes replacing MAD by CTR, considering the process of overcoming MAD to have already started with the US-Russian cooperative nuclear programme in 1991:

> By the end of October 2000, CTR programmes in the former Soviet Union had secured the deactivation of 5,014 nuclear warheads, destroyed 407 intercontinental ballistic missiles (ICBMs) and 366 ICBM silos; eliminated 68 strategic bombers and 256 launchers from ballistic missile-carrying submarines; destroyed 148 submarine-launched ballistic missiles, 17 ballistic missile-carrying submarines, and 204 long-range cruise missiles; and sealed 194 nuclear test-tunnels ...[725]

US Senator Lugar, one of the co-authors of the CTR programme, rightly demands a globalization of cooperative threat reduction programmes.[726] This is only possible in an adequate multilateral framework.[727] Similarly, Europe has strengthened efforts to make the Hague Code of Conduct against Ballistic Missile Proliferation (HCoC) more universal by seeking to include a greater number of states with missile technology, in particular China, Pakistan, India, Iran and Israel.[728] An extension of these programmes alone, however, would not suffice to overcome nuclear deterrence. All measures need to be additionally embedded in a comprehensive system of common security. Naturally, however, this can only be achieved incrementally.

Since the peaceful use of outer space is a preoccupation not only for present, but even more so for future generations, the claim of the international community for common security will become stronger. In accordance with mankind's interest in the peaceful use of outer space, these interests will have to take priority over national interests, especially with regard to military uses of outer space and the eventual deployment of a space-based missile defence, since the issue raises the question of mankind's very survival.

7.5   CONCLUSIONS

Generally, the principles of common security are recognized in relations between the nuclear-weapon powers. Their manifestation with regard to security in outer space, however, needs further clarification with respect to the question of military use of the common space, and in particular a cooperative settlement of the issues linked to the possible introduction of a strategic missile defence. The mankind clause of the Outer Space Treaty obliges space powers to pursue cooperative efforts in respecting the interests of all states. As a result, states are thus required to establish common security as the expression of the security interests of the international community according to the mankind clause and in compliance with the nuclear disarmament obligations of the NPT.

The solutions to such a strategic transition could form the content of cooperative/common security in outer space, which is the focus of the next section of the present study.

PART IV

A multilateral agreement and an International Organization for Common Security in Outer Space

The unhappy fact is that, thus far, whenever we (or others) have sought to solve our national security dilemma by technical means, we have in the end only made matters worse.

Herbert F. York
1985[729]

Those advocating the aggressive use of space often overlook how the rule of law embodied in verifiable arms control agreements may provide greater levels of national security through reduced levels of threat.

P. J. Baines
1998[730]

CHAPTER 8

PROPOSALS FOR THE IMPLEMENTATION OF THE PRINCIPLE OF THE PEACEFUL USE OF OUTER SPACE

8.1 IMPLEMENTING THE PRINCIPLE OF THE PEACEFUL USE OF OUTER SPACE AND THE PREVENTION OF AN ARMS RACE IN OUTER SPACE[731]

Since the 1970s a number of delegations from around the world have submitted proposals to the various United Nations fora to create special treaty rules that would ensure the peaceful use of outer space, fill the gaps of the Outer Space Treaty regarding new military uses of outer space, and eliminate the existing legal uncertainties in securing outer space for the benefit of mankind. In addition to confidence-building measures and immunity rules for civil space uses, the proposals concentrate on an explicit prohibition of active military uses of outer space through an express space weapons ban, in particular of ASAT and BMD weapons. In the CD's Ad Hoc Committee on PAROS, it was hoped that by agreeing first on confidence-building measures, it would be easier to win subsequent US support[732] for specific treaty rules on the prohibition of space weapons.[733]

8.1.1 PROPOSALS FOR A BAN ON ACTIVE MILITARY USES OF OUTER SPACE

8.1.1.1 Proposals for the prevention of an arms race in outer space

To date, the proposals submitted in this regard range from those containing specific additional rules for the Outer Space Treaty, to comprehensive drafts for a separate treaty on the peaceful use of outer space. Several states have considered the easiest and most feasible solution to be the extension of the prohibition on the deployment of WMD in outer space, as stipulated in Art. IV of the Outer Space Treaty, to cover any type of space weapon through the inclusion of the phrase "any kind of weapon" to the Treaty's phrasing in para. 1. Italy first proposed this idea in 1968[734] and again in 1978[735] at the United Nations General Assembly. In 1979 Italy submitted a draft for such an additional protocol to the Outer Space Treaty to the CD.[736] The draft is based on the distinction between passive military uses, which should continue to be permitted (explicitly Art. 1, para. 2 of the draft with regard to verification satellites), and active military uses of a destructive nature in outer space, which were to be explicitly banned. The prohibition of active uses in the form of an explicit ban on space weapons should be controlled by multilateral verification. For this purpose, the draft supports the French proposal on the establishment of an International Satellite Monitoring Agency (ISMA).[737] Venezuela proposed a similar addition to the Outer Space Treaty in 1987.[738] Peru considered it necessary to also prohibit ASAT weapons that were not deployed in space.[739] The proposals submitted by Venezuela and Peru also included the prohibition of the development, production and testing of space weapons, which represented a precedent for outer space law. A development ban is also included in most proposals for a separate treaty on the prohibition of space weapons.

The initiative for a separate treaty came from the Soviet Union in 1981 at the United Nations General Assembly[740] and in 1982 at the CD,[741] which submitted a "Draft Treaty on the Prohibition of the Stationing of Weapons of Any Kind in Outer Space". Referring to the Italian proposal, Art. 1 of this draft contained a general prohibition of space weapons. Article 3 provided for a general prohibition "to destroy, damage, disturb the normal functioning of, or change the trajectory of space objects of other States Parties".[742] The United States did not find the draft acceptable due to, among others, the provision in Art. 1 to prohibit the deployment of weapons on "reusable manned space vehicles", since this could be understood as an attempt to limit the US shuttle programme.[743] In addition, delegations criticized the formulation—not the concept itself—of the principle of "non-interference" with regard to other space objects, as it was perceived to be prone to misunderstanding.[744] The second Soviet draft of 1983 pursued a broader approach, which was also reflected in its title: "Draft Treaty on the Prohibition of the Use of Force in Outer Space and from Space Against the Earth".[745] It took account of several of the points that had been criticized by a number of mainly Western states in the first draft,[746] and provided for international means of verification beyond "national technical means".[747] In particular, it stressed cooperative elements of security in space especially with regard to provisions on cooperation and consultation, which would be supported by the proposed establishment of a Consulting Committee modelled on the bilateral examples in the SALT and ABM Treaties. This draft was generally received more positively,[748] finding support also among the group of Western states.[749]

At the beginning of 1985 China tabled a far-reaching working paper aimed expressly at a complete ban on any militarization of space, in particular a prohibition of "space weapons with actual lethal or destructive power and military satellites of all types".[750] By also trying to limit passive military uses of outer space, the Chinese draft went beyond the great majority of previous proposals. While China has reaffirmed this position in principle to this date through statements at the CD, it views the prior agreement on a non-weaponization of space as the most urgent interim measure towards its complete de-militarization.[751]

Canada submitted early on a conceptual paper on arms control in outer space,[752] and like France, made proposals on the procedural and institutional measures necessary to guarantee the peaceful use of outer space,[753] including draft treaties on a prohibition of space weapons.[754] The paper also elaborated on the distinction between passive military uses with potentially stabilizing effects, such as verification or early warning satellites, and destabilizing systems, among which it included ASAT systems or other types of space weaponry.

India favoured consolidating the moratorium on the testing of ASAT systems that had previously been unilaterally declared by the Soviet Unions and was also *de facto* respected by the United States due to the support of the US Congress, in a multilateral treaty.[755] This was additionally complemented by an explicit provision to destroy existing systems. In the same vein, Pakistan proposed a multilateralization of the ABM Treaty, including a prohibition on the development of such systems, a package of confidence-building measures and immunity rules for satellites.[756] While Sri Lanka favoured a ban on ASAT systems, distinguishing between "low-orbit" and "high-orbit" systems,[757] India preferred to distinguish between near-Earth orbit, higher-Earth orbit and geosynchronous orbit.[758]

Sweden has consistently called for a comprehensive ban on space weapons that would include their development, production and the destruction of existing land- or air-based ASAT systems, within both the CD and the United Nations General Assembly.[759] On 21 January 1988, the heads of Government of Sweden, Greece, Mexico, Tanzania, Argentina and India called for such a comprehensive prohibition of space weapons through the adoption of the "Stockholm Declaration",[760] deemed urgent for the prevention of an arms race both in outer space and on Earth.

With its proposal of 1978 for the establishment of ISMA, France took a leading role in space disarmament,[761] and additionally submitted draft proposals on the prohibition of space weapons, including—along the same lines as Germany[762]—an explicit ban on ASAT systems. However, France did not consider an ASAT ban to be sufficient to secure the "fundamental principles of the present space regime" of the peaceful use of outer space, the non-discrimination and the prohibition of national appropriation.[763] Rather, on the basis of the principle of "non-interference" it deemed it necessary to agree to a "code of conduct" for all space activities,[764] which should be based on the distinction between passive and active military uses of space.[765] The principle of non-interference and immunity of satellites was, however, problematic for the non-aligned states, which rejected any military use of outer space.[766]

Germany concentrated its proposals on questions of definition, confidence-building measures and an immunity regime for satellites as well as on multilateral verification issues.[767] These would complement an agreement on the ban of ASAT systems to be achieved first bilaterally between the United States and the Soviet Union.

None of these proposals have been negotiated in detail since the United States continues to take the position that an arms race in outer space is not imminent, and that additional multilateral treaty stipulations on the military use of outer space are not necessary. In contrast to the US Administration, the US Congress more or less imposed from 1983 until 1995 a ban on the testing of ASAT systems,[768] as long as Soviet Union/ Russia adhered to such a ban as well. The US House of Representatives had adopted in February 1983 a resolution that called on the President to negotiate a comprehensive ban on space weapons, including the testing of such systems.[769]

In the late 1990s, despite US opposition to the re-establishment of the Ad Hoc Committee on PAROS, new initiatives were undertaken at the CD and the United Nations for a multilateral space weapons ban and for safeguarding the peaceful use of outer space. In early 2000, Russia, China and Canada tabled new working papers at the CD, where they reconfirmed their previous proposals for a prohibition of space weapons and additional confidence-building measures, and adapted them to the most recent developments.[770] The Chinese paper of February 2000 proposed both strengthening existing legal instruments (Outer Space Treaty and ABM Treaty) and creating new instruments,[771] including the prohibition of the testing and deployment of space weapons systems and their components in outer space, and restrictions on the current uses of satellites for military purposes. In June 1999, Russian President Putin made a proposal at the Group of 8 summit in Cologne to set up a "Global Missile and Missile Technologies Non-Proliferation Control System" that would effectively counter the "missile threats" of "rogue states" without abandoning the ABM Treaty, and would thereby contribute to the prevention of an arms race in outer space.[772] In a subsequent proposal, Russia suggested holding a United Nations conference on the prevention of the militarization of outer space and the promotion of the peaceful use of outer space in February 2001,[773] calling again for the urgent conclusion of a multilateral agreement on the prevention of an arms race in outer space. Russian Foreign Minister Igor Ivanov made yet another proposal, which combined the previous drafts, at the United Nations General Assembly on 24 September 2001,[774] calling for the start of negotiations on a comprehensive multilateral agreement to prevent an arms race in outer space, the prohibition of space weapons of any kind, and a moratorium on the deployment of such systems in outer space. In the case of a reciprocal adherence to such a moratorium by other space powers, Moscow declared that it was prepared to undertake a unilateral obligation to that extent.

In February 1999 and again in February 2001 Canada submitted working papers at the CD for action on outer space, in which it reaffirmed its proposal to negotiate a multilateral convention for the non-weaponization of outer space, proposing that:

> ... a CD Ad Hoc Committee on Outer Space be established with the mandate to negotiate a convention for the non-weaponisation of outer space. ... There is no current multilateral agreement banning the deployment of weapons other than weapons of mass destruction. There is thus need for the international community to address this problem, and to do so multilaterally, particularly in view of the growing number of states with the capacity or near-capacity to place objects into orbit. ... We accept the current military uses of outer space for surveillance, intelligence-gathering and communication. Our focus is on the *non-*

weaponisation of outer space, i.e. no positioning of actual weapons in outer space [emphasis in the original].[775]

Dennis Kucinich, a US Democrat member of Congress, introduced in October 2001 a draft bill entitled the "Space Preservation Act", aimed at supporting an international initiative for a "World Treaty to Ban Space Weapons".[776] The draft bill announced its aim in the preamble "to preserve the cooperative, peaceful uses of space for the benefit of humankind by permanently prohibiting the basing of weapons in space".[777] According to Section 4:

> The President shall direct the United States representatives to the United Nations and other international organisations to immediately work toward negotiating, adopting, and implementing a world agreement banning space-based weapons.[778]

The European states, while demanding the re-establishment of the Ad Hoc Committee on PAROS and recalling their previous draft treaty proposals, have not, at the time of writing the present study, undertaken new initiatives.[779] A joint European initiative to preserve outer space for peaceful purposes would provide a strong backing in support of the international community to prevent an arms race in outer space, and improve its chances of success to a considerable extent.

8.1.1.2 Non-governmental proposals

In "Resolution No. 1" of 27 August 1988, the International Law Association adopted the following urgent proposals on the regulation of military uses of outer space *de lege ferenda*, demanding that the two space powers prolong the ABM Treaty,[780] particularly also in view of the start of service of the space station and a possible manned space flight:

1. Recognizing the destabilizing nature of the use of ASAT weapons, stresses the need of reaching, both on a bilateral and multilateral basis, an agreement on an extended ban on the testing of these weapons.
2. Referring to the harmful consequences of the present absence of definite legal rules regarding the military uses of or on these stations;
3. Submits that there is an urgent need for a definition of impermissible categories of military uses of or on these stations [emphasis in the original].

The US-based Union of Concerned Scientists submitted in May 1983 a draft treaty prepared by Kurt Gottfried, Richard Garwin and Len Meeker on the prohibition of anti-satellite weapons to the US Senate Foreign Relations Committee.[781] The draft was a proposal for a bilateral US-Soviet agreement, which was from the vantage point of the US scientists understandable given the imminent ASAT developments in the two countries. In the same vein, representatives of the US Air Force continue to support a treaty explicitly banning space weapons. Thus, after a detailed analysis of the capabilities of space weapons, Major William Spacy II,[782] concluded that the strategic objectives of the US Space Command over "space control, defensive counterspace, offensive counterspace, force application" could be achieved equally by land-, air- or sea-based systems. Further, Spacy concluded that it would be in US interest to renounce the development of space weapons. This would be necessary, he argues, in view of the international legal prohibition of active military uses of outer space and the international reactions to be expected from a unilateral deployment of space weapons. The Former Deputy Assistant Secretary of Defence of the Reagan Administration, Lawrence J. Korb, also speaks of an "international norm prohibiting the weaponization of space" and hence opposes a deployment of NMD in outer space.[783]

In Germany, the Göttinger Initiative of Scientists is heralded for being the first to propose a comprehensive "Draft Treaty on the Limitation of Military Uses of Outer Space".[784] The draft was deliberated at the initiative of the Social Democratic parliamentary group in autumn 1984 in the German Bundestag, but was, however, rejected by the then governing Conservative and Free Democratic Parliamentary groups.[785] The main objective of the draft was to limit military uses of outer space to activities with stabilizing effects, and at the same time to protect civil space uses.[786] As a result, the draft provides for a prohibition of any kind of active military uses of a destructive nature. Thus, Art. 1 provides a general prohibition to destroy, damage or disturb the orderly functioning of space objects in any way. This is specified in Art. 2 by a prohibition to develop, test or deploy weapons or weapon systems in outer space, on Earth or in the air, which would serve such purposes. The eventual destruction of existing ASAT systems is also foreseen. The draft goes beyond a prohibition of active military uses, inasmuch as Art. 9 also prohibits the use of any system in space for the direct guidance of nuclear weapons. Although this does not affect the potentially stabilizing use of satellites for reconnaissance, navigation and communication, it would no longer permit the use of precise positioning and speed data by satellites for the direct guidance of nuclear weapons. This could raise problems of verification and other passive military uses, which, however, the drafters considered to be solvable.[787]

A further feature of the draft is its stipulation in Art. 4 of a minimum distance between space objects, which serves on the one hand to protect civil space objects, and on the other hand would prevent the otherwise difficult to control deployment of space mines.[788] In keeping with the multilateral character of the treaty, the draft provides, in addition to "national technical means" for verification, for the transfer of such means to an international organization, since otherwise the verification and monitoring of the treaty's implementation would lie exclusively in the hands of the few space powers. However, due to the still pervasive East-West rivalry at the time, the draft initiators did not provide for the transfer of military reconnaissance and navigation satellites to international control although deemed necessary.[789]

In light of the large number of proposals made in the international legal and arms control literature, the following will highlight only a few of these proposals. In 1977, Stephen Gorove proposed a treaty that took the approach of explicitly enumerating the permitted space activities in the security field as opposed to prohibition norms.[790] According to Gorove, this had the advantage of presuming that everything not permitted is therefore forbidden, which would thus apply to new technological developments in the military field.[791] S. Sanders proposed combining the ABM and SALT I Treaties with a prohibition of ASATs, which would together:

> ... constitute a new step in arms control for outer space, as for the first time they address themselves not only to the extension of weapon systems existing on Earth to outer space but also to the protection of technologies which—if we assume that national technical means of verification includes satellites—are typical for the space environment only.[792]

Rebecca Johnson suggested a "Treaty to Prohibit Weapons and War in Space" consisting of three elements:

- A ban on the deployment and use of all kinds of weapons in space, thereby extending and strengthening the 1967 Outer Space Treaty's prohibition on weapons of mass destruction in space ...;

- Banning the testing, deployment and use of anti-satellite (ASAT) weapons, whether earth-based or space-based;
- Establishing a code of conduct for the peace-supporting, non-offensive and non-aggressive uses of space.[793]

With a view to preventing an arms race in outer space, Eileen Galloway proposed in 1982 the establishment of an international group of experts tasked with the clarification and integration of the principle of peaceful use of outer space and Art. IV of the Outer Space Treaty.[794] This proposal has since become even more urgent. Such a group of experts could prepare an eventual international treaty conference on the establishment of a multilateral regime securing the peaceful use of outer space, including the submission of a draft treaty.

8.1.2 PROPOSALS FOR CONFIDENCE-BUILDING MEASURES IN OUTER SPACE AND AN IMMUNITY REGIME FOR SATELLITES

A number of states have submitted mainly to the CD, but also occasionally to COPUOS, comprehensive proposals for confidence-building measures either as part of an arms control regime in space, or as a separate contribution to security in outer space.[795] Their objective is to establish transparency and predictability and to facilitate information exchange as well as a technology transfer given the dual-use capabilities of space technologies.[796] With a view to the specific problems in outer space, the traditional confidence-building measures were complemented by proposals for a special immunity regime for satellites as well as "rules of the road" in the form of a so-called "space code of conduct".[797] However, given the US position,[798] according to which satellites are already sufficiently protected by the prohibition of the use of force, even these confidence-building measures have not been negotiated so far in earnest.

Both Germany[799] and France[800] made elaborate proposals on confidence-building measures that would be part of a cooperative security order for outer space. On behalf of the German delegation, Kries underlined in a presentation before the CD the necessity of a cooperative approach in military or other security-related uses of outer space to be pursued in the framework of confidence-building measures.[801] In his function as "Friend of the Chair", A.V. Voroblev summarized the discussions on confidence-building measures in "Draft Guidelines regarding Measures on Confidence Building and Predictability in Outer Space

Activities".[802] Voroblev tabled these proposals in the form of a draft resolution for the United Nations General Assembly; however, Russia did not introduce the draft officially at the General Assembly, presumably to avoid provoking the United States, which continued to reject any negotiation of concrete security measures for outer space.[803]

In 1986 Germany proposed a multilateral immunity regime for satellites as well as a package of further confidence-building measures and a prohibition of ASATs.[804] By contrast, some authors consider an immunity regime for satellites to be an alternative to an ASAT ban, should such a ban be unattainable.[805] In order to improve the information on space activities, Germany made an additional proposal in 1991 that every launching state should annually publish a list of all of the space launches and a description of their purposes.[806] As part of a regime "bestowed upon registered objects by international agreement" safety margins and the introduction of "keep-out" zones were considered as further protective measures for communication satellites in particular.[807] In the same year France had proposed strengthening the Convention on Registration of Objects Launched into Outer Space, introducing safety margins, and establishing security zones wherein passing space objects should be subject to a compulsory prior notification.[808] While these proposals for rules over security zones also use the term "keep-out" zones, they differed fundamentally from proposals for such zones around space-based components of an NMD system since they want to exclude active military uses from the benefit of immunity. The "keep-out" zones envisaged for space-based components of weapons systems are considered to run counter to the principle of non-appropriation and occupation since they aim at exclusive control of part of outer space.[809] By contrast, the security zones for civil satellites would normally not pose the risk of leading to a military occupation.

France[810] and Germany[811] additionally made elaborate proposals for a "Space Code of Conduct" with the threefold objective to improve the security of civil space activities, to prevent the use of outer space for non-peaceful uses, and to create an immunity regime for satellites. The proposals met with broad support at the CD with the exception of the United States.[812] In view of a general protection for military surveillance satellites, France was also seeking a multilateralization of the "non-interference" exchanged mutually by the United States and the Soviet Union with regard to each other's surveillance satellites under the heading of "national technical means of verification" in the ABM Treaty and in SALT I and II.[813] Such a principle should be applied to all satellites that do not have capabilities to destroy or damage other space objects. France proposed to strengthen the immunity regime institutionally by establishing an International Trajectory Centre as well as an International Launch Notification Centre to be put under the aegis of the United Nations.[814] The former would receive all relevant data about the projected orbit of space objects to prevent eventual collisions, while the latter would serve as a mechanism for the notification of all space launches of satellites and ballistic missiles, which France and Germany had proposed to be obligatory.[815]

These proposals at the CD are accompanied by a number of suggestions made by space institutions and individual authors.[816] The contribution by H. Feigl, who presented a German proposal to the CD entitled "Confidence and Security Building in a Protection Regime for Outer Space, Observance of Behaviour vs. Monitoring Weapons", is of particular interest.[817] It foresaw a set of confidence-building measures in outer space as part of a concept of cooperative security in outer space consisting of three main elements:

* Extension of the registration and notification procedures;
* Rules on orbital behaviour in space ("rules of the road"); and
* Surveillance measures.

The proposal is premised on the assumption that independent of the risk of an arms race in outer space, there is an urgent need to fill the regulatory vacuum for the protection of civil space activities. This requires a consensus on international legal safeguards for the use of outer space on the basis of multilateral agreements.[818] The objective of such a "gradual elaboration of a satisfactory security *structure*" [emphasis added] are concrete measures in the framework of a legal regime for the immunity of space objects that would result in increased security for space activities and would inevitably lead to a treaty banning space weapons.[819]

Richard DalBello from the Office of Technology Assessment of the US Congress proposes the following measures as possible "rules of the road":

* New, stringent requirements for advance notice of launch activities;
* "Keep-out" zones around satellites;
* Rights of inspection;

- Minimum separation distance between satellites;
- Registration of low-orbit overflight;
- Limitations on high-velocity fly-bys or trailing;
- "Hotline" for space activities.[820]

Agreeing to such comprehensive confidence-building measures and security rules for the civil use of outer space could be a propitious step to prepare the ground for a cooperative approach to the question of space-based missile defence.

8.2   PROPOSALS FOR A JOINT DEVELOPMENT OF A GLOBAL MISSILE DEFENCE

When President Reagan surprised the world in 1983 with his suggestion to share the results of SDI with the Soviet Union, and to jointly make nuclear weapons "impotent and obsolete", quite a few considered this to be an exercise in public relations.[821] However, the United States indeed made a concrete proposal at the CD for both sides to open their research laboratories to each other for this very purpose.[822] Thus, Reagan gave a strong impulse to the process of a fundamental review of the strategic relationship of the two countries and, in fact, of developing new cooperative security structures that continued into the post-Cold War era. In 1992 the defence ministries of the two countries set up a US-Russian Concepts Working Group so that concrete steps towards common security could be envisaged. President Yeltsin's response to President Bush Sr.'s offer to participate in GPALS, the more limited successor of SDI, was probably the most far-reaching step towards envisaging a common defence system.[823] Then Chairman of the Foreign Relations Committee of the Duma and later Russian Ambassador to Washington, Vladimir Lukin, explained the thinking of the Russian leadership as follows:

> The United States is extending a hand to us for real alliance in the nuclear sphere and the strategic defence system. If we agree on this, we could be talking about creating a strategic defence system for the whole of mankind—that is, a situation will arise where we, together with the United States, Europe, and all democratic countries, will protect ourselves from people such as Saddam [Hussein] and others capable of destroying mankind ...[824]

For that purpose, Jewgenij Velikhave, member of the Russian Academy of Sciences,[825] presented a comprehensive cooperative global defence as part of a broad non-proliferation regime, starting first with bilateral then multilateral early warning and verification. The Russian idea that a joint defence system should be put under the aegis of an international organization was viewed, however, by the United States with scepticism. In addition, Russia insisted that such a system should not include space-based interceptors or other space weapons.[826]

In early 2000 President Putin referred to his predecessor's proposals as a reaction to the reinforced NMD plans, in suggesting, primarily to the Europeans, to cooperate in the development of a first tactical missile defence system in addition to a global non-proliferation regime for ballistic missile technology.[827]

The US-Russian "Joint Declaration on the New Strategic Partnership" of 24 May 2002 marked a significant step towards an enhanced bilateral cooperation in an eventual joint development in particular of tactical missile defence systems.[828] Although the divergent positions on the issue of space-based systems are not resolved, the declaration, together with the institutional cooperation in the new NATO-Russia Council, could nevertheless open an avenue for cooperatively overcoming the risks of the antagonisms of the missile defence issue.

Various proposals for an internationalization of missile defence have been made in the literature, based also on the legal argument that the interest of mankind in the peaceful use of outer space could only be safeguarded through appropriate multilateralization.[829] In this vein, Edward Finch pleads for an "International Strategic Defence Initiative":

> If outer space is to be used for peaceful purposes, any measure adopted to prevent the arms race in outer space must apply to all parties, be verifiable and enhance stability and security ... Thus what seems to be needed is an International Strategic Defence Initiative (ISDI), which would be used to defend the whole planet, including both superpowers. It appears that space technology would better serve its purpose if it was to be developed with the participation of the *international community* by means of an *international depoliticised agency*, which would also be responsible for the operation and control of the ISDI [emphasis added].[830]

Scott March has also proposed a joint deployment of the US SDI system and a Soviet BMD system in a cooperative framework, including technology transfer as a means to overcome nuclear deterrence.[831]

Particularly with regard to the close link of missile defence and non-proliferation to the new threats concerning the enhanced risks within and from the South, missile defence is no longer a question of a US-Russian duopoly, but rather concerns the entire international community. This has led to proposals for a jointly developed defence system under the aegis of the United Nations. For outer space, the requisites for non-proliferation are particularly acute given the dual-use capabilities of most of civil space technologies. For this purpose, Olivier de Saint Lager combines the general considerations of space law and the security and arms control rationale, and suggests setting up a world space organization.[832] The organization would have specific security functions, in particular with regard to the non-proliferation control of sensitive technology, and would also consider multilateral satellite verification capabilities. In the same sense, George Paul Sloup suggests setting up an international peacekeeping capability including space-based components and an international BMD system under the aegis of the United Nations Security Council and the United Nations General Assembly.[833]

Although these proposals might appear utopian to many, the idea that a missile defence deployed in outer space concerns the interests of all mankind is fully justified. The international community is therefore entitled to take the issue beyond bilateral relations between states to the multilateral level by proposing to negotiate on common security in outer space. With the issue of a missile defence in outer space, the prospect of not only the peaceful use of the common space in general is at stake but also the non-proliferation of weapons of mass destruction.

8.3 PROPOSALS FOR A COMPREHENSIVE SECURITY ORDER TO SAFEGUARD THE PEACEFUL USE OF OUTER SPACE

In 1990 the United Nations General Assembly mandated a group of governmental experts (from Argentina, Brazil, Bulgaria, Canada, China, Egypt, France, India, Pakistan, Russia, the United States and Zimbabwe) to work out proposals for confidence-building measures in outer space.[834] In its comprehensive report, the group not only made an analysis of confidence-building measures, but also addressed the whole range of proposals submitted at the CD aimed at preventing an arms race in outer, space including procedural and institutional repercussions.[835] According to the report, a great number of states see a prohibition of space weapons as the most important confidence-building measure in outer space.[836] Referring to the numerous existing proposals and to their significance for a prevention of an arms race in space and thus for the safeguarding of the peaceful use of outer space,[837] the group suggests the following measures to be agreed at the CD and COPUOS:

- Transparency measures concerning dual-use technology to secure its use for exclusively peaceful purposes;[838]
- Access to space technology and information;[839]
- Strengthening the Registration Convention;[840]
- Multilateral use of satellite remote sensing in the interest of the international community,[841] as well as the creation of an international early warning system concerning accidents in outer space;[842]
- Drafting "rules of the road" including safety margins between space objects;[843]
- Use of space technology for preventive diplomacy, crisis management, and peaceful settlement of conflicts in the framework of the United Nations;[844]
- Re-examination of the proposal to establish an International Satellite Monitoring Agency and an International Space Monitoring Agency;[845]
- Examination of a coordinating mechanism, including a world space organization, to promote confidence building and cooperation in outer space on such issues as remote sensing, environmental monitoring, crisis prevention and forecasts of natural catastrophes.[846]

In a similar vein, Peter Jankowitsch, speaking of the need for a new security agenda for outer space, also proposes a comprehensive set of confidence-building measures, including a ban on space weapons and an immunity regime for satellites to be agreed upon in a treaty governing new security principles in outer space:

> A new "Magna Carta" has to be drafted which not only encompasses what has happened in outer space over the last 20 years but which can also avert the imminent danger of an arms race in outer space ... which will also bring a new sense of security to this environment ... to leave the option of peaceful development open.[847]

The main actors, according to Jankowitsch, have to contribute to this objective in the understanding that:

> ... their best interests ... will not be served by the mindless translation of conventional means to achieve security in outer space but by the patient search for a new security agenda which will bear dividends not only for themselves but also for the rest of mankind.[848]

In January 2001, the German journal *Wissenschaft und Frieden* published a memorandum of renowned representatives of the Union of German Scientists, offering a dynamic proposal countering the risk of an arms race on Earth and in space through:[849]

- Maintaining the arms control regime, including in particular the non-proliferation regime by preserving the ABM Treaty (in the meantime denounced by the United States) and by convincing commitments of Washington, Moscow and Beijing to the objective of non-proliferation of WMD;
- Creating an international early warning and control system for ballistic missiles and space weapons as well as measures of confidence building, risk reduction and timely notification of space launches as part of preventive arms control;
- Maintaining a similar initiative with regard to the potential proliferating countries such as Iran, Iraq, Syria and Libya in a gradually extending "Southern sphere of European responsibility".

Theresa Hitchens has elaborated an ambitious agenda to address transparency, confidence-building and "rules of the road" as major elements of a cooperative order for future security in outer space.[850]

These concepts, taken together with a package of confidence-building measures in outer space, would form an auspicious basis for the negotiation of a multilateral agreement on common security in outer space, which could effect the paradigmatic change in international law towards elevating the interest of mankind above that of single states, and thus safeguard the peaceful use of the common space.

CHAPTER 9

A COMMON SECURITY IN OUTER SPACE TREATY TO IMPLEMENT THE OUTER SPACE TREATY IN THE FIELD OF SECURITY

9.1 FOUNDATIONS AND PREMISES

9.1.1 IMPLEMENTATION OF THE INTEREST OF MANKIND IN THE AREA OF SECURITY IN OUTER SPACE

The paradigmatic change that validates the interest of mankind, which the Outer Space Treaty set in motion in the security field, provides the necessary basis for common security in outer space. For that purpose, a multilateral Treaty on Common Security in Outer Space, in short a CSO Treaty, should be negotiated as soon as possible. The international legal foundations for such a treaty would first of all be the common status of outer space as CHOM, based on the Outer Space Treaty's inclusion of the mankind clause and the principle of cooperation in Art. I, para. 1 and Articles II and III, and the principle of due account of the interests of other states in Art. IX, as well as the obligation of the nuclear-weapon states under Art. VI of the NPT to negotiate an agreement on general and complete nuclear disarmament. The CSO Treaty would thus at the same time create the multilateral basis on which the United States and Russia could solve the issue of a "strategic transition" raised by missile defence by replacing the strategy of MAD with a new strategy of "mutual assured security" based on CTR[851] and "strategic reassurance measures".[852]

In terms of arms control such a treaty seems urgent, since with the exception of the bilateral ABM Treaty of 1972, which has now been denounced by the United States, out of the whole range of the numerous multilateral and bilateral treaty rules on demilitarization, arms control, disarmament and non-proliferation, outer space is nearly completely absent.[853]

According to Michael Krepon, the United States has a choice between pursuing unilateral strategic dominance based on the weaponization of space, or a strategy of international cooperation, which would keep outer space free of weapons. According to international law, this alternative does not exist. The Outer Space Treaty requires that a qualitatively new use of space will have to take into account the interest of mankind and other states. New strategic uses of outer space therefore require a multilateral framework. Of course, the multilateralization of nuclear strategic issues can only take place gradually and with circumspection. Therefore, the institutional arrangements of the CSO Treaty would have to grant special status to the nuclear-weapon powers. Thus, a standing Consultative Committee, which would in particular be entrusted with the elaboration of strategic reassurance measures and CTR measures, could be restricted in its membership to the nuclear-weapon powers meeting bilaterally according to subject matters. While the multilateral obligations would thus be limited to a reporting system, this would nonetheless have an important confidence-building impact on the other states.

The primary function of the CSO Treaty would be to heed the security interests of all states in space by replacing the pursuit of unilateral or selective security with the concept of cooperative security.[854] The Treaty would prohibit transgression towards active military use of outer space by specifying the legal standards of peaceful use and of the principles and mechanisms of cooperative security. At the same time, the Treaty would create an international disarmament mechanism with regard to outer space, which could gradually take charge of the passive (and stabilizing) military functions of satellite surveillance and of verification and early warning that are at present carried out on a national level only. In putting the ban on active military uses of outer space within a comprehensive concept of common security that also includes the general protection of civil space uses, the Treaty would have an important value-added in comparison to the proposals made so far that concentrate solely on a weapons ban. By leading to defensive force configurations and cooperative denuclearization, common security would help overcome the strategy of nuclear deterrence. The Treaty would include a comprehensive protection regime for civil uses of outer space, including "rules of the road" as well as containing institutional provisions in the form of ISMA for international cooperative verification. The convergence of these elements reinforcing each other would lead to new cooperative security structures in outer space, which correspond to its legal status as CHOM and, in turn, to the structural order underlying this community status. In the long-term, the community status of outer space as CHOM would be best served by a complete demilitarization such as currently in force for the Antarctic and the celestial bodies. Therefore, the Treaty should contain a clause obliging the parties to make efforts to conclude a treaty on complete demilitarization once a successful strategic change and nuclear disarmament have been achieved.

9.1.2 COMPARISON OF A PROHIBITION OF SPACE WEAPONS WITH THE CWC

A model for the CSO Treaty could be the Chemical Weapons Convention (CWC), which entered into force on 29 April 1997 and was the first multilateral agreement to ban a whole category of weapons and to provide for an organization entrusted with its implementation.[855] In addition, the agreement provides adequate mechanisms for dealing with dual-use technology to guarantee that the development of the chemical industry for civil purposes is not adversely affected.[856] On the basis of Art. II, para. 11, and Art. VIII of the Convention, the Organization for the Prohibition of Chemical Weapons (OPCW) was established with nearly universal membership, including all states with a significant chemical industry, among them the major nuclear-weapon powers and more than 120 states from all over the world. The CWC links the complete ban on chemical weapons with the obligation to cooperate in the field of the peaceful use of the chemical industry. Article XI of the CWC calls upon parties to exchange, to the greatest extent possible, chemicals, equipment as well as scientific and technical information with regard to permissible civil activities. This clear commitment to the scientific and technological development of states parties and of international cooperation in the chemical domain allowed the chemical industry within the state parties to support the agreement. The agreement, supported through an effective verification regime, could thus be considered a model for providing a workable distinction between prohibited military and permitted peaceful uses. This model is particularly relevant for a space agreement, which in view of widespread dual-use technologies, has to organize the details of the ban on active military uses in space in such a way that the civil use for peaceful purposes is not affected.

The negotiating process of the CWC also has instructive parallels for the space issue. Given the complexity of the issue, the multilateral CWC was preceded by tedious bilateral negotiations dating back to the BTWC in

1972. Once Gorbachev came to power in the Soviet Union and opened cooperative verification, including on-site inspection, the bilateral US-Soviet agreement on the destruction of their chemical weapon arsenals was concluded in 1990.[857] As explicitly stated in its title, this bilateral agreement was meant to lead to the conclusion of a multilateral agreement. With regards to outer space, a CSO Treaty could build on the prior bilateral negotiations that have been conducted between the United States and Russia since the mid-1970s,[858] and on similar negotiations between the United States and China due to the latter's particular strategic and space capabilities. In the preamble, the CWC is explicitly put in the broader context of general and complete disarmament. This connection would be even stronger for a CSO Treaty, which could adopt in its general provisions a stipulation comparable to Art. VI of the NPT that would provide for a genuine reduction of nuclear weapons leading to general and complete nuclear disarmament.

The CWC also lays down an ambitious prohibition on the development and production of chemical weapons, which although optimal from the perspective of disarmament is, however, from the point of view of the technological development and economic uses in the chemical industry, not without problems.[859] Given that such an ambitious provision was possible in the chemical field, where the immense economic interests of the chemical industry are at stake, it should be pursued at least as an objective with regard to space weapons. In addition to confirming the obligation to nuclear disarmament, the CSO Treaty would refer to the main elements of the CWC in another area as well, which involves the complete destruction of existing chemical weapons arsenals. The practical experience gained by the OPCW in this regard could be used in the implementation of a comparable obligation to destroy existing ASAT capabilities.

9.2   PRINCIPLES OF THE CSO TREATY

Taking into account the recommendations of the report of the Palme Commission[860] and the report of the United Nations Group of Experts on Confidence-building Measures in Outer Space,[861] the CSO Treaty should contain the following principles in its preamble, as the foundation of common security in outer space.

9.2.1 COMMON/COOPERATIVE SECURITY

The CSO Treaty would be based on the application of the concept of common security to outer space.[862] It would implement the obligation of the Outer Space Treaty on the use of outer space in the interest of mankind in the security field. At the same time, it would reinforce the necessary nuclear strategic change towards "mutual assured security" in an adequate multilateral framework, which the nuclear-weapon powers have to set in place in order to fulfil their disarmament obligation under Art. VI of the NPT. The concept of common security must be complemented by specific strategic elements going beyond the classic confidence-building measures. In particular, the multilateralization of the US-Russian CTR programmes would lay the ground for a global system of cooperative threat reduction and an effective non-proliferation regime.

9.2.2 TRANSPARENCY AND CONFIDENCE-BUILDING MEASURES

The CSO Treaty idea is based on the principles of transparency and confidence building in the use of the common space in the security interests of mankind as a whole. It thus complements existing confidence-building provisions in the Outer Space Treaty, and those in the Registration Convention, in particular by introducing a "pre-launch registration" and on-site inspection of launch sites as well as new strategic confidence-building measures and further cooperative security elements for outer space in the form of immunity and traffic rules for satellites.

9.2.3 NON-OFFENSIVE FORCE CONFIGURATIONS, COOPERATIVE STRATEGIC CHANGE AND NUCLEAR DISARMAMENT

Structurally non-offensive force configurations whereby armed forces are organized and equipped in such a way that does not permit offensive military action in outer space entail that no active military uses of space would be permitted. A structurally non-offensive force configuration in outer space is thus best achieved by an explicit prohibition of active military uses of a destructive nature. It can also contribute to structurally non-offensive force configurations and nuclear disarmament on Earth by putting an end to the strategy of nuclear deterrence.[863]

The CSO Treaty would create the necessary conditions for a cooperative nuclear strategic transition. The strategic change would thus be oriented in accordance with the mankind clause of the Outer Space Treaty towards the creation of common security for all states in the interest of mankind and guarantee at the same time that outer space will remain free of weapons. It would thus only allow a space-based missile defence as insurance against missile attacks that violate the non-proliferation regime or against accidental or unauthorized attacks.[864] Such a system would be put under international surveillance, and would not need any space-based weapons components apart from sensor satellites. So long as deterrence has not been completely replaced by a system of common security, a quantitative limitation on unilateral BMD systems would be necessary so that other nuclear-weapon powers do not feel forced to increase their nuclear offensive systems to maintain their deterrence capability.[865] By limiting the number of ICBMs in accordance with Art. VI of the NPT, the risk of unauthorized and accidental attacks would be considerably restrained, and thus the necessity of space-based defence systems further reduced.[866] The Treaty would thus lead in the long term to complete nuclear disarmament, to be monitored by cooperative verification including reliable on-site inspections in particular.

9.2.4 PREVENTIVE ARMS CONTROL THROUGH A BAN ON ACTIVE MILITARY USES OF OUTER SPACE

A main principle of the CSO Treaty would be the preservation of the weapons-free status of the common space by prohibiting the active military use of outer space. Thus, it would fulfil the objectives of preventive arms control,[867] which has particular importance for space technology.[868] The development of space weapons would trigger both a quantitative and especially a qualitative arms race.[869] By creating legal clarity as to the prohibition of the development, production and deployment of space weapons, the Treaty would prevent a new arms spiral in both variants in keeping with the objectives of preventive arms control and to the benefit of mankind as a whole. Even if a ban on the development and production of space weapons could turn out to be too ambitious, an explicit prohibition of the deployment of space weapons in a multilateral treaty would have a strong effect in slowing down, if not stopping altogether, the development of space weapons. Thomas Petermann, Martin Socher and Christine Wennrich have explained, in their report submitted to the German Bundestag, that the creation of cooperative structures and political cooperation alone would not suffice to prevent an arms race if they were not complemented by preventive arms control measures for technological developments.[870] Completely new and unforeseeable arms control and non-proliferation problems would arise with the continuous advancement of new technologies that preventive arms control would effectively curb.[871]

9.2.5 THE PRINCIPLE OF EQUALITY

Respect for the principle of equal security laid down in the United Nations Charter (Art. II, para. 1) would be more than a formal legal aspect in a CSO Treaty. The main purpose of the Treaty would be to prevent the aggravation of security inequalities that would arise from resort to active military uses of outer space, by setting up a system of common security. This dovetails with the material understanding of equality in the CHOM principle. At the same time, the Treaty would also fulfil the criteria the US Administration set for effective arms control treaties (that they should be "clearly defined, significant, equitable and verifiable"[872]) as it would provide for an internationally verifiable prohibition of a whole weapons category and be equally binding on all states.

9.3 THE MAIN ELEMENTS OF THE CSO TREATY

The essential elements of a cooperative security structure in outer space have already been proposed in principle in one form or another at the CD and also partly in the bilateral US-Soviet/Russian arms control treaties. Therefore, the main task ahead is to combine the individual elements in a mutually reinforcing manner to build a coherent cooperative security system. In particular, the principles of common security in outer space have to be developed in terms of both substance and procedure with regard to the following main elements:

9.3.1 PRINCIPLES OF COOPERATIVE SECURITY IN OUTER SPACE

9.3.1.1 General provisions on cooperative security and specific nuclear-strategic questions

It is necessary to distinguish between general provisions on cooperative security and specific issues of nuclear strategy, since in the nuclear-strategic field the main responsibility for filling the cooperative security structures lies undoubtedly in the bilateral relations of the US, Russia and China. Therefore, with regard to a "new strategic framework" and a "cooperative strategic transition" in the relationship between defensive and offensive weapons it would be difficult to regulate these in detail in the multilateral CSO Treaty. Such a far-reaching multilateralization of the nuclear-strategic questions would certainly not be acceptable at present to the nuclear-weapon powers. Thus, it would suffice to provide the general principles and procedures regarding the necessary interface of these issues with the general security interests of the international community, including a flexible institutional arrangement.

9.3.1.2 Particular provisions on cooperative security in outer space

Transparency and confidence building

The state parties should commit themselves to be guided in all their military space activities by the principles of transparency and confidence building.

Structural non-provocation and defensive configurations

The state parties should commit themselves to conduct space activities in a way compatible with the principle of structurally non-offensive force configurations. A Consultative Committee would elaborate on the details of this qualification.

Non-proliferation and disarmament

The state parties should commit themselves to keeping all military activities in outer space in conformity with the objectives of non-proliferation and disarmament under Art. VI of the NPT.

Protection against unauthorized missile launches and attacks

For this specific purpose only and in the interest of legal clarity, the deployment of sensor satellites in the framework of a cooperative development of a limited NMD system to combat ballistic missiles in the boost phase ("boost-phase NMD") should be allowed *expressis verbis*. The tasks of such a system should be enumerated and thus limited to the protection:

- Against unauthorized and accidental missile launches; and
- Against missile attacks in violation of the non-proliferation regime for ballistic missile technology and WMD.

The implementation of the system would have to be secured by a multilateral monitoring and verification mechanism.[873] A standing Consultative Committee should work out the details of such a consensual NMD deployment.

9.3.1.3 Correspondence of the general provisions on cooperative security with the prerequisites of bilateral cooperation

The general principles of the concept of common security in outer space are found congruently in the prerequisites for a cooperative approach in the NMD issue and in new nuclear-strategic relations between the United States and Russia as well as the United States and China, which have been detailed by US experts.[874]

This concerns the question of whether a missile defence system should be limited to the boost phase, which would imply the renunciation of destructive components in outer space,[875] or whether the interception should also be effected during mid-course, which would involve the destruction of attacking warheads in outer space. For a number of reasons, most experts consider that only a limited boost-phase defence would be compatible with a cooperative approach with Russia and China.[876]

This congruence is in addition also valid for the criterion of structurally non-offensive force configurations. According to Charles Glaser and Steve Fetter, Russia and China may fear the negative impact of an NMD system on their second-strike capability, and thus fear the risk of a US first strike capability:

First, Russia may fear that limited NMD would undermine confidence in its retaliatory capability of its current forces.[877]

As an alternative they propose, therefore, a cooperative approach:

The simplest way to avoid provoking Russia would be to deploy an NMD system that lacked capability against Russian missiles. The key example of such an NMD is a land- or sea-based boost-phase system, which could destroy only missiles launched within a limited distance where it was deployed.[878]

As a safeguard, the United States should commit itself not to deploy any space-based system of a "layered defence that would add mid-course systems".[879] Such a renunciation would correspond to the international legal standards of peaceful use of outer space, and could be enshrined in a multilateral prohibition.

Further, with regard to the fear of a sudden expansion of an initially limited NMD system, or "breakout",[880] the answer again lies in a cooperative approach to the relationship of offensive/defensive systems in a binding arms control agreement:

> Russia likely fears that the planned limited deployment would provide the United States with the infrastructure and experience to field a larger and more advanced NMD system in the future.[881]

The international community would share this fear since such an extension would have to be made in any case through the deployment of space-based systems of a destructive nature. Glaser and Fetter suggest instead that:

> ... the United States should pursue co-operative policies to reduce the threat posed by the NMD system it deploys. An arms control agreement that integrated limits on offensive and midcourse defensive forces would reduce, if not eliminate, a number of Russia's key concerns. Such an agreement would set a ceiling on the number of deployed warheads plus the number of deployed interceptors.[882]

Thirdly, this congruence is also valid for the concern of effective non-proliferation and nuclear disarmament, which according to Glaser and Fetter, could only be safeguarded in the context of NMD by adopting a cooperative approach. Disarming both warheads and launchers by the two major nuclear-weapon powers would best work to curb the proliferation of ballistic missiles in other states. With a cooperative mix of defensive/offensive systems, the uncertainty of other states over the sufficiency of the arms control measures would be greatly diminished, and their preparedness to agree themselves to non-proliferation and disarmament measures enhanced.

Fourthly, this congruence is also valid for the objectives pursued in the US National Missile Defense Act of 1999—a limited NMD deployment for protection against missile attacks by states of concern. According to Glaser and Fetter, this objective would again be better achieved cooperatively than unilaterally.[883] The inclusion of these objectives in a CSO Treaty would contribute to an effective policy of non-proliferation of ballistic missile technology. Confidence building and transparency in the framework of a CSO Treaty could have positive effects on states of concern, and thus contribute to the containment of those risks,[884] as the types of risks that would stem from such states of concern would more likely take another form than ballistic missiles and thus would occur beyond the protection of even the most optimal NMD system.[885]

Fifthly, this congruence is valid also for protection against "accidental, erroneous and unauthorized attack".[886] To achieve this second objective of the US National Missile Defense Act of 1999 a limited NMD deployment would again be facilitated by a cooperative approach. Indeed, according to a widespread view, the desired protection could only be achieved through such cooperation. A first step in this direction was the bilateral US-Russian agreement to set up a joint early warning centre in 2000 that provides explicitly for the possibility of the multilateralization of missile defence.[887] Glaser and Fetter show in detail that in the absence of a cooperative framework, the deployment of an NMD system would increase the risk of such attacks.[888]

9.3.2 A BAN ON ACTIVE MILITARY USES OF A DESTRUCTIVE NATURE

A central provision of the CSO Treaty should be an explicit prohibition of active and destructive military uses in outer space in order to achieve the necessary legal clarity with regard to the implementation of the principle of the peaceful use of outer space. This principle would thus be confirmed and specified through a ban on space weapons, namely by explicitly banning space-based ASAT and BMD weapons. Canada has rightly stated that even without a general space weapons ban the prohibition of the use of force would also protect against the deployment of space weapons.[889] Deployment would run counter to the community purpose of the peaceful use of the common space.

Concerning a prohibition of space weapons, in particular a ban on space-based BMD and ASAT systems, five issues need to be tackled:[890]

1. Definition: the issue of so-called "non-dedicated systems", i.e., the distinction between prohibited ASAT systems and permitted civil space

objects that could be misused such as through collision or docking, in an ASAT function;[891]

2. Verification: especially given the possible residual ASAT capability of "non-dedicated systems" an effective international verification is necessary, including of missile launch pads *in situ*;

3. Applicability of the prohibition also in the case of conflict;

4. Verifiable destruction of existing ASAT capabilities, which should be complemented also by limiting the number of military satellite launches;[892]

5. Immunity of satellites: an explicit prohibition of ASATs should also ban non-space-based ASAT systems and thus guarantee a complete protection of all peaceful satellites.

The Treaty stipulation prohibiting space weapons, referring to the definition of active military use of outer space, could read as follows:

> The States Parties commit themselves to refrain from any deployment or use of any object in space or on Earth, *that was designed or modified specifically for the purpose to inflict permanent physical damage on any other object through the projection of mass or energy respectively.* In particular, the deployment of *BMD* and *ASAT* systems in outer space are prohibited, except for a system put under the aegis of the United Nations for the purpose of implementing and enforcing a non-proliferation regime and for the purpose of protecting against unauthorized and accidental missile launches on the decision of the United Nations Security Council and the United Nations General Assembly [emphasis added].[893]

In addition, a prohibition of the development and production of space weapons would serve preventive arms control and confidence building and effective non-proliferation.[894]

Such a prohibition of active military uses of outer space corresponds to the requirements of a cooperative approach in the NMD issue. Thus, numerous US studies have shown that a space-based missile defence system to intercept warheads in their mid-course in outer space would not be viewed as cooperative by Russia and China, but rather as destabilizing.[895] Only the deployment of a missile defence limited to a boost-phase defence (and thus renunciation of the deployment of interceptors in outer space) in tandem with additional requirements is considered to be compatible with a cooperative approach to BMD. In particular, offensive and defensive systems will have to be limited in number; for instance, an equilibrium will have to be established between permitted defensive and offensive weapons. However, according to Glaser and Fetter,[896] the risks that a cooperative approach with Russia or China or with both could fail should not be underestimated, inasmuch as the proponents of missile defence pursue different objectives within the programme, among them some directed against Russian and Chinese nuclear assets.

For these reasons, an explicit treaty provision on the prohibition of space-based BMD systems, with the exception of non-destructive sensor satellites, is indispensable to not only safeguard the principle of the peaceful use of outer space as a prerequisite for common security in outer space, but also to permit the necessary cooperative approach with regard to the nuclear-strategic and arms control questions raised by missile defence.

9.3.3 DESTRUCTION OF EXISTING ASAT WEAPONS AND CAPABILITIES

According to the current state of knowledge, existing ASAT systems have only the capability to destroy satellites in near-Earth orbit. The strategically important satellites used for early warning, navigation and precise guidance systems are all stationed in the geostationary orbit or on other high-Earth orbits, and are thus considered to be not yet at risk.[897] However, low-Earth orbit satellites fulfil important functions in crisis situations such as photographic reconnaissance, ocean surveillance and electronic intelligence. Furthermore, as in the Gulf War, they deliver real-time intelligence to all military operations. In a crisis situation the fear that an opponent may destroy one's satellites can represent an "irresistible temptation ... to remove such satellites from the sky".[898] It is, therefore, necessary to provide for the destruction of existing land- and air-based ASAT systems not only as a matter of congruence with the prohibition of space-based ASAT systems, but also to safeguard security in outer space in crisis situations.

9.3.4 CONFIDENCE-BUILDING MEASURES

In view of the recognized contribution of confidence-building measures to the establishment of cooperative security structures,[899] they should be one of the major elements of the proposed CSO Treaty. For this purpose, the detailed preparatory work accomplished at the CD and in the arms control literature could be a valuable resource.[900] Due to the representative membership of the United Nations Group of Experts of 1994,[901] their proposals should be granted a special role as one of the basis for negotiating the CSO Treaty.

The Treaty would also facilitate the strengthening and possible extension of the various control regimes for missile technologies and WMD, including the regulation of the transfer of sensitive technologies with military applications by, for instance, enhancing and extending the current MTCR and HCoC regimes. The use of multilateral satellite monitoring could encourage the considerable number of states potentially acquiring ballistic missile technology to join such control regimes. A stimulus for this would be the prospect of possible access to space technology for civil space activities, which could open up as a result of the establishment of a multilateral cooperative security order for outer space.[902]

As a model for concrete confidence-building measures for outer space the international community could again take the bilateral cooperation agreed in 1982 by the United States and Russia for the development of a joint Russian-American Observation Satellite, which is supposed to carry out civil functions, but could also be used for such military tasks as early warning and verification. This cooperation is unthinkable without the exchange of sensitive technologies. On the US side, the project is led by the Ballistic Missile Defense Organization, whose former director, Air Force Lieutenant General Ronald Kadish, expressly called the project a "confidence-building effort" with Russia in the context of NMD plans.[903] The joint US-Russian satellite could be the nucleus of a multilateral satellite early warning and verification system for the benefit of arms control and disarmament.

9.3.5 A REGIME TO PROTECT CIVIL SPACE OBJECTS AND PASSIVE MILITARY USES OF A NON-DESTRUCTIVE NATURE

The creation of an immunity regime for civil space objects and satellites with passive military tasks of a non-destructive nature would be an important part of the confidence-building measures. Such a regime is also necessary in light of the lack of legal clarity concerning the admissibility of military space uses. By determining the range of the satellite uses protected under the immunity regime, the necessary legal clarity as to the admissibility of these uses would be achieved. The United States believes that the prohibition of the use of force would be sufficient to protect existing satellite uses.[904] This, however, does not take into account that a number of states have voiced doubts as to the admissibility of even the existing passive military uses.[905] This concerns in particular the use of satellites as precise guidance systems for nuclear weapons. Given the possibility that these states could claim the illegality of these space uses, in particular with regard to the law of reprisals and the controversial issue of the use of force as a means of reprisal,[906] such a clarification over the legality of certain satellite uses is indispensable, and would be an important contribution to confidence building. An immunity regime is all the more necessary as the dual-use capabilities of most satellites may cause civil space objects to become targets of interference or even attacks by ASAT weapons in a crisis situation.[907]

An immunity regime for satellites, which would be specified by "rules of the road" in the framework of a "space code of conduct", would be an important contribution to "traffic security" in the near-Earth and geostationary orbit, and becomes urgent in view of the rapid growth in commercial satellite launches.[908] An important element of such traffic rules would be to respect certain security distances as well as provisions to avoid collisions,[909] which become necessary also for environmental protection against the proliferation of space debris.

Concerning the range of satellite uses to be included in an immunity regime, it is possible to distinguish a functional approach as favoured by Germany,[910] France,[911] Australia[912] and Pakistan,[913] and a more comprehensive approach proposed by the former Soviet Union[914] and Poland,[915] that would include all civil and passive military satellites.[916] According to the so-called "damage potential" method, all satellites with the capability "to interfere actively with other satellites" would have to be excluded from the immunity regime.[917] For promoting multilateral verification in the framework of cooperative security, according to a proposal by Australia, monitoring and verification satellites would explicitly be included in the immunity regime.[918]

9.3.6 Mechanisms of implementation control: monitoring and verification

The CSO Treaty would have to contain appropriate mechanisms of implementation control through multilateral monitoring and verification.[919]

Péricles Gasparini Alves defines monitoring as the general collection of data on the implementation of the treaty.[920] Verification is a concrete review of the implementation of the specific arms control, non-proliferation or destruction provisions.[921] The monitoring and verification provisions of the CSO Treaty should provide for the control of the comprehensive ban on active military uses of outer space of a destructive nature, in particular of space weapons, as well as of the protection regime, including the immunity rules for space objects used for peaceful purposes. Given the enormous potential of dual-use technologies for civil, in particular commercial purposes, it will be important to provide for mechanisms that guarantee at the same time both the necessary confidentiality and the protection of civil interests.[922]

A space weapons regime is arguably verifiable. Already in the 1980s in the context of the various proposals at the CD for international verification mechanisms, which were supposed to have recourse to satellite reconnaissance,[923] it was shown that such a space weapons agreement could be reliably verified.[924] Given the progress made since on questions both of verification technology and policy, today the verifiability of arms control and non-proliferation regimes for outer space in principle is beyond doubt, even though the details of technical and procedural implementation will require the highest standards.[925]

Even more important for verification than technological progress is the breakthrough reached during the early 1980s in discussions on the verification aspects of a space weapons ban. Today it enables the drafters of arms control treaties to strive for a comprehensive system of cooperative monitoring and verification, in accordance with the principles of cooperative security.[926] With the Soviet change of policy under Gorbachev,[927] who gave up the traditional Soviet refusal of on-site inspections such that elaborate cooperative verification rules became possible in the INF Treaty in 1987,[928] an excellent starting point exists for elaborating reliable cooperative verification rules for a CSO Treaty. The range of possible verification measures now spans from, as defined by Rafael Biermann, the classic "national technical means" (national military reconnaissance satellites) to both "passive cooperative" and "active cooperative" verification such as on-site inspections in the form of "continuous monitoring", "clarification inspections" or "challenge inspections" (anytime-anywhere inspection).[929] The high standard of cooperative verification achieved with the INF Treaty between the United

States and Russia should be upheld in a future multilateral arms control agreement for outer space. This would also test the preparedness of the other potential military space powers, in particular China and India, to accept the standard. Next to the bilateral INF Treaty, the elaborate multilateral verification mechanisms of the CWC[930] and the CTBT[931] could also serve as models.

In addition to a "space-to-ground" verification, outer space has a special requirement for "ground-to-space" and "space-to-space" verification methods.[932] For the monitoring of the proposed protection regime for civil space objects such as for safety margins, a "space-to-space" verification seems indispensable. As Jürgen Scheffran demonstrated, "space-to-space" could also be used for the monitoring of a space weapons ban, and for this purpose be complemented by inspections of missile launch pads *in situ*.[933] The satellites used for this type of verification could, according to Jasani,[934] ideally form "multilateral technical means" for the verification of a space weapons ban. They could additionally be used to provide the still lacking multilateral verification of the PTBT of 1963.[935] In the meantime, civil and commercial satellites have also reached a level of technological development capable of supporting verification.[936]

The special advantage of cooperative verification rules in a CSO Treaty would not be limited to the monitoring of the agreement itself. Rather, the eventual use of satellite data for international verification purposes, be it through an international verification agency's satellites or by having verification data and imagery of national satellites at its disposal, would open the way for fulfilling a long-standing hope for a general international verification for bilateral and multilateral arms control, non-proliferation and disarmament treaties. The monitoring and verification mechanism of the CSO Treaty could thus also be used for monitoring the compliance of further arms control and non-proliferation treaties, in particular of the CTBT and the NPT, as well as for crisis prevention purposes.

9.3.7 CODIFICATION OF THE LEGAL STANDARDS OF THE PEACEFUL USE OF OUTER SPACE

In a further step, in addition to the principle of cooperative security and the prohibition of active space uses of a destructive nature, further legal standards of the peaceful use of outer space could be codified in the CSO Treaty, in particular the standards of environmental protection and beneficial economic use for all countries and of future generations.[937] This would permit taking full account of the entire structural feature of the status of outer space as CHOM, laying the foundations for a comprehensive security order for outer space in accordance with the peaceful purpose principle and also covering the economic and environmental dimensions. Should such a comprehensive approach be too ambitious to be carried out in one step, a clause of intention as an objective for a future review conference could be foreseen.

9.4   APPROPRIATE NEGOTIATING INTERNATIONAL FORA

Since the arms issue in outer space was raised, there has been a continuous debate over whether COPUOS or rather the multilateral arms control fora would be the appropriate venue to eventually negotiate an agreement.[938] The Western states have argued against treating the issue in COPUOS, referring primarily to the potential risk of the forum to become politicized. By contrast, the non-aligned states always underlined the close link between limiting military uses and promoting peaceful cooperation in outer space, and therefore were of the opinion that the arms control issue should be dealt with at the CD and within COPUOS.[939]

In the meantime, the issue of military uses of outer space has taken on significance for all future space activities. Active military uses of outer space would have considerable repercussions for the safety of civil and particularly commercial uses of space. Further, the impact of such a transgression on international security in terms of nuclear armaments, the balance between defensive and offensive weapons, and the entire bilateral and multilateral arms control, non-proliferation and disarmament regimes, make it necessary to treat the issue comprehensively from all angles. Therefore, the convocation of a separate international state conference under the aegis of the United Nations to negotiate a CSO Treaty would seem to be appropriate. Such a multilateral conference of plenipotentiary state representatives could potentially break the impasse currently witnessed at the CD by negotiating the necessarily comprehensive treaty with sufficient authority and effect with regard to new trade-offs towards a complete security order for the space powers with regard to their civil space uses. This agreement should, as with the Outer Space Treaty and the specialized space agreements, be approved by the United Nations General Assembly for its adoption by the international community. One could also consider including non-governmental organizations and the numerous international scientific organizations dealing with space and disarmament issues at an early stage of the process.

On 5 February 2001 Canada reaffirmed its commitment to convene a review conference on the Outer Space Treaty with the objective of negotiating an additional protocol on the military use of outer space.[940] The proposal for a CSO Treaty, as an implementation agreement of the Outer Space Treaty, could be tabled at such a conference.

9.5   EFFECT ON THIRD-PARTY STATES

By applying the legal analysis of Tomuschat,[941] two main strands of argument can be used for an international order to apply to third party states with regard to the peaceful use of outer space and the proposed CSO Treaty, so long as this order is based on a sufficiently broad consensus of states that view its rules as a quasi-legislative act of the international community. First, the Outer Space Treaty's inclusion of the mankind clause in Art. I, para. 1, and the principle of taking due account of the interests of other states in Art. XI, provide explicit legal references as to its binding effect on third party states. Inasmuch as the mankind clause requires that the use of outer space has to be "in the interest of all states and mankind as a whole", it automatically requires third party states to take into due account the specification of this interest in an international order that is created by the great majority of states. Thus, inasmuch as the international community specifies the mankind clause and the principle of the peaceful use of outer space when it lays down principles such as transparency, adequate registration of space launches and reliable verification with regard to military uses of outer space, it can require compliance with this order with regard to third party states.

By specifying the existing principles and norms of outer space law in a new order and treaty that gives substantial and legal credibility to the peaceful use of outer space, the CSO Treaty would also have recourse to elements of customary space law such as the legal standard of prevention of an arms race in outer space,[942] which is derived from the principle of the peaceful use referred to by the ICJ in the "Gulf of Maine" case.[943] If treaties can, as Tomuschat argues, develop "general principles of order specifying customary international law" that have a binding effect on third party states,[944] then such a specification based on a general treaty such as the Outer Space Treaty, as well as on international customary law principles such as the prevention of an arms race in the common space and the CHOM principle is valid a *fortiori*.

A second line of argument is premised on the hypothesis that military uses of a destructive nature in space directly affect "fundamental legal principles of the international community"[945] as the resort to active military uses would be detrimental to the security interests of all states when considering that they could endanger the survival of mankind, and affect the interest of present and future generations in the preservation of the environment of outer space. In this context, recourse can be made to Tomuschats' conclusion concerning the definition of "international crimes" in the "Draft on State Responsibility" of the ILC of 1980[946] over a "massive pollution of the atmosphere or the seas":

> The material need for such a regulation as an actualisation of the customary international rule to defend against a serious disturbance of the international coexistence in connection with procedural justice allows drawing the conclusion that the draft treaty order is also binding for outsiders. [947]

Paulus has detailed that one of the main corollaries of the community-oriented "law of the international community" is its capacity to lay down law with the consent of its "essential components".[948] Thus, given its fundamental significance for world security and international stability, the fulfilment of the principle of the peaceful use in the Outer Space Treaty and thus of common security in outer space would also be binding for third party states.

However, it could be argued that a comparison with other serious infringements on fundamental international legal rights of the international community such as aggression or violations of human rights, indicates that a violation has to be imminent to justify its binding effect on third party states. With regard to military uses of outer space, this would mean that an outsider would only be bound by the prohibition of the use of outer space weapons as opposed to their mere deployment. Apart from the fact that such a prohibition on the use of space weapons is already universally binding due to the general ban on the use of force, the binding effect on imminent violations is indispensable for an international order meant precisely to prevent such violations from occurring. In view of the extraordinary importance of the interest of mankind that is potentially affected, the binding effect is thus necessary for the preventive rules creating the international order of peaceful use of outer space.

9.6 UNIVERSALITY OF THE PRINCIPLE OF COMMON SECURITY AND US AND EUROPEAN INTERESTS

The current US opposition to the elaboration of a multilateral order concerning the military uses of outer space in general, and of negotiating a PAROS agreement in particular, raises the question of whether or not the international community's security interests in outer space could be achieved and protected without the foremost space power. The international order to safeguard the peaceful use of outer space could be established with effect *erga omnes* by an overwhelming majority of states if it included a sufficiently wide grouping of states representing the international community as a whole; if the content would adequately fulfil the common interest clause contained in Art. I, para. 1 of the Outer Space Treaty; and if the participants were acting in the interest of all states and mankind as a whole. These prerequisites are fulfilled in reference to the claim of the international community to negotiate a multilateral treaty on the prevention of an arms race in outer space. If under the aegis of the United Nations the great majority of states participated in the negotiation of such a treaty, it would be guaranteed that such "a normative order ... would not be based on a one-sided ponderation of interests".[949]

Nevertheless, it would undoubtedly be preferable to have all major powers participate in the elaboration of a cooperative security regime from the very beginning, which will depend largely on the concrete content and modalities of implementation of the security regime. A system of cooperative security in outer space should be in the enlightened national security interest even of the most powerful states. Thus, it could be hoped that the convening of a special state conference attended by the overwhelming majority of the international community with the purpose of negotiating a multilateral agreement on the prevention of an arms race in outer space as the foundation for a common security regime in space, would eventually also influence states that currently prefer a unilateral course. Notwithstanding the possible effect with regard to third party states, the CSO Treaty could fulfil its political objective of establishing an order of common security in outer space in the "interest of all mankind" by aiming at universal membership that would include the big space and nuclear-weapon powers participating in the institutional arrangements for its implementation. The possibility that the United States would see its security interests best preserved in a space order of common security should not be excluded *a priori*, since the CSO Treaty would not prohibit the deployment of a limited missile defence system (that excludes space-based interceptors) in a cooperative framework. It would be important even for the biggest power to weigh the benefit of a verifiable arms control regime that would keep an effective check on nuclear threats and proliferation against the value of shielding against nuclear weapons, whereby safety could not be entirely guaranteed and would come at the cost of international security. As Stephen Pullinger aptly states:

> In other words, of course it is preferable to be able to shoot down a proportion of attacking nuclear warheads than none at all. However, as the consequences of even a single warhead landing on a city is so catastrophic one's ability to mitigate an attack is of far less relevance than the overwhelming imperative of preventing the attack in the first place.[950]

The prevention of an arms race in outer space by a CSO Treaty would probably be the most important step towards an active non-proliferation policy and therefore would be in the particular interest of the states most threatened by nuclear proliferation. With regard to US interests in missile defence and the military use of outer space, Steven Miller, the Director of Harvard University's International Security Program of the Belfer Centre for Science and International Affairs reached the following conclusion:

> At present, the answer seems to be that missile defences represent a high-cost remedy to a threat that is speculative, distant in time and uncertain in scale and character. Very expensive and very limited missile-defence capabilities will be acquired at the risk of provoking a variety of adverse diplomatic and strategic consequences. It is not at all clear that the net effect will be an improved security order for the United States.[951]

Glaser and Fetter describe the US interests as follows:

> Even though the United States is the dominant military power, it should nevertheless strongly prefer a world in which all of the major powers are

secure. ... Increased insecurity would fuel the arms competition and a breakdown of Cupertino, which would further strain relations and create military dangers. ... Although Russia is now too weak economically to engage in a major build-up, this is unlikely always to be true. In any case, the United States has important co-operative programs with Russia, designed to improve Russian control over its nuclear weapons and weapon materials that could be interrupted or terminated if the United States pursued NMD... The key counter argument to the above analysis is that the deterrent and damage-limitation benefits of a highly effective NMD would more than offset the dangers that would flow from increased Russian and Chinese insecurity. We believe that under current conditions this case for nuclear superiority is flawed. Given that U.S. relations with Russia and China are in formative transition stages and that co-operative policies might help advance and cement peaceful relations, our judgement is that forgiving large-scale NMD seems preferable to risking what at best would be a new Cold War. This conclusion is reinforced by the near certainty that U.S. efforts to achieve effective NMD against Russia and China would fail, in which case the United States would get all the costs but none of the benefits of full-scale NMD.[952]

Jack F. Matlock, Jr., former US Ambassador to Moscow and current Professor at the Institute for Advanced Study, Princeton University, assesses the repercussions of the newest US NMD plans as follows:

... the concept [of a national missile defence] raises the question of whether such a system, even if technologically feasible, would enhance the security of American citizens ... it is a concept that, at the moment, cannot be justified on either technical or diplomatic grounds...

... America's security depends on the strength of its alliances and the wisdom of its diplomacy as much as it does on capable armed forces. To undermine our alliances and encourage a renewed arms race in pursuit of a still dubious technological fix to a largely non-existent threat would be sheer folly. It would, in fact, undermine many of the benefits we have gained from the end of the Cold War and leave the American people significantly less secure than they are today.[953]

Looking at European and in particular German interest, it is clear that Germany as a non-nuclear-weapon state would be a credible candidate to propose a CSO Treaty as part of an active non-proliferation policy, which in the future will have to include outer space. It could do this together with

European partners, such as France, which is very active in outer space arms control questions, as well as Italy and Sweden, which have both repeatedly made proposals on the prevention of an arms race in outer space. Such a proposal for cooperative security in outer space would correspond to Germany's interest in a security policy that enhances cooperative security structures as well as strengthens multilateralism. As Germany has no plans for its own active military use of outer space, but does have an economic interest as one of the leading technological powers and a main contributor to the exclusively civil ESA, it has an eminent interest in strengthening security in space and enhancing the safety of civil uses of outer space.

CHAPTER 10

AN INTERNATIONAL WORLD SPACE ORGANIZATION FOR SAFEGUARDING THE PEACEFUL USE OF OUTER SPACE

10.1 CURRENT PROPOSALS FOR AN INTERNATIONAL SPACE ORGANIZATION

10.1.1 EARLY PROPOSALS

The majority of the early proposals in the literature foresaw the granting of a regulatory or even an executive power on the use of outer space to the United Nations. In particular, in the years following the adoption of the Outer Space Treaty, proposals for an institutional cooperation in outer space intensified, which either also included the security domain in a comprehensive approach, or were exclusively targeted at the institutionalization of security and arms control cooperation in outer space.[954]

Probably the first to propose the establishment of an international space commission, which should exercise international control to safeguard the exclusively peaceful use of outer space, was the French international lawyer Joseph Kroell in 1952, five years before the first satellite was launched.[955] In the United States, Philip Jessup and Howard Taubenfeld presented three options for the structural and institutional order of outer space.[956] One option was to transfer the trusteeship over outer space to the United Nations; the second to create a separate international organization; and the third to have a "direct international administration" with at least also legislative competencies "over all technical, legal, governmental, and security matters in space" [emphasis added].[957] They considered an "organized multinational action in the common interest" in one of the three forms as indispensable for international security:

> The motivations have been as various as the forms—political, economic, technical, ideological, humanitarian. In recent years a still stronger

171

motivation—human survival—has been added. The need and the incentive have never been greater than now. Steadily the trend on the face of the earth has been toward organized multinational action in the common interest. There will be no reversal of that trend as man moves on into outer space.[958]

The second Secretary-General of the United Nations, Dag Hammerskjöld, formulated in May 1958 the motivation of the later Outer Space Treaty as "the overriding interest of the community of nations in the peaceful and beneficial use of outer space", and expressed the expectation that "[t]he General Assembly would ... initiate steps for an international machinery to further this end ... of the use of outer space for the benefit of all".[959]

Remarkably, the first proposals by the two space powers in 1958 were motivated by security reasons, and aimed at an institutional safeguard for the peaceful use of outer space by providing for international "inspection systems".[960]

The French proposal presented to the First Special Session of the United Nations General Assembly on Disarmament in 1978 to establish ISMA was the beginning of a number of similar proposals, pursuing the same objective of harnessing the potentiality offered by satellite technology for arms control and disarmament purposes.[961] In particular, it was hoped that the transfer of reconnaissance and early warning functions of satellites to an international organization would not only contribute to the prevention of an arms race in outer space, but also to the achievement of disarmament objectives on Earth.

10.1.2 CRITICISM OF PROPOSALS AND INTERNATIONAL SECURITY NEEDS

Proposals for new international institutions have received considerable criticism due to neoliberal qualms over intergovernmental and bureaucratic institutionalism and the relevant financial costs.[962] However, their necessity in principle as "magnifiers of concern, facilitators of agreement, and builders of capacity"[963] could not be denied, and thus the need for an institutional underpinning of security and cooperation in outer space has increased as a result of the lack of achievements made to safeguard the peaceful use of outer space without such institutionalization. Consequently, there has been a renewal of institutional proposals that are aimed at creating "lean" organizational structures. A study undertaken by the Centre d'études et de recherches sur le droit de l'espace in 1992 exemplifies this trend towards a lean structure by concluding that *"l'organisation mondiale de l'espace devrait être modeste pour garantir son réalisme et son efficacité"*.[964] In the same vein, Andrew Young raises doubts as to whether a comprehensive international space organization would be achievable, calling it an "universalist's pipe-dream", and favours instead concrete measures such as the right to inspections of space stations.[965] Yet, at the same time Young still considers specialized global institutions "which should function to ameliorate the individual excesses of nations operating in space through timely and appropriate legislation" to be indispensable. As a *quid pro quo* for the transfer of legislative powers to such institutions, commercial uses of space should be promoted in a democratic process through the pragmatic and broad inclusion of developing countries in the civil uses of space.

The proposals made by states at the CD and the suggestions made in the literature will be examined to determine whether they offer appropriate elements for the eventual creation of an Organization for Cooperative/Common Security in Outer Space. Such a security organization can draw on successful examples of international organizations regulating the civil use of outer space such as INTELSAT, inasmuch as it can relate to the promotion of cooperative structures in the peaceful civil use of space.[966] Outside the space area, but directly in the field of disarmament, the OPCW represents an institutional precedent, which directly fulfils tasks with respect to the implementation of the comprehensive prohibition of a new weapons category, including the destruction of existing arsenals.

10.1.3 SPACE RESEARCH AGENCY

Early proposals to create a space research agency already contained security implications through stipulations that unilateral military endeavours in outer space should be banned from the outset in the interest of allowing the institutionalization of peaceful international space research. In this vein, the US Senator Alexander Wiley made a proposal on 24 December 1957 to establish an international space research agency, which should guarantee the exclusive peaceful use of outer space.[967] Myres McDougal and Leon Lipson noted that this suggestion might have influenced the proposal made a month later at the United Nations by Soviet Foreign Minister Andrei Gromyko, albeit without explicit reference to the US Senator.[968] Gromyko proposed on 15 March 1958 at the United Nations General Assembly the inclusion in its agenda of the following item:

> The banning of the use of cosmic space for military purposes, the elimination of foreign bases on the territories of other countries, and international co-operation in the study of cosmic space.[969]

However, given that the Soviets linked the ban on military space activities with the issue of foreign military bases, this proposal was not accepted largely owing to its strategic implications for the United States and the European allies.[970] Unfortunately, the chance to institutionalize the international cooperation in the exploration of outer space was lost in the 1960s due to the increased tensions of the Cold War.

10.1.4 COMPREHENSIVE SPACE ORGANIZATION

The proposals to set up a comprehensive space organization are based on the perceived need for an integrated approach to the various space uses. Additionally, there are advantageous synergies to be expected from such a comprehensive approach. Starting from the community status of outer space and its resources as "world public services", Jenks has emphasized the need for an institutional structure as a prerequisite of effective space use in the interest of mankind:

> An effective law of public world services presupposes more than the renunciation of sovereignty in space and the dedication of space for the benefit of all mankind. It presupposes *an organised world community* taking a major collective responsibility for developments in space [emphasis added].[971]

To avoid duplication with the evolving global and regional institutions dedicated primarily to the civil uses of outer space, it is proposed to either limit the suggested comprehensive space organization to coordinating functions or to assimilate existing institutions into the new encompassing space organization. The former chairman of the Institute of International Space Law of the International Astronautical Federation, Isabella Diederiks-Verschoor,[972] and the Polish space lawyer Andrzej Gobriel,[973] stress the need for coordination, which should be carried out by a world space organization. Diederiks-Verschoor underlined:

As outer space activities are growing in number and applications are getting many-sided, there is a need for new rules and a co-ordinating institution coping with these new situations in outer space.[974]

Going a step further, C. Horsford deems it necessary to grant full executive powers to a future space organization, in contrast to the loose competencies of the International Civil Aviation Organization:

... intervening where necessary to police infringements of space law and its own regulations, with powers to do so, vested in a formal Council and Secretariat.[975]

Early on, the non-aligned countries in particular pursued the objective of creating a space organization. At their summit meeting in Belgrade in 1961, the Heads of State and Government of the Non-aligned Movement spoke in favour of an international organization to promote the peaceful use of outer space.[976] In 1966, the United Arab Republic tabled such a proposal in the Legal Subcommittee of COPUOS.[977] In 1967, the United Arab Republic, Austria and Iran explained in a joint paper to COPUOS their motivations for the establishment of a world space organization. Iran proposed creating an "executive body on the lines of the International Atomic Energy Agency" for outer space.[978]

At the beginning of the 1980s, building on the French proposal for the creation of ISMA and in view of developing plans for an active military use of outer space, a number of non-aligned states renewed their proposals for a comprehensive space organization. Chile put its proposal explicitly in the context of the objective "to prevent it [outer space] from becoming militarized".[979]

Following on and complementing its draft treaties for a prohibition of space weapons of 1981 and 1983,[980] the Soviet Union made in 1985 a far-reaching proposal to set up a broad world space organization to safeguard the peaceful use of outer space.[981] However, it did not receive widespread support outside the group of socialist and of non-aligned countries for two reasons. The first was its link with the draft treaties aimed against SDI and, hence its unacceptability for the United States. Second, its organizational features were expansive and as such were also criticized by Russian space lawyers.[982]

Establishing an international world space organization with global rules for safety and good practices in outer space was called for at the first Asia-Pacific Conference on Multilateral Cooperation in Space Technology and Applications of 1994 held in Bangkok.[983] The organization was supposed to take over and combine the functions of INMARSAT, INTELSAT and the International Telecommunication Union (ITU) in the area of the distribution of radio frequencies and orbital positions. By bringing the various tasks together in one service, it was argued the costs could be reduced.

There appears to be a renewal of interest in the political and legal literature in the creation of a world space organization.[984] Monserrat Filho is of the opinion that without the creation of such an organization, there cannot be an effective implementation of the principle of cooperation in the Outer Space Treaty.[985] In a similar vein, A.J. Emmanouel, a member of the Greek Astronautical Society and Barrister of the Supreme Court of Greece, maintains that the international community's interest in "mankind's common space effort" can only be safeguarded through an independent institutional basis, and thus stresses such an institution as a "contribution to the idea of world peace".[986] O.M. Ribbelink and P.H. Tuinder consider a world space organization to be a feasible mechanism to counter the growing number of space actors and increasingly contradictory public and private interests in regulatory processes.[987]

In addition, an increasing number of writers see the need for an international institution to have coordinating, if not regulatory, functions for the preservation of the space environment.[988] This is based in particular on the argument that specialized international organizations require the recognition of legislative competencies in order to protect the general interest of the international community.[989] In a contribution to the 1999 colloquium on "International Organisations and Space Law" in Perugia, a member of the Russian Academy of Sciences, Alexander Yakovenko, favoured a streamlined version of the previous Soviet proposal for a world space organization, suggesting instead an organization "with limited purposes", which in addition to the promotion of international cooperation in large-scale space projects of mankind such as missions to Mars and the regulation of technology transfers, should also fulfil the task of coordinating environmental monitoring by satellites and all security-related issues of dual-use capabilities of space technology.[990] According to Yakovenko, in light of the worldwide dissemination of information and the growth of a "global village", the time has come to embark, with adequate institutional support, on joint projects of mankind in outer space.[991] Similarly, Patrick-André Salin envisions a world space organization with a flexible structure based on a "global space activities regulation" that would coordinate the various space activities.[992] Salin refers to the experience of the ITU to show that no contradiction exists between "market competition" and institutional cooperation. Simone Courteix, in her contribution on the occasion of the 30th anniversary of the Outer Space Treaty in 1997, refers to the proposals of the Centre d'études et de recherches sur le droit de l'espace, arguing forcefully for a world space organization that should aim at having broad functions, and yet at the same time a lean structure.[993] On the one hand, it would have enormous effects in promoting the peaceful use of outer space for the benefit of mankind; on the other hand it would meet the urgent need in the security field for an institutional safeguard of the peaceful use of space in view of the dual use of space technologies. Courteix proposes in particular:

> ... that a political drive, at the highest level, should be given to mobilise states to this initiative, possibly taking the form of a solemn statement by heads of states setting out objectives and prospects for the long term.[994]

Eileene Galloway proposes examining the "creation of new international institutions, including a world space agency" in the review of the Outer Space Treaty as a special agenda item in the framework of COPUOS.[995]

10.1.5 INTERNATIONAL SATELLITE MONITORING AND VERIFICATION AGENCIES

In the security domain a number of proposals on the institutional safeguard of the peaceful use of outer space concentrate on the creation of multilateral satellite agencies for monitoring and verification purposes.[996]

10.1.5.1 Monitoring and verification agencies

With a view to safeguarding the peaceful use of outer space, Myers McDougal proposed in 1957 the establishment of an international satellite agency at which states should register any satellite launch as well as declare their readiness to accept international inspections, thus allowing the agency to ensure that the satellite equipment corresponds to the registered purpose of the flight.[997] In 1958, he complemented this proposal by suggesting that states should launch satellites under the auspices of a special space agency of the United Nations, to be created for that purpose. The satellites should undertake international functions determined by the United Nations, including the surveillance of the peaceful use of the common space.[998] In view of the technological progress in satellite remote sensing and reconnaissance that had been achieved in the meantime, Bruce Murray and Merton Davies put forward in 1972 the general idea of international satellite surveillance under the aegis of the United Nations for arms control and crisis prevention purposes, and included in their suggestions detailed technical discussions for its implementation.[999] In the same way, Jasani proposed in 1973 the use of satellite remote sensing for the purpose of arms control verification.[1000]

Building on these proposals, Abram Chayes, William Epstein and Theodore Taylor appealed to the space powers at the 26th Pugwash Conference on Science and World Affairs in 1976 to promote international confidence and cooperation in space by making the data collected from their satellites available to all states:

> The key to arms control and disarmament is openness of information about military activities. Knowledge removes fear and suspicion and creates confidence ... We think it would create a climate of confidence that would contribute to international peace and security if the information from satellite surveillance of military activities was published and universally available to all countries.[1001]

For this purpose, a consortium of 12 non-nuclear-weapon states from around the world should set up a "satellite system for the surveillance of the military activities of all countries" that would report to the United Nations.[1002]

These proposals paved the way for a French initiative at the United Nations in 1978 on the occasion of the First Special Session of the United Nations General Assembly on Disarmament that proposed in a special memorandum the establishment of ISMA.[1003] This new international organization would serve as a specialized United Nations agency in the security field, with far-reaching monitoring and verification functions in arms control agreements through the use of data received through satellite remote sensing. The organization would also be equipped with an arbitration commission for dispute settlement. The explicit objective of the initiative was that:

> ... dans le cadre des efforts de désarmement ... cette nouvelle méthode de contrôle soit mise au service de la communauté internationale.[1004]

The organization would be set up in three phases. In the first phase, ISMA would include a centre for assessing the collected data. By the second phase it would receive its own network of relay stations. And in the third phase it would acquire its own surveillance satellites. This proposal was positively evaluated in two studies and received widespread support at the United Nations General Assembly.[1005] However, the United States rejected the proposal for security as well as institutional reasons.[1006] The security objections were based on the lack of confidence between the superpowers in light of the Cold War. Institutionally, the proposed institution would have no specific treaty-related verification function. Such "treaty specificity" was viewed as an indispensable element for justifying the creation of a multilateral verification agency.[1007] Another objection, which was shared by other industrialized countries, referred to the high costs of the project. The Soviet Union, while not commenting on the French initiative,[1008] submitted similar proposals in the following years.[1009]

Only in 1988 did France come back to its proposal, reducing it to the creation of a multilateral centre entrusted with merely assessing relevant data. Foreign Minister Roland Dumas proposed to the United Nations General Assembly:

> ... the constitution, within the United Nations, of an agency for the processing and interpretation of images obtained from space.[1010]

In view of the persistent refusal of the United States as the major military space power to participate in such an initiative, the suggestions turned towards setting up regional satellite centres, which could then become the basis for eventually creating a universal system. Thus in June 1991, given the new verification needs emerging from the previous year's conclusion of the CFE Treaty, the Western European Union (WEU) member states set up a regional Satellite Centre at Torrejon near Madrid.[1011] This Centre, which is a special agency of the European Union, effectively carries out the same verification tasks in the field of security that were foreseen in the former French proposal submitted to the United Nations. In accordance with the original phased plan, the centre has started to train experts in the evaluation of satellite images for verification purposes. In addition, the WEU Council of Ministers has decided to commission a feasibility study on the creation of a European verification satellite.[1012]

According to a concept paper for the Satellite Centre, the general mandate of the Centre also includes "treaty verification, arms control and proliferation control".[1013] The Centre has already carried out such tasks by using satellites of the ESA and other commercial satellite images.[1014] It could eventually be integrated into a comprehensive European satellite system with wide remote sensing as well as navigation capabilities that would include verification and early warning. Should other regions develop such institutions,[1015] the necessary foundation for finally setting up a universal ISMA would be effectively laid.[1016] Ruitaro Hashimoto rightly sees the successful work of the European Union Satellite Centre, particularly with regard to arms control treaty verification, as a compelling reason to re-examine the establishment of ISMA.[1017]

At the CD as well, a number of delegations[1018] have called for a re-examination of the French initiative, in particular in the context of discussions on PAROS. At the last session of the Ad Hoc Committee on PAROS in 1994 several delegations, including the German delegation, suggested re-evaluating the French proposal. The final report of the Ad Hoc Committee thus states:

> Germany and Algeria felt that the time was right to put into practice the concrete proposals made by France, the former USSR, and Canada, with regard to the setting up of international agencies under the auspices of the UN, entrusting them with monitoring functions in outer space.[1019]

At the Third Special Session of the United Nations General Assembly on Disarmament in 1988, the Soviet Union proposed setting up a Space Image Processing and Interpretation Centre.[1020] It was suggested that the agency not only engage in confidence-building measures but also carry out monitoring and verification functions with regard to arms control agreements for outer space and nuclear matters, for conventional armaments (CFE Treaty), and with a view to a future chemical weapons agreement. In addition, the organization should also fulfil remote sensing functions for the forecast of natural and other catastrophes. Although the envisaged structure of the organization as a specialized agency of the

United Nations is along the same lines as the earlier French memorandum, the Soviets envisaged that the Centre, which would be part of the Secretariat, would include only experts from those countries capable and willing to provide the organization with satellite remote sensing facilities.

10.1.5.2 Pure verification agencies

In 1987 and 1988 at the CD, the Soviet Union proposed the creation of an International Space Inspectorate for the exclusive verification of a space weapons ban that would consist of a permanent international team conducting on-site inspections of launching pads.[1021] Foreign Minister Eduard Shevardnadze declared the Soviet Union's readiness to extend the on-site inspections to "storage facilities, industrial plants, laboratories, testing centres, etc.", should a complete weapons ban be agreed.[1022] A main objective of the Inspectorate would be the verification of non-declared space launches by granting each party the right to demand explanations about every space launch and, in the case of continued doubts over the nature of launched space object, to call for challenge inspections by the team of inspectors of the agency.[1023]

Canada, having long since taken a leading role in questions of arms control and verification in outer space within the CD and the United Nations, submitted in 1986 a proposal for entry into service of international verification satellites, PAXSAT A and B, accompanied by an International Space Data Centre that would assess and evaluate their images.[1024] While PAXSAT B was meant for the "space-to-ground" verification of regional conventional arms control agreements, PAXSAT A envisaged the use of "space-to-space" verification satellites. The verification satellites would be treaty-specific, in that they would accompany a multilateral agreement on the prohibition of space weapons to be concluded. Two options for this treaty-specific verification of a space weapons ban were proposed. The first foresaw the launch and use of PAXSAT satellites only for the concrete verification of a space object already launched into space, while the second envisaged the permanent deployment of satellites in space to allow them to "to co-orbit and keep station with the target over a reasonably lengthy period of time".[1025] Both variants excluded, however, a permanent space surveillance, providing for an inspection "on challenge" that was to be decided in each case by a treaty consultative authority.[1026] A data acquisition and processing centre would be attached to this authority with the task to assess the confidential satellite data.

In a comparative assessment of the proposals by France, Canada and the Soviet Union for multilateral satellite verification, Gasparini Alves comes to the conclusion that they each have similar objectives as well as similar task descriptions, and that it would be possible to combine them into a comprehensive proposal.[1027]

The idea of establishing a comprehensive multilateral disarmament organization with global verification tasks under the aegis of the United Nations was introduced by the two space powers in their proposals for general and complete disarmament in the early 1960s in the US-Soviet McCloy-Zorin declaration.[1028] Jozef Goldblat writes:

> The United States envisaged the establishment of an international organisation to ensure that all obligations were observed during and after implementation of general and complete disarmament; inspectors of the organisation would have unrestricted access to all places necessary for the purpose of effective verification.[1029]

To the extent that the increasingly unrealistic objective of complete disarmament was replaced by partial arms control agreements, the idea of a global arms control and verification organization lost ground. Instead, treaty-specific organizations were preferred—the IAEA being one of the main examples in the area of controlling the use of nuclear energy.

With the enhanced capabilities of satellite remote sensing and with the French ISMA proposal, the idea of a global verification agency became attractive once more. Perhaps the time will come when both objectives will be combined, such that satellite remote sensing will be used in the security interest of mankind for treaty-specific and global verification of a CSO Treaty as a decisive contribution to both the prevention of an arms race in outer space and to nuclear disarmament on Earth.

10.1.5.3 International legal assessment of multilateral satellite verification

From the perspective of international law, a multilateralization of satellite remote sensing for monitoring and verification through the establishment of ISMA would be a positive step. During an assessment of the original French ISMA proposal at the 61st session of the International Law Association in 1984,[1030] all members of the Space Law Committee called it without exception an important contribution to the prevention of an arms race in outer space. There are no international legal objections to such a proposal. Quite to the contrary, such a multilateralization would represent an appropriate implementation of the common purpose clause contained in Art. I of the Outer Space Treaty and of the "Principles Relating to Remote Sensing of the Earth from Outer Space", adopted by consensus by the United Nations General Assembly in 1986.[1031] Principle VI of the latter encourages states to provide joint facilities for the collection and evaluation of satellite sensing data through an international agreement. Although the document is commonly held to be applicable only to civil uses, given that it explicitly states that only "positive goals" (such as best use of resources and land, environmental protection) should be supported by remote sensing methods (Principle I (a)),[1032] it does not preclude its application for multilateral satellite verification for disarmament and non-proliferation purposes. In contrast to the national use of satellite remote sensing for reconnaissance, such multilateral satellite verification would qualify as a "positive" activity according to the "Principles Declaration" of 1963 as it would be in the general interest of the international community.[1033] The transfer of verification to a multilateral competence would additionally represent an adequate procedural manifestation of the mankind clause in Art. I of the Outer Space Treaty. Furthermore, such a multilateral competence is in line with the Environmental Modification (ENMOD) Convention of 1977 (Art. V, para. 1) and the Moon Treaty (Art. 15, para. 1), both of which make reference to "appropriate international procedures within the framework of the United Nations", which has become a standard clause in many multilateral arms control provisions, and also includes, in accordance with recent practice, the setting up of new verification mechanisms.[1034]

The legal controversy at the time of the first proposals for a multilateralization of satellite remote sensing questioned whether the collection and in particular the use of satellite images of a foreign territory was compatible with the principles of sovereign equality and territorial integrity of states.[1035] Considering the already mentioned declaration on the principles of remote sensing, the issue has been positively resolved. According to Principle IV, data collection by remote sensing is in principle admissible without the prior consent of states, as long as their legitimate interests and rights are not affected. According to Principle XII, states have a right to access the obtained data on the basis of non-discrimination.[1036]

The ISMA would according to Art. VI of the Outer Space Treaty also be entitled to conduct its own activities in outer space.

The controversy over the admissibility of military satellite reconnaissance was resolved earlier by the recognition in state practice of "national technical means" in bilateral and multilateral arms control agreements.[1037] Nevertheless, there is a persisting sense of uneasiness particularly within the developing world about the unilateral possession of sensitive data collected by the space powers concerning their territory.[1038] A multilateralization would contribute to reducing these reservations. In addition, the reliable verification of the non-proliferation of space weapons and of WMD is a vital security interest for the international community.[1039] Furthermore, a multilateralization would increase the willingness of states to accept comprehensive controls necessary for an effective non-proliferation policy. In building a treaty for ISMA, guidelines governing multilateral verification could specify the general principles on remote sensing.

In his monograph of 1987, Claus Dieter Classen argues for the creation of an international remote sensing organization that covers the military domain,[1040] as it would guarantee a balanced dissemination of information and could contribute to the reduction of military spending in the developing countries.[1041]

In conclusion, the multilateralization of satellite remote sensing for verification and its institutional implementation would not only correspond to the general trend in arms control policy that increasingly gives responsibility to international organizations for multilateral verification, but would also be a step towards constituting the international community as a bearer of legal rights and trustee of the security interests of mankind in outer space and with regard to disarmament and non-proliferation.[1042]

10.1.5.4 Conclusions

An institutional mechanism, along the lines of the proposals submitted to the CD, is needed in order to achieve the desired cooperative multilateral satellite verification and monitoring necessary for the implementation of the proposed CSO Treaty. The proposals to establish an international agency for satellite monitoring and/or verification are an excellent basis for the procedural and institutional implementation of the

CHOM principle in the security domain to guarantee the peaceful use of space, and thus for negotiations of the CSO Treaty with regard to its institutional as well as control mechanisms.[1043] The old objection to ISMA, that it would lack "treaty specificity" and would not have clearly defined functions, would no longer hold true given the specific control, monitoring and verification tasks of the CSO Treaty. The great potential of ISMA for the verification of further multilateral disarmament and arms control treaties working in combination with an active global non-proliferation policy could lead to a broader acceptance of other elements of common security in outer space. Such proposals could become increasingly appealing and thus also acceptable to the United States, in light of the demise of the Cold War on the one hand, and the urgency of a universally acceptable non-proliferation policy due to new threats from "states of concern" on the other. As a necessary instrument of, and at the same time the institutional framework for "multilateral technical means" of cooperative verification, the creation of ISMA is not only a precondition for the prevention of an arms race in outer space, but also for a successful non-proliferation regime for ballistic missile technology and WMD.

From the point of view of international law, instituting a multilateral satellite verification system would be the first step towards fulfilling the CHOM principle in space law and protecting the security interests of the international community in the exclusively peaceful use of outer space.

10.2 CREATION OF AN ORGANIZATION FOR COMMON SECURITY IN OUTER SPACE

10.2.1 AN INSTITUTIONAL MECHANISM TO SAFEGUARD THE PEACEFUL USE OF OUTER SPACE

In the same way Friedmann generally emphasized the institutional requirements of the changing structure of international law towards cooperation, underlining in particular:

> ... the quest for a more effective international order of security [and] the continued pursuit of the creation of an effective international organisation able to control and, if necessary, effectively stamp out wars;[1044]

the structural principle of CHOM equally calls for an institutional implementation. For the sake of security this implementation can no longer be delayed. Tomuschat states:

> ... institionalisation provides the key to the substance of what is referred to as the international community [and] [i]t is obviously much to be preferred to see common interests of mankind handled by institutions duly established for that purpose.[1045]

Institutionalization is also for Simma,[1046] Paulus,[1047] and Roberto Ago[1048] essential for consolidating the evolving "law of the international community". This institutional need is more pressing when considering the common territories beyond national jurisdiction such as outer space, since the international community is the true trustee of the common interest and the legislator and guarantor of its realization.[1049] With regard to the Outer Space Treaty in particular, a number of authors rightly emphasize the need for an institutional basis.[1050] According to Ago, institutionalization becomes indispensible when the security interests of mankind are at stake.[1051]

In the security field, however, institutionalization is confronted with strong national reservations, which prove difficult to overcome. Matte's analysis of the existing international organizations for outer space, which he classifies as "'traditional' international organisations", such as the United Nations and ITU, and "'new' operational organisations", such as the International Telecommunications Satellite Organization, Intersputnik International Organization of Space Communications, INMARSAT and ESA, concludes that states have recognized a "diminution from the absoluteness of sovereignty ... as a consequence of the procurement of practical benefit" including majority decisions of the organization and the weighing of votes.[1052] While this has been achieved mainly for organizations in the more technical areas, Matte states that in the political field similar solutions have yet to be found. Especially in relation to security, enormous political efforts will be required to overcome the existing tendencies of states to put their national security above international security. This will depend in particular on the common understanding that in the era of common security an antagonistic juxtaposition of national and international security is wrong, and that an institutional structure is needed to give all states the feeling that their national security is best served by an institutional safeguard of cooperative security in outer space.

Not only because of budgetary constraints, but also in the interest of rapid decision-making, a "lean" organizational structure should be adopted that should also accommodate the inclusion of the private sector by, for instance, using commercial satellite images, as well as of scientists and of civil society representatives. The budgetary constraints of Member States would be met most effectively by the enormous savings in terms of a security dividend, since OCSO would effectively prevent an arms race in space and would contribute to disarmament on Earth.

Although Matte considered the creation of a comprehensive world space organization to be premature in 1987, he did simultaneously emphasize the need to gradually implement the CHOM principle in the area of outer space and favours an international agency for satellite remote sensing as a first step in this direction:[1053]

> Such an agency could develop as a mechanism for managing specific and operative space-related peaceful uses of outer space, such as environmental protection and even possibly remote sensing activities. In this way, the agency would be acting as a *guardian for peace*, as well as promoting development. ... The major space powers ... should prove their sincerity toward humanity and *provide a gradual aerospace system and organisation according to the heralded CHOM principle* ... the common effort ... may well prove to be a gigantic step on the path to establishing a new order of international co-operation—indeed, in this era of total destruction—a new international order for survival [emphasis added].[1054]

The institutional underpinning of the Outer Space Treaty and the community status of outer space as established by the CHOM principle can no longer be delayed. Both the imminent advances towards active military uses of outer space and the established need for confidence building make an institutionalization of the CHOM principle in outer space law urgent. In the same way as the creation of an international regime governing the exploitation of natural resources of celestial bodies according to Art. 11, para. 5 of the Moon Treaty, the preservation of CHOM in the security field requires the establishment of international norms reinforced by necessary institutional mechanisms, before the threshold to active, destructive uses of outer space is passed.

In addition, there are several particular reasons that make an institutional structure to safeguard the peaceful use of the common space indispensable. The impossibility to distinguish military from purely civil technology renders a multilateral surveillance of "sensitive" technologies necessary, which would be hardly imaginable without a corresponding institution for securing monitoring and verification. Such an institutional framework will enable the non-proliferation of space technology for active military uses of space on the one hand, and the promotion of peaceful cooperation for civil and scientific purposes on the other.[1055] In the deliberations of the International Law Association regarding restrictions on military space uses, the Polish branch emphasized that genuine disarmament measures in outer space would particularly require an effective international institutional framework.[1056]

Firmly establishing the principle of the peaceful use of outer space, for instance, within a multilateral agency for satellite monitoring, verification and remote sensing, would create the structural prerequisites for implementing the central elements of four key areas of the CHOM principle in outer space:

- The preservation of the environment in the interest of present and future generations. The multilateral collection and evaluation of satellite images would promote favourable environmental conditions in the common space (and on Earth);[1057]
- The strengthening of international security whereby the security interest of the international community would be strongly enhanced;[1058]
- The "institution-building" process would have in itself positive effects on confidence-building, on safeguarding the peaceful use of space and on compliance with the ban on active military uses of outer space; similarly, it would have a positive influence on building the capacity of developing countries;[1059]
- The promotion of the economic use for the benefit of the international community and support for North-South cooperation in view of the dual-use capabilities of space technology.[1060]

While the CSO Treaty would be tasked with establishing a regime of common security in outer space, it would also be directly linked to a global system of common security, as was convincingly laid out by Abram Chayes, emphasizing that:

... a robust and vigorous institutional base will be necessary to accomplish the many tasks ... in the context of a co-operative security regime.[1061]

The regime would need to cover in particular the complex management tasks for the collection and evaluation of satellite data, their use for verification, and the diligent coordination of confidence-building measures, transparency and cooperative denuclearization. According to Chayes:

> The case for institutional strength together with continuing party involvement is even stronger in the context of a co-operative security regime. The starting point—and perhaps the end point—of such a regime is a network of arms control, non-proliferation, and regional security treaties. Co-ordination among a number of organisations addressing particular facets of the overall problem of co-operative security will be essential. ... If countries are to be assured not just that threats from a particular source or weapons system have been eliminated but that their security needs overall will not be compromised, the implementing organisations must be capable of cooperation at a technical and expert as well as at a policy level.[1062]

With a view to the prevention of an arms race in outer space and on the occasion of the strongly welcomed consensus to establish the Ad Hoc Committee on PAROS in 1985, the United Nations General Assembly has specifically supported the examination of adequate institutional steps.[1063] The proposed CSO Treaty would have to take account of these institutional requirements for effective implementation of the peaceful purpose principle by providing for the establishment of OCSO.

10.2.2 THE AREAS OF ACTIVITY OF THE ORGANIZATION

The organization's scope should correspond to the major elements of the CSO Treaty and guarantee their implementation.

10.2.2.1 Cooperative security and confidence building

The structural elements of cooperative security need institutional safeguards. A Consultative Committee within OCSO, whose membership could initially be limited to the permanent members of the United Nations Security Council or to the major military space powers, could ensure the necessary transparency of activities in outer space and strengthen confidence-building. The committee should, therefore, from the very beginning be accountable to an annual conference of state parties.

10.2.2.2 Monitoring and verification

Monitoring and verification are undoubtedly the most important activities of an international organization of cooperative security in outer space. The current proposals range from merely granting states the right of access to satellite images collected by "national technical means", to the obligatory notification of all missile launches through space, and to the establishment of multilateral verification satellites. The increasing availability of commercial satellite images, which have since the mid-1980s with the French SPOT satellites also covered the military field, points to the need for international regulation. To the extent that every interested state can freely acquire satellite and even military images on the open market, regulations to cover these images are imperative to ensure the security interests of all states. Satellite images obtained through commercial means could also be used for military purposes. In the Gulf War, for instance, both sides had commercial satellite images of the battlefield at their disposal. OCSO could regulate the use of satellite images with regard to the monitoring and verification of the CSO Treaty, and eventually also the entirety of the multilateral arms control and disarmament regime.

The proposed comprehensive prohibition of active military uses of outer space requires a broad range of passive and active verification measures, ideally including the possibility of on-site inspections of launching pads.[1064] OCSO, as an implementation and monitoring organization, could best guarantee their neutral and regular implementation. Likewise, the elaborate institutional verification mechanisms of the CWC and the CTBT, both providing for the creation of a special implementation organization, could serve as a model. The verification mechanism of the CWC is based on data provided willingly by the state parties and is far-reaching in terms of the scope and intensity of inspection rights and the obligation to destroy existing chemical arsenals. The mechanism of the CTBT only covers the monitoring of the test ban and thus is limited in its scope, being, however, more developed than the CWC mechanism in terms of its multilateral nature as it provides for a genuine international monitoring system. Under Art. IV of the CTBT and Part I of the CTBT Protocol, all states have an obligation to contribute to the multilateral inspection system by putting at its disposal seismological stations that are combined into a global network by the International Data Centre under the authority of the Secretariat.[1065] The proposal by China and Pakistan to include satellite data in the CTBT system was rejected allegedly for budgetary reasons.[1066] The monitoring system is institutionally designed to guarantee that all of the data obtained is available to all state parties.[1067] In contrast to the older IAEA safeguard system, which strictly respected state sovereignty, the CTBT monitoring system is no longer dependent on a state's ad hoc cooperation in being inspected. Thus, the CTBT's monitoring system is a model for a multilateral arms control inspection mechanism, and could be applied to satellite verification of the proposed CSO Treaty. A CSO satellite verification system could in turn support the inspection tasks of the CTBT monitoring system, and could further cooperate institutionally with the future CTBT Organization (CTBTO).[1068] Consequently, this would underline the close link between cooperative security in outer space and the nuclear-weapon powers' disarmament obligation under Art. VI of the NPT, for which a comprehensive ban on nuclear tests is indispensable.

10.2.2.3 Early warning and protection against unauthorized and accidental missile attacks

OCSO should include a multilateral JDEC, similar to the one outlined in the US-Russian memorandum of September 2000 with regard to early warning and notification of missile launches.[1069]

The protection against "accidental missile launches" and unauthorized attacks by missiles in the hands of terrorists is a multilateral affair *par excellence*. A multilateral data exchange centre as well as further cooperative arrangements such as "post-launch destruction" measures could provide an effective protection for both nuclear-weapon powers and other threatened states that would preclude the necessity of NMD systems.[1070] If the United States would nevertheless consider NMD to be necessary, a limited combined BMD/TMD system, similar to GPALS without space-based destructive components as envisaged by the Clinton Administration, would be sufficient.[1071]

The multilateral integration of the system could be achieved by establishing, under the aegis of OCSO, a network of early warning satellites under continued national authority that would guarantee a worldwide early warning capability. The data would be collected and assessed by an internationally staffed JDEC that would also employ military experts seconded by members of the Consultative Committee. The interceptors would continue to be under national control of the deploying state parties. Given the need for immediate reaction, the decision to activate interception would also rest with the member states. The operational and technical modalities of the system could follow closely the already mentioned bilateral early warning agreement between the US and Russia of 2000. The advantages of the multilateral linkage through the proposed integration with OCSO would be twofold. Firstly, the deployment of the system could not be misused as a pretext for taking offensive measures or for breaking out from the nuclear non-proliferation regime. Thus, the major purpose of OCSO, namely to prevent an arms race in outer space, would be achieved. Secondly, the international network of early warning satellites would also benefit states that would not otherwise have the capability to develop or maintain satellites for early warning, thereby contributing to the promotion of international security according to Art. III of the Outer Space Treaty and universal protection against nuclear terrorism.

10.2.2.4 Additional task in the area of military and civil space security

Another important task of the organization would be to promote an active global non-proliferation policy, which could be prepared by the Consultative Committee in collaboration with the experts from the various existing control regimes.

The two special committees of COPUOS could be entrusted with the task of elaborating the details of the immunity regime for civil satellites, the "rules of the road" and the security rules. The committees could make recommendations as to the implementation rules and procedures to OCSO, which would be responsible for the implementation and monitoring of the immunity and traffic stipulations.

10.2.2.5 Possible long-term functions of the Organization

The creation of OCSO would be an important step towards institutionalizing the CHOM principle in outer space.[1072] It could also draw on the discussion on reforming the United Nations Trusteeship Council, which, according to the Commission on Global Governance, should take an overall responsibility "for the governance of the global commons".[1073] The environmental field also considers the institutional implementation of the

CHOM principle to be critical for outer space.[1074] This corresponds to the general trend in international environmental law towards a universalization of the responsibility for the global environment.[1075] The inclusion of environmental protection among the tasks of the future OCSO would dovetail with the broad notion of security and correspond to "eco-security" and the Commission on Global Governance's appeal "to acknowledge that the security of the planet is a universal need to which the UN system must cater".[1076] The close linkage between the peaceful use of outer space and the preservation of the environment in space reinforces the value of joint institutional arrangements. In addition to the effects of space debris caused by weapon tests in space,[1077] the numerous security-related questions regarding the use or misuse of solar and nuclear energy in space[1078] necessitate an international regime for safeguarding environmental and military security in space.

10.2.3 INSTITUTIONAL STRUCTURE OF THE ORGANIZATION

By framing the primary functions of the proposed OCSO in terms of arms control and non-proliferation, institutional solutions can be drawn from existing treaty regimes in this field, such as OPCW, while keeping in mind the specific needs of a cooperative security regime in outer space. Comparable to the IAEA and the envisaged CTBTO, the OPCW consists of an annual Conference of the States Parties, an Executive Council with 41 members and a Technical Secretariat, in accordance with Art. VIII of the CWC. The members of the Executive Council are elected by the Conference of the States Parties on the basis of regional representation, the importance of their chemical industry and their political and security interests. The structure of OCSO could follow this basic pattern of an annual Conference of the States Parties, a Secretariat and an Executive Council whose members could be granted special voting rights based on their space (and nuclear-weapon) capabilities.[1079] In addition, there should be additional provisions allowing for flexibility in setting up possible ad hoc committees and involving national experts as needed.

A standing Consultative Committee—perhaps modelled on the multilateral Consultative Committee of the ENMOD Convention, which covers both security and environmental matters—comprised of the nuclear-weapon powers would form a fourth institutional segment of OSCO. Responsible primarily for the elaboration of global CTR and "security reassurance measures", the Committee would report to the annual

Conference. Depending on the subject addressed, and especially when considering the active non-proliferation of missile technology and WMD, *de facto* and potential nuclear-weapon powers would be included as well. The Consultative Committee could also assume, depending on its task, a bilateral or trilateral only format (United States/Russia/China). The CSO Treaty would ensure the organizational structure's necessary flexibility. A cooperative security structure for outer space requires an adequate balance between a multilateral approach to addressing the strategic questions related to the use of outer space, and the predominantly bilateral treatment of the strategic transition towards a new mix of defensive and offensive weapons. These issues cannot be separated from one another, as the nuclear strategic transition necessarily requires the regulation of security in outer space.

Finally, an IDC should be attached to the Secretariat, which would supervise the launch notifications and be tasked with the collection and analysis of the verification data. An ISMA modelled on the successful European Union's Satellite Centre, which should eventually have its own verification satellites along the lines of the Canadian PAXSAT proposals, could also be added.

10.2.4 CONCLUSIONS

In view of the close structural as well as substantive link between the prevention of an arms race in outer space and the promotion of civil uses of space, the long-term goal of a comprehensive world space organization should be to cover all activities falling under the CHOM principle. This would also correspond to the original approach suggested by A.A. Cocca for outer space,[1080] and Pardo for the seabed,[1081] according to which the international regime and the envisaged international institution should not only be entrusted with regulating the exploitation of resources, but also with safeguarding the principles of non-appropriation and the peaceful use of the common space in the interest of mankind. The world space organization could also become a model for a general international organization for common security, which could be set up in the long run under the aegis of the United Nations. The international community, having overcome the Cold War and turning towards a more pragmatic approach in North-South relations, is in a better position than ever to undertake such an endeavour. If, for the time being, there are no realistic chances for a universal participation in such a comprehensive world space organization, a gradual approach has to be set in place by creating first a world space organization limited to the security field (OCSO), where the necessary institutional safeguard of the peaceful use of outer space proceeds without further delay.

PART V

Conclusion

Just as the water of the streams we see is small in amount compared to that which flows underground, so the idealism which becomes visible is small in amount compared with what men and women bear locked in their hearts ... To unbind what is bound, to bring the underground waters to the surface: the mankind is waiting for such as can do that.

Albert Schweitzer
1963[1082]

For the time being, there are no weapons deployed in outer space. The military uses of outer space are limited to those of a passive quality by satellites without destructive effect. This represents an unambiguous and clearly definable threshold, up to which the international community is, and has so far been, prepared *nolens volens* to accept the military use of the common space. However, there is now an increasing possibility of a drift towards active military uses of outer space, which could spur an arms race, should space weapons be deployed. The international community has from the very beginning of such plans raised serious objections, referring to the status of outer space as a "common heritage of mankind" according to the mankind clause in Art. I, para. 1 of the Outer Space Treaty. The space powers have been repeatedly called upon within the CD and the United Nations General Assembly to refrain from any action that could lead to an arms race in outer space, asking them in particular to refrain from any active military uses in space. A large number of non-aligned states would also like to prohibit the present passive military uses by satellites, arguing that these contribute to destructive effects on Earth and are capable of extending the nuclear arms race into outer space. The present (and ambiguous) acceptance of tests for the development of destructive space systems does not imply the international community's readiness to accept permanent active military uses of outer space, as long as these tests are not linked to clearly announced intentions to deploy the systems. While the current testing in the framework of the NMD plans of the G.W. Bush Administration could lead to a deployment in the next ten years, even though the technical feasibility is still doubtful, the United States has not been unequivocal in its announcements that it will deploy, apart from satellite sensors, active military components of a destructive nature in outer space.

According to the Outer Space Treaty of 1967, the space powers are to participate in the elaboration of an international order so as to safeguard the peaceful use and to preserve the common status of outer space according to the CHOM principle. Such an international order that specifies the principle of the peaceful use of outer space is urgently needed to prevent an arms race in outer space. In light of the Outer Space Treaty's inclusion of the mankind principle, substantiating the principle of the peaceful use and the prevention of an arms race in the common space is a legal obligation as it is a corollary of the mankind clause and of the community status of outer space. It is based on the development of the full meaning of the principle of the peaceful use by interpreting it in light of the mankind clause as a central element of the CHOM principle, which, as a structural principle of outer space law, constitutes the status of outer space as a "common heritage of mankind". In the framework of the current negotiations at the CD, several delegations have repeatedly referred to the CHOM principle as an obligation to prevent an arms race in outer space. Thus, in state practice an *opinio juris* is developing that as a result of CHOM's applicability to outer space, there are ensuing legal consequences obliging states to refrain from any measures that could cause an arms race in space.

The influence of the CHOM principle on the structure of outer space law is significant. On the one hand, the principle leads to a presumption in favour of the interdependence of states taking precedence over national sovereignty. Contrary to classic international law, the common space is not open for states to exclusively pursue their own interests, but rather states also have to act in pursuance of the common good of the international community. The CHOM principle as a structural principle of outer space law is a binding guideline for interpretation as well as for creating norms *de lege ferenda* to fill the *lacunae* in the treaty regime, as well as for the procedural and institutional implementation of the legal principles governing outer space and the harmonization of community interests with individual state interests.

As the central element of the CHOM principle, the mankind clause together with the principle of cooperation in outer space law forms the legal foundation for common security in outer space. The principles of common security are recognized on a general plane by the major space and nuclear-weapon powers. As such, they compel the space powers to pursue cooperative solutions regarding the military use of space in the security interests of all states and in compliance with the nuclear disarmament obligations under Art. VI of the NPT.

Just as the peaceful use of outer space is an essential constituent of the CHOM principle, so the preceding analysis has shown that the various dimensions of "peaceful use" reflect the main legal principles of the Outer Space Treaty. In turn, the CHOM principle is manifested in outer space law through the Outer Space Treaty. International law has undergone, and continues to undergo, a structural change with regard to outer space. Fulfilling the content of the CHOM principle in state practice additionally reinforces Art. I of the Outer Space Treaty, as the implementation of the common interest clause in the security field leads to a customary international legal obligation to prevent an arms race in outer space. This obligation can be adequately implemented by a multilateral prohibition of space weapons and the establishment of a protection regime for peaceful uses of outer space. The refusal to regulate the active military use of space in a multilateral agreement would contradict the obligation of the nuclear-weapon powers according to Art. VI of the NPT to conclude a nuclear disarmament agreement, as the ICJ confirmed in its "Advisory Opinion on the Legality of the Threat or Use of Nuclear Weapons", which also applies to outer space. Thus, the unilateral deployment of missile defences with active military components in space would not be admissible under international law. Rather, the international community would have to be adequately involved in a consensual multilateral framework. Hence, the unilateral or antagonistic deployment of a comprehensive missile defence system that includes space-based weapons to defend against missiles in mid-course would constitute an unlawful use of the common space.

Procedures are urgently needed to determine the common interest in the field of space security. A minimum requisite is the creation of an international norm governing the military use of outer space. Since the existing regulation of military uses is insufficient in the Outer Space Treaty with regard to procedural guarantees, and given that the controversy over the interpretation of the principle of the peaceful use of space has persisted for more than 30 years, there is a normative need to define the principle's content and to establish guarantees for compliance with it. This need coincides with the general necessity for nuclear disarmament affirmed by the ICJ. The overriding interest of mankind in outer space is in the promotion of world peace and international stability as well as international understanding and cooperation in accordance with Art. III of the Outer Space Treaty. States, thus, have an obligation to provide the necessary substantive as well as procedural safeguards for the peaceful use of the common space. Negotiating a multilateral treaty on common security in outer space, including adequate institutional mechanisms, would fulfil this obligation and provide the necessary safeguards. Substantively, such an agreement could build on the structural and legal standards for the peaceful use of outer space, which could in turn be manifested by explicit rules of prohibition and prescription to enhance legal clarity and predictability. The legal standards derived from the principles of cooperation and peaceful use of outer space are: common/cooperative security; prevention of an arms race in outer space; prohibition of military occupation; prohibition of the deployment of nuclear and other WMD in space; the complete demilitarization of celestial bodies; positive effects for world peace and international security as well as international cooperation and understanding (Art. III of the Outer Space Treaty); the benefit of all mankind and of all states with particular consideration of the developing countries (Art. I, para. 1 of the Outer Space Treaty); and the preservation of the environment in the common space for present and future generations (Art. I, para. 1, IX of the Outer Space Treaty and Art. 4 and 7 of the Moon Treaty).

The peaceful purpose and mankind clause in the Outer Space Treaty would best be manifested through a multilateral CSO Treaty. In turn, the Treaty could establish the foundation for a cooperative strategic transition that would render nuclear deterrence obsolete and would allow for an active non-proliferation policy through the adoption of "strategic reassurance measures". The main tenets of such a CSO Treaty could be categorized as follows:

1. Principles of cooperative security in outer space:
    (a) Transparency and confidence building;
    (b) Defensive force configuration;
    (c) Non-proliferation and disarmament; and
    (d) Protection against unauthorized and accidental missile attacks and attacks in violation of non-proliferation regimes;
2. Prohibition of active military uses of destructive effect in outer space;
3. Destruction of existing ASAT systems;
4. Confidence-building measures;
5. Protective regime for civil space objects and passive military uses of a non-destructive nature in outer space;
6. Implementation of multilateral monitoring and verification (ISMA);
7. Codification of further legal standards of the peaceful use of outer space.

The evolving community-oriented law of the international community and of cooperation in the security field, arising from an underlying structural change of international relations and international law, offers the opportunity to safeguard the peaceful use of outer space by setting the foundation for common security in outer space that would open the way towards establishing an effective order of preventive peacekeeping. The alternative to this perspective is an understanding of the unrestricted freedom of military use of outer space as a "last frontier" pursued in an antagonistic competition of states and based on the traditional structures of classic international law. Through continuing and even extending the arms competition into outer space, the international community would be faced with a new arms race that would undermine the hope of limiting and finally ending arms races on Earth. An arms race in space would go in tandem with a race in high technology used for weapons, demanding financial resources to a degree hitherto unknown.

The obligation of the nuclear-weapon powers to conclude an agreement on complete nuclear disarmament necessitates a renunciation to extend the arms race into outer space. If the introduction of defensive systems into outer space is meant to be part of a strategic transition that aims to overcome the strategy of nuclear deterrence and to establish a strategic environment more amenable to nuclear arms control and disarmament, then technological solutions alone are not sufficient. Such a strategic transition is only possible in a cooperative framework that would also guarantee the exclusion of any military uses of a destructive nature in outer space. This cooperative framework, based on the status of outer space as CHOM according to the Outer Space Treaty of 1967, must be a multilateral one, given that the security interests of all states are affected by the military use of outer space. Disarmament and the prevention of an arms race in outer space only stand a chance through a cooperative strategic transition.

An international order governing the use of outer space in accordance with CHOM and the new structure of space law could be a model for the evolving structure of cooperative international law that would enhance the community orientation of the international system, which would favour the community values embodied in the CHOM principle and corresponding to disarmament, economic development and democracy essential for overall international security.[1083] In this regard, the establishment of a legal framework for common security in outer space, thereby preserving and enhancing civil uses of space in the interest of all states, would also be an important contribution to the "law of international welfare". Having the prohibition of active military uses in outer space in combination with the international community's vested right to prevent an arms race in outer space embodied in a cooperative framework of common security would be both an adequate implementation of the mankind clause in the security field and an important step towards general and complete disarmament on Earth. Such a regime would thus fulfil the Outer Space Treaty's objective expressed in the preamble that the use of outer space has to serve the interests of mankind as a whole.

The resulting outcome in attempting to develop this regime will demonstrate how much credence the space powers are willing to assign to the "rule of law" in questions of international security. It will also show whether the objective of the Outer Space Treaty to reserve the common space exclusively for use in the interest of mankind can be preserved and its underlying structure strengthened; or whether instead it has to accommodate the uninhibited unilateral control and use in the national interest by one or a few states. Unilateral control of space would severely undermine the community status of the common territory beyond national jurisdiction, as well as the structural change of the international system thus far achieved, given its fragility and reversibility from the lack of central institutional safeguards, thus allowing the establishment of a "space power hierarchy" with the inherent trend for "space sovereignty" of a few powerful states.

The international community is at a crossroads: either the very basis of the structural change of international law with regard to the common space can be secured by a multilateral order safeguarding the peaceful use of outer space, or an unbridled power rivalry to expand into outer space will erupt. Even at the height of the Cold War, both major space powers respected the peaceful purpose standards in the use of outer space. It would be an irreparable setback for the international community to now lose the peaceful purpose standard in outer space, and risk having space become the new arena for an arms race for the sake of unilateral military "space control" ambitions and the transgression towards active military uses of a destructive nature. If met successfully, the challenge will inspire mankind's hope that the common space will be governed by an internationally agreed upon *pax cosmica*.

Modern international law has rightly abandoned the "legal indifference towards war" that was characteristic of classic international law.[1084] It is thus called upon to consolidate the structural foundations of the community status of outer space and safeguard the principle of its peaceful use to avert an arms race in space and war. If a multilateral agreement to safeguard the peaceful use of outer space is not concluded soon, Montserrat Filho, a Brazilian space lawyer, drawing a parallel with the legality of nuclear weapons, suggests putting the question of the peaceful use of outer space before the ICJ for an advisory opinion.[1085]

The Outer Space Treaty with its inclusion of the mankind and peaceful purpose clauses has laid the far-sighted foundation for the establishment of a regime of common security in outer space. The role of international law "at the heart of which is the overriding consideration of humanity", as in the formulation of the ICJ,[1086] is to protect the common heritage of mankind and to preserve the common peaceful status of outer space. The conclusion of a multilateral agreement and the creation of an international organization for the common security in outer space would help meet this challenge. It would at last be an appropriate answer to the challenging question raised by the US diplomat and winner of the peace prize of the Deutscher Buchhandel, George F. Kennan:

> Can we not at long last cast off our preoccupation with sheer destruction, a preoccupation that is costing us our prosperity and preempting the resources that should go to the solving of our great social problems?[1087]

206

Notes

1   W. Friedmann, *The Changing Structure of International Law*, London, 1964, p. 3.

2   Speech on the national defence policy, 18 December 1967, quoted in D. Goedhuis, "An Evaluation of the Leading Principles of the Outer Space Treaty of 27th January 1967", *NTIR*, vol. 15, 1968, p. 40.

3   J. Schell, *The Abolition*, New York, 1984.

4   For an analysis of foundations of common security in general international law see H. Fischer, *Völkerrechtliche Normenbildung und sicherheitspolitische Konzeptionen. Aktuelle Rechtsquellenprobleme und die Implementation Gemeinsamer Sicherheit*, Bochum, 1987, and H. Fischer, "Koexistenz und Kooperation im modernen Völkerrecht—'Gemeinsame Sicherheit' und die Struktur des Rechts der Friedenssicherung" in E. Bahr and D. S. Lutz (eds), *Gemeinsame Sicherheit—Idee und Konzept*, Baden-Baden, 1986, p. 55.

5   W. Friedmann, op. cit., 1964; G. Dahm, J. Delbrück and R. Wolfrum, *Völkerrecht. Die Grundlagen. Die Völkerrechtssubjekte*, Berlin, 1989, p. 452.

6   H. Mosler, *The International Society as a Legal Community*, Alphen aan den Rijn, 1980; C. Tomuschat, "International Law: Ensuring the Survival of Mankind on the Eve of a New Century", *RdC*, vol. 281, 1999, p. 72; B. Simma, "From Bilateralism to Community Interest in International Law", *RdC*, vol. 250, 1994, p. 217; B. Simma and A. Paulus, "The 'International Community': Facing the Challenge of Globalization", *EJIL*, vol. 8, 1997, p. 276; A. Paulus, *Die internationale Gemeinschaft im Völkerrecht. Eine Untersuchung zur Entwicklung des Völkerrechts im Zeitalter der Globalisierung*, Munich, 2001.

7   UN Doc., A/S-10/AC.1/7, 1 June 1978.

8   *ICJ Reports 1996*, p. 264.

9   Ibid., S. 42, p. 100.

10   The then Senator in the US House of Representatives Albert Gore emphasized at the United Nations General Assembly on 12 March 1962: "It should be easier to agree not to arm a part of the environment that has never been armed than to disarm parts that have been armed"; reprinted in *AJIL*, vol. 57, 1963, p. 429.

11   Quoted in Goedhuis, op. cit., 1968, p. 27.

12 For the genesis of the principle of peaceful use of outer space see P.K. Menon, *The United Nations' Efforts to Outlaw the Arms Race in Outer Space. A Brief History with Key Documents*, St. Paul, 1988, p. 40; M.N. Andem, *International Legal Problems in the Peaceful Exploration and Use of Outer Space*, Rovaniemi, 1992; P.C. Jessup and H.J. Taubenfeld, *Controls for Outer Space and the Antarctic Analogy*, New York, 1959, p. 252; E. Galloway, "The United States and the 1967 Treaty on Outer Space", Proceedings from the 40th Colloquium on the Law of Outer Space, 1998, p. 18; P. Sontag, *Der Weltraum in der Raumordnung des Völkerrechts. Hoheitsrechte im Weltraum*, Cologne, 1966, p. 133; M.S. Vázquez, *Cosmic International Law*, New York, 1965, p. 149; C.W. Jenks, *The International Law of Outer Space*, New York, 1965, p. 44; I.A. Vlasic, "The Legal Aspects of Peaceful and Non-Peaceful Uses of Outer Space" in B. Jasani (ed.), *Peaceful and Non-Peaceful Uses of Space: Problems of Definition for the Prevention of an Arms Race*, 1991, Geneva, p. 39; Vlasic, "Disarmament Decade, Outer Space and International Law", *McGill Law Journal*, vol. 25, 1981, p. 135; T. Beer, "Der Weltraum und seine militärische Nutzung in Friedenszeiten im Lichte des Völkervertragsrechts", dissertation, 1987; P.M. Stadler, "Rechtliche Schranken der militärischen Tätigkeiten im Weltraum und auf den Himmelskörpern in Friedenszeiten", dissertation, 1975, p. 54; G.C.M. Reijnen, *The United Nations Space Treaties Analysed*, Gif-sur-Yvette, 1995, p. 41; B.C.M. Reijnen, "The Prevention of an Arms Race in Outer Space" in M. Benkö, W. de Graaff and G.C.M. Reijnen (eds), *Space Law in the United Nations*, Dordrecht, 1985, p. 181; G.W. Rehm, *Rüstungskontrolle im Weltraum*, Bonn, 1965, p. 91; H. Taubenfeld, "Consideration at the United Nations of the Status of Outer Space", *AJIL*, vol. 53, 1959, p. 405; N. Jasentuliyana, *International Space Law and the United Nations*, Boston, 1999, p. 24; M. Benkö and K.-U. Schrogl, "The UN Committee on the Peaceful Uses of Outer Space" in M. Benkö and K.-U. Schrogl (eds), *International Space Law in the Making: Current Issues in the UN Committee on the Peaceful Uses of Outer Space*, Gif-sur-Yvette, 1993, p. 7; R. Wolfrum, "The Problems of Limitation and Prohibition of Military Use of Outer Space", *ZaöRV*, vol. 44, 1984, p. 784; M.G. Marcoff, "Sur l'interprétation juridique de l'Article 4 du Traité régissant les activités spatiales des États", *Revue générale de l'Air*, vol. 31, 1968, p. 42; G.M. Marcoff, "Disarmament and 'Peaceful

Purposes' Provisions in the 1967 Outer Space Treaty", *JSL*, vol. 4, 1976, p. 11; C.-J. Cheng, "Military Use of Outer Space: Article IV of the 1967 Space Treaty Revisited" in C.-J. Cheng and D.H. Kim (eds), *The Utilization of the World's Air Space and Free Outer Space in the 21st Century*, The Hague, 2000, p. 309; M. Filho, "Total Militarization of Space and Space Law: The Future of the Article IV of the 1967 Outer Space Treaty", Proceedings from the 40th Colloquium on the Law of Outer Space, 1998, p. 358; H.-J. Heintze, "Peaceful Uses of Outer Space and International Law" in W. Bender, R. Hagen, M. Kalinowski and J. Scheffran (eds), *Space Use and Ethics*, vol. 1, Munster, 2001, p. 243; M.N. Andem, "Implications of the 1967 Outer Space Treaty in the New Millennium: A Brief Reflection on the Implications of Proposed Missile Defense Systems", Proceedings from the 43rd Colloquium on the Law of Outer Space, 2001, p. 275; J.W. Heath, "Mahan's Legacy: How Will a New Generation of Weapons fit into Competing Visions of Outer Space", Proceedings from the 43rd Colloquium on the Law of Outer Space, 2001, p. 298.

[13] The Soviet Union launched Sputnik I, the first satellite launched into space, in October 1957. The United States followed with Explorer I in January 1958 and France in 1965. In 1968 the first European research satellite was launched, with a leading contribution by Germany. Japan followed in 1970, China in 1971, India in 1980, and Great Britain in 1982. W. Buedeler, *Geschichte der Raumfahrt*, Künzelsau, 1982.

[14] W. von Kries, "Weltraumforschung" in K.-H. Böckstiegel (ed.), *Handbuch des Weltraumrechts*, Berlin, 1991, p. 254; R. Wolfrum, *Die Internationalisierung staatsfreier Räume*, Berlin, 1984, p. 276.

[15] US memorandum submitted to the First Committee of the United Nations General Assembly, 12 January, 1957, UN Doc. A/C.1/738, printed in Department of State, "Documents on Disarmament 1945-1959" (1960, publication 7008), vol. 2, p. 733; Jessup and Taubenfeld, op. cit., 1959, p. 252; generally on the role of the United States in the introduction of the principle of peaceful use of outer space see Galloway, op. cit., 1998, p. 18; Váquez, op. cit., 1965, p. 149; Wolfrum, op. cit., 1984, p. 275.

[16] Ibid.

[17] See the US position on the regulation, limitation, and balanced reduction of all armed forces and armaments, UN Doc. A/C1/783 submitted to the United Nations General Assembly in 1957.

18 R. Handberg, *Seeking New World Vistas: The Militarization of Space*, New York, 2000, p. 44.

19 UN Res. 1148, 14 November 1957; Jenks, op. cit., 1965, p. 44; Vlasic, op. cit., 1991, p. 39; Heintze, op. cit., 2001, p. 243.

20 Department of State, "Documents on Disarmament 1945-1959", printed in Reijnen, op. cit., 1995, p. 41.

21 Section 102 (a), National Aeronautics and Space Act, House Resolution, H.R. 12575, Public Law 86-568, 85th Congress, First Session, 29 July 1958, p. 5.

22 UN Doc. A/3818, Annexes, 17 March 1958, printed in Reijnen, op. cit., 1992, p. 47; G. Zhukov and Y. Kolosov, *International Space Law*, New York, 1984, p. 58; Jessup and Taubenfeld, op. cit., 1959, p. 252; G.W. Rehm, *Rüstungskontrolle im Weltraum*, Bonn, 1965, p. 91; Taubenfeld, op. cit., 1959, p. 405; Wolfrum, op. cit., 1984, p. 784; Wolfrum, op. cit., 1984, p. 275; according to Goedhuis, op. cit., 1968, p. 23 the Soviet draft with the provision of a prohibition of the deployment of any weapons in outer space and—in accordance with the US proposal—of an international control of this prohibition, was the expression of the fact that both super powers were at the beginning even aiming for a complete demilitarization of outer space.

23 Rehm, op. cit., 1965, p. 7.

24 Galloway, op. cit., 1998, p. 18 offers the following assessment of the US efforts at the UN during the early years: "The United States pursued policies in the United Nations that strengthened peaceful uses..."

25 UN Doc. A/C.1/L.220 Rev.1, 13 November 1958.

26 UN Res. 1348 (XIII), 13 December 1958.

27 UN Doc. A/4141, 14 July 1959.

28 UN Res. 1472 (XIV), 12 December 1959.

29 Reijnen, op. cit., 1995, p. 20.

30 Ibid.

31 Jasentuliyana, op. cit., 1999, p. 24; Benkö and Schrogl, op. cit., 1993, p. 7. The members are: Albania, Argentina, Australia, Austria, Belgium, Benin, Brasil, Bulgaria, Burkina Faso, Cameroon, Canada, Chad, Chile, China, Columbia, Cuba, Czech Republic, Ecuador, Egypt, France, Germany, Greece, Hungary, India, Indonesia, Italy, Japan, Iran, Iraq, Kazakhstan, Korea, Kenya, Lebanon, Mexico, Mongolia, Morocco, Nicaragua, Netherlands, Niger, Nigeria, Pakistan, Peru, Philippines, Poland, Portugal,

Romania, Russian Federation, Senegal, Sierra Leone, Spain, Sudan, Sweden, South Africa, Syria, Turkey, Ukraine, United Kingdom, United States, Uruguay, Venezuela, Vietnam and FR Yugoslavia. In 1993 the International Telecommunication Union, International Atomic Energy Agency and United Nations Educational, Scientific and Cultural Organization were granted observer status.

32 The Austrian Chairman of the Space Committee, Franz Matsch, reported to the United Nations General Assembly in 1962 that the Committee had agreed "to conduct the Committee's work in such a way that it would be able to reach agreement in its work without need for voting". UN Doc. A/5181, 27 September 1962, p. 2.

33 The Legal Subcommittee and Scientific and Technical Subcommittee.

34 Treaty on Principles Governing the Activities of States in the Exploration and Use of Outer Space, including the Moon and other Celestial Bodies (Outer Space Treaty), entered into force 10 October 1967; Agreement Governing the Activities of States on the Moon and other Celestial Bodies (Moon Treaty), entered into force on 12 July 1984; Convention on the Registration of Objects launched into Outer Space (Registration Convention), entered into force on 15 September 1976; Agreement on the Rescue of Astronauts, Return of Astronauts and the Return of Objects launched into Outer Space (Rescue Agreement), entered into force on 3 September 1968; Convention on International Liability for Damage caused by Space Objects (Liability Convention), entered into force on 1 September 1972; Resolution of 3 December 1986 on Principles Governing Remote Sensing of the Earth from Outer Space; Resolution of 3 December 1986 on Principles of Direct Satellite Broadcasting.

35 Kewenig, Menschheitserbe, Konsens und Völkerrechtsordnung, EA, vol. 36, 1981; Wolfrum, "The Principle of the Common Heritage of Mankind", ZaöRV, vol. 43, 1983, p. 336.

36 UN Res. 1721 (GV XVI), 20 December 1961.

37 UN Res. 1802 (GV XVII), 14 December 1962.

38 UN Res. 1962, (GV XVIII), 13 December 1963.

39 W. von Kries, op. cit., 1991, p. 329; Wolfrum, op. cit., 1984, p. 799; Wolfrum, op. cit., Berlin, 1984, p. 275; S. Hobe, Die rechtlichen Rahmenbedingungen der wirtschaftlichen Nutzung des Weltraums, dissertation, 1992, p. 104 underlines that both great powers had linked the mankind clause in outer space law primarily

with this arms control objective and that the discussion about its content had only in later years turned to the question of the distribution of economic benefits from space use.

40   Jenks, op. cit., 1965, p. 192. Similarly, the Institute of International Law in *Annuaire de l'Institut de Droit International*, vol. 50 II, 104 states in its resolution on the subject that it is not sufficient to lay down the principle of peaceful use of outer space in particular pending clarification of its meaning merely as an objective and not an operative legal principle in order to clearly prohibit all military uses.

41   Hobe, op. cit., 1992, p. 104.

42   S. Welck and R. Platzöder, *Weltraumrecht*, Baden-Baden, 1987, p. 602.

43   Stated by the Soviet Union on 12 July 1962 in the Legal Subcommittee of COPUOS, UN Doc. A/AC.105/C.2/SR.57; N.M. Matte, "The Common Heritage of Mankind and Outer Space", *AASL*, vol. 12, 1987, p. 318.

44   On the close link between the space issue and the process of multilateral disarmament negotiations see Vlasic, op. cit., 1991, p. 39; Jenks, op. cit., 1965, p. 46; Jasentuliyana, op. cit., 1999, p. 24; Sontag, op. cit., 1966, p. 133; Menon, op. cit., 1988, p. 39.

45   Printed in *Disarmament Diplomacy*, no. 22, 1962.

46   Rehm, op. cit., 1965, p. 45.

47   UN Doc. ENDC/19/Rev.1, 6 April 1962 and Statement by the Honourable Howard Green, Secretary of State for External Affairs of Canada, UN Doc. ENDC/17, 28 March 1962; P. Gasparini Alves, *Prevention of an Arms Race in Outer Space: A Guide to the Discussions in the Conference on Disarmament*, Geneva, 1991, p. 3.

48   ENDC/98, 21 June 1963; Rehm, op. cit., 1965, p. 38; Menon, op. cit., 1988, p. 40; Gasparini Alves, op. cit., 1991, p. 3.

49   ENDC/98, 21 June 1963.

50   P.D. O'Neill, Jr., "The Development of International Law Governing the Military Use of Outer Space" in W.J. Durch (ed.), *National Interest and the Military Use of Space*, Washington DC, 1984, p. 173.

51   Printed in *EA*, April 1963, D.

52   "Partial Test Ban Treaty", *BGBl*, vol. II, 1964, p. 906 (ratification as of January 2001: 126 parties).

53   "Nuclear Test Case", *ICJ Reports 1974*, p. 253 qualified a unilateral declaration as legally binding. This is true when unilateral declarations are exchanged with the express intent of creating a binding obligation. N. Singh and E. McWhinney, *Nuclear Weapons and Contemporary International Law*, (2nd. ed.), Dordrecht, 1989, p. 235.

54   UN Res. 1884 (XVII), 17 October 1963; Jenks, op. cit., 1965, p. 50.

55   UN Doc. A/5549/Add.1, 27 November 1963, pp. 21 and 28.

56   Antarctic Treaty, 1 December 1959.

57   See also Art. 2 of the Statute of the International Atomic Energy Agency.

58   UN Res. 2749 (XXV), 17 December 1970.

59   G. Fahl (ed.), *Internationales Recht der Rüstungsbeschärnkung*, Lose-Blatt-Sammlung, 1975.

60   Wolfrum, op. cit., 1984, p. 347; R. Wolfrum, "Restricting the Use of the Sea to Peaceful Purposes: Demilitarization in Being?", *GYIL*, vol. 24, 1975, p. 201; P.B. Payoyo, *Cries of the Sea. World Inequality, Sustainable Development and the Common Heritage of Humanity*, The Hague, 1997, p. 313; M. Virally, "Les utilisations militaires des espaces et leur limitation par le Droit International", *RGDIP*, vol. 88, 1984, p. 5.

61   For a comparison between the provisions of peaceful use for territories beyond national jurisdiction including the high seas and in outer space law see Wolfrum, op. cit., 1984, p. 346.

62   S. Courteix, "Le Traité de 1967 et son application en matière d'utilisation militaire de l'espace", *Politique Étrangère*, vol. 36, 1971, p. 257; N. Poulantzas, "The Outer Space Treaty of January 27, 1967: A Decisive Step Towards Arms Control, Demilitarization of Outer Space and International Supervision", Proceedings from the 10th Colloquium on the Law of Outer Space, 1968, p. 213.

63   ABM Treaty of 26 May 1972, Welck and Platzöder, op. cit., 1987, p. 62.

64   UN Doc. A/RES/2222 (XXI), 19 December 1966.

65   C.-G. Hasselmann, "Weapons of Mass Destruction, Article IV Outer Space Treaty and the Relationship to General Disarmament", Proceedings from the 25th Colloquium on the Law of Outer Space, 1983, p. 103.

66   UN Doc. A/AC.105/32, 17 June 1966.

67   UN Doc. A/6352, 16 June 1966.

68   P.G. Dembling, Negotiating Issues in Forming the 1967 Treaty on Outer Space, Proceedings from the 40th Colloquium on the Law of outer Space, 1997, p. 37; Courteix, op. cit., 1971, p. 257.

69   Articles 8 and 9 of the US draft, UN Doc. A/AC.105/35, Annex I.

70   UNGA Committee I, 17 December 1966 in *Department of State Bulletin*, 9 January 1967, p. 78.

71   Kries, "Die militärische Nutzung des Weltraums" in Böckstiegel (ed.), op. cit., 1991, p. 316.

72   Kries, "Die militärische Nutzung des Weltraums", op. cit., 1991, p. 316.

73   P. Jankowitsch, "From Cold War to Detente in Outer Space: The Role of the United Nations in Outer Space Law Development", Proceedings from the 40th Colloquium on the Law of Outer Space, 1998, p. 45.

74   UN Doc. A/AC.105/C.2/SR. 66, 25 July 1966.

75   Summary of Foreign Policy Aspects of the U.S. Outer Space Program, attached to Memorandum from McGeorge Bundy, Chronology of Development of U.S. Policy with Respect to Outer Space, pp. 8-10.

76   P.B. Stares, *The Militarization of Space: U.S. Policy, 1945-1984*, New York, 1985, p. 54. Emphasis in the original.

77   Handberg, op. cit., 2000, p. 192.

78   K-H. Böckstiegel, Grundlagen des Weltraumrechts in Böckstiegel (ed.), op. cit., 1991, p. 11.

79   J.E.S. Fawcett, *Outer Space: New Challenges to Law and Policy*, Oxford, 1984; O.O. Ogunbanwo, *International Law and Outer Space Activities*, The Hague, 1975, p. 214; D. Wolter, "Völkerrechtliche Grundlagen 'Gemeinsamer Sicherheit' im Weltraum", *ZaöRV*, vol. 62, 2002, p. 943.

80   Poulantzas, op. cit., 1968, p. 213.

81   According to Cheng, op. cit., 2000, p. 309, the two space powers pursued their objectives in different ways. While the Soviet Union "... pretended that it did not use satellites for military reconnaissance...", the United States admitted this openly, but "... here is where its diplomats, advised no doubt by their nimble-minded legal advisers, started to re-invent the word 'peaceful', turning its meaning from 'non-military' to 'non-aggressive' so that all its military space missions, not being aggressive, would also be for peaceful purposes".

82   For instance, a Soviet draft of 1958 talks of "... directing the latest achievements of science and engineering towards peaceful uses for the good of mankind...", UN Doc. A/3818, para. 2, 15 March 1958.

83   A. Bueckling, "Grundbegriffe und Grundprinzipien des Weltraumrechts" in Böckstiegel (ed.), op. cit., 1991, p. 99; for the contrary view, see Hobe, op. cit., 1992, p. 104; Kries, "Die militärische Nutzung des Weltraums", op. cit., 1991, p. 329; Wolfrum, op. cit., 1984, p. 275; Vlasic, op. cit., 1981, p. 135; Marcoff, op. cit., 1976, p. 11.

84   "There was universal agreement on confining the use of outer space to 'peaceful purposes', a concept already expressed by the General Assembly". Jessup and Taubenfeld, op. cit., 1959, p. 252. Also, J. Dean, "Future Security in Space: Treaty Issues", *Information Bulletin des International Network of Engineers and Scientists Against Proliferation*, no. 20, August 2002, p. 16 wrote: "This language points to the fact that, during the thirty-year existence of the Outer Space Treaty, a powerful norm has emerged against the weaponisation of space, and for ensuring the peaceful use of space."

85   Rehm, op. cit., 1965, p. 7.

86   A. Verdross and B. Simma, *Universelles Völkerrecht. Theorie und Praxis*, Berlin, 1984.

87   Article 23, para. 1, Vienna Convention on the Law of Treaties, 22 May 1969.

88   Section 102 (a), National Aeronautics and Space Act, op. cit., 1958, p. 5.

89   "Temple of Prehar Case", *ICJ Reports 1962*, p. 39.

90   Stares, op. cit., 1985, p. 55; P.B. Stares, "Space and U.S. National Security" in Durch (ed.), op. cit., 1984, p. 38; Wolfrum, op. cit., 1984, p. 793.

91   P. Magno, "How to Avoid the Militarisation of Outer Space", Proceedings from the 26th Colloquium on the Law of Outer Space, 1984, p. 222.

92   Kries, "Die militärische Nutzung des Weltraums", op. cit., 1991, p. 327.

93   "... new international organizations have evolved which place less emphasis on the sanctity of State sovereignty and equality ... Outer space has become a proving ground for international cooperation and mutual assistance. The emphasis has been drawn away from

94   the sovereign State and directed towards the international community as a whole". N.M. Matte, "Outer Space and International Organizations" in R.-J. Dupuy (ed.), *Manuel sur les organisations internationales*, Leiden, 1998, p. 752.
M. Lachs, "International Academy of Aeronautics", *I.I.A.*, vol. II, 1970, p. 2. From the traditionally voluntarist approach of Soviet theory of international law emphasizing state sovereignty and freedom, Soviet international lawyer V.S. Vereshchetin stated "... the unqualified assertion on the legality of everything not directly prohibited in the sphere of military activities runs counter to the general principles of international law..." and "... as well as the norms of international morality prompt, in our nuclear and space age, a need for states' self-limitation...", which is quite remarkable. V.S. Vereshchetin, "Against Arbitrary Interpretation of Some Important Provisions of International Law", Proceedings from the 30th Colloquium on the Law of Outer Space, 1987, p. 154.

95   J.F. Galloway, "Limits to Sovereignty: Antarctica, Outer Space and The Seabed", Proceedings from the 41st Colloquium on the Law of Outer Space, 1999, p. 84.

96   Tomuschat, op. cit., 1999, p. 168; Jasentuliyana, op. cit., 1999, p. 33 goes even further in claiming a complete abolition of state sovereignty in outer space: "the Treaty was also one of the first multilateral instruments in which the centuries-old international law concept of sovereignty of States gave way to the modern concept of internationalisation of the Global Commons [emphasis added]."

97   Andem, op. cit., 1992, pp. 210-214.

98   J. Delbrück (ed.), *Friedensdokumente aus fünf Jahrhunderten - Abrüstung -Rfistungskontrolle - Kriegsverhütung*, vol. I, Kehl, p. 13.

99   Galloway, op. cit., 1998, p. 20.

100   From the literature on the early military uses of outer space see H.F. York, "Nuclear Deterrence and the Military Uses of Space", *Daedalus*, vol. 114, no.2, 1985, p. 17; Gasparini Alves, op. cit., 1991, p. 12; R. Witzel, "Von ABM zu SDI. Die Raketenabwehrdebatte" in den USA ab 1955 in B.W. Kubbig (ed.), *Die militärische Eroberung des Weltraums*, vol. 1, Frankfurt, 1990, p. 23; D.E. Lupton, *On Space Warfare: A Space Power Doctrine*, Alabama, 1988; Stares, op. cit., 1985, p. 57; P.B. Stares, *Space and National Security*, New York, 1987, pp. 8-72; Kries, "Die militärische Nutzung des Weltraums", op. cit., 1991, p. 328;

Marcoff, op. cit., 1968, pp. 33-62; also see references in H.G. Brauch and R. Fischbach, *Militärische Nutzung des Weltraums. Eine Bibliographie*, Berlin, 1988.

[101] Several delegations at the CD have made proposals to define destructive space capabilities using notions such as "weaponization" (China, CD/579, 19 March 1985) "militarization" (France, CD/579, 19 March 1985), "space strike weapons" (Venezuela, CD/709/Rev.1, 22 July 1986 and CD/851 with a draft for a supplement to Art. 1 of the Outer Space Treaty to define "space weapons"); Italy, CD/PV.167, 30 March 1982, p. 32; Sweden, CD/PV.252, 22 March 1984; German Democratic Republic, CD/927, 26 June 1989 as well Canada, CD/716, 16 July 1986.

[102] Vlasic, op. cit., 1981, p. 149; C.Q. Christol, "Outer Space: Battle-Ground of the Future?" in M. Cohen and M.E. Gouin (eds), *Lawyers and the Nuclear Debate*, Boston, 1988; R.M. Bowman, "The Militarization of Space? The Real issue is the Weaponisation of Space", paper submitted to the International Progress Organization, 24 September 1984, p. 2; International Law Association, *Report of the Sixty-Third Conference*, London, 1988, p. 308; I.I. Kuskuvelis, "The Method of Genetic Effectiveness and the Future of the Military Regime of Outer Space" in T.L. Zwaan, W.W.C. Vries, P.H. de Tuinder and I.I. Kuskuvelis (eds), *Space Law: Views of the Future*, Deventer, 1988, p. 91; A.J. Young, *Law and Policy in the Space Stations Era*, Boston, 1989, p. 202; Gorove, *Studies in Space Law*, 1977, p. 90 and S. Gorove, "Limiting the Use of Arms in Outer Space: Legal and Policy Issues", Proceedings from the 25th Colloquium on the Law of Outer Space, 1983, p. 96; Reijnen, op. cit., 1985, p. 181; Kries, "Die militärische Nutzung des Weltraums", op. cit., 1991, p. 317; B. Jasani, "Introduction" in Jasani (ed.), op. cit., 1991, p. 24; M.L. Smith, "Legal Implications of a Space-Based Ballistic Missile Defense", *California Western International Law Journal*, vol. 15, 1985, p. 54.

[103] Gasparini Alves, op. cit., 1991, p. 24; Stares, op. cit., 1985, p. 55; Marcoff, op. cit., 1968, p. 25; F.R. Cleminson, "Banning the Stationing of Weapons in Space Through Arms Control: A Major Step in the Promotion of Strategic Stability in the 21st Century" in J.M. Beier and S. Mataila (eds), *Arms Control and the Rule of Law: A Framework for Peace and Security in Outer Space*, Proceedings of

the Fifteenth Annual Ottawa NACD Verification Symposium, Toronto, 1998, p. 35.

104 The acronyms NMD, BMD and ABM systems are often used interchangeably for defence systems against strategic ballistic missiles. In Art. II of the ABM Treaty, 26 May 1972, ABM systems are defined as "a system to counter strategic ballistic missiles or their elements in flight trajectory, currently consisting of: (a) ABM interceptor missiles, which are interceptor missiles constructed and deployed for an ABM role, or of a type tested in an ABM mode; (b) ABM launchers, which are launchers constructed and deployed for launching ABM interceptor missiles; and (c) ABM radars, which are radars constructed and deployed for an ABM role, or of a type tested in an ABM mode." TMD systems are defensive systems against "theatre missiles" or "tactical missiles". In the US-Russian Demarcation Agreement of 26 September 1997 concluded according to Art. VI (a) of the ABM Treaty in order to clarify the delimitation between permissible and non-permissible missile defence systems, "tactical missiles" are defined as ballistic missiles with a reach of less than 3,500 km. In this study, the acronym NMD is used, when the vantage point of a nation-wide defense against strategic missiles is emphasized or when reference is made to specific former or current US plans named NMD. When reference is made in a more general way to missile defense against strategic missiles, the acronym BMD or ABM is used.

105 York, op. cit., 1985, p. 24.

106 G. Steinberg, "The Militarization of Space: From passive support to active weapons systems", *Futures*, October 1982, p. 379.

107 Ibid., p. 390.

108 B. Jasani, *Outer Space: Battlefield of the Future?*, New York, 1978, p. 432.

109 Jasani, op. cit., 1991, p. 24; Gasparini Alves, op. cit., 1991, p. 18.

110 Vlasic, op. cit., 1981, p. 149.

111 Christol, op. cit., 1991, p. 57.

112 Young, op. cit., 1989, p. 202.

113 Bowman, op. cit., 1984, p. 2.

114 D. Goedhuis, "Some Observations on the Attitude of West-European Governments to the Development of Defensive Weapons in Outer Space", *JSL*, vol. 15, 1987.

115 Kries has voiced doubts as to the notion of "passive uses" in as far as there are at least indirect active military effects of satellites on

Earth as "force enhancers". However, he refers at least indirectly to this distinction when he distinguishes current military uses from the possible future "introduction of armed space objects" expressing the hope that the space constitution as a peace-oriented universal order [die "friedensbestimmende Weltraumverfassung vermittels ihrer universellen Trägerschaft"] will prevent such a development. Kries, "Die militärische Nutzung des Weltraums", op. cit., 1991, p. 348.

116   Jasentuliyana, op. cit., 1999, p. 68.

117   Some states wanted these activities to be included in a general condemnation of military activities in outer space, while others pointed to the stabilizing effects of these systems for verification of arms control agreements.

118   On which the Conference gave the specifically recommended to the United Nations General Assembly to urgently take the necessary steps for the conclusion of a multilateral agreement on the prohibition and control of space weapons.

119   CD/375, 14 April 1983.

120   "Additional Protocol to the 1967 Treaty on Principles Governing Activities of States in the Exploration and Use of Outer Space, Including the Moon and Other Celestial Bodies' with a view to preventing an arms race in outer space", CD/9, 26 March 1979. The Swedish representative at the CD emphasized the passive nature of remote satellite sensing in contrast to space weapons: "Although the civilian exploitation of outer space is increasing, the vast majority of satellites perform military functions ... These satellites ... have stabilising functions ... Mention could be made of reconnaissance satellites with photographic, electronic or ocean surveillance tasks. In principle, all these satellites can have important functions in connection with weapons systems on earth. Their military role, however, is of a passive nature". CD/PV.516, 11 July 1989.

121   CD/9, 26 March 1979. Article 1, para. 2 of the Italian draft provides that its rules of prohibition do not refer to "... any control system to be established in order to ensure compliance with disarmament and security agreements".

122   UN Doc. A/36/192, 11 August 1981.

123   UN Doc. A/38/194, 23 August 1983 and CD/476, 20 March 1984.

124   CD/579, 19 March 1985.

125   Venezuela has submitted for this purpose a definition of space weapons building on proposals of China, Bulgaria, Hungary, Sri Lanka and the Soviet Union, CD/709/Rev. 1, 22 July 1986; CD/851; CD/PV.398, 19 March 1987.

126   Sri Lanka , CD/PV.254, 29 March 1984.

127   Peru, CD/939, 29 July 1989; CD/PV.472; CD/PV.544.

128   India, CD/PV.262, 26 April 1984.

129   CD/OS/WP.70; see also CD/OS/WP.71 and CD/OS/CRP.16 and Corr. 1: "Résumé by the Friend of the Chair of Proposals and the Course of Discussions on Confidence-Building Measures in Outer Space"; as well as Gasparini Alves, op. cit., 1991, pp. 12-20.

130   Venezuela, CD/OS/WP.14/Add.1, 21 July 1986.

131   UN Doc. A/36/192, 11 August 1981.

132   Bulgaria and Hungary, CD/OS/WP.14/Add.1, 21 July 1986.

133   German Democratic Republic, ibid.

134   China, ibid.

135   Sri Lanka, ibid.

136   CD/1487, 21 January 1998. The paper is based on previous Canadian papers in the Ad Hoc Committee on PAROS, which are described in Cleminson, op. cit., 1998, p. 35.

137   "... the non-weapon components of a space-based military system (e.g. navigation, communication and observation components) would not be prohibited, because these elements per se do not actually inflict the physical harm on the target object. Only the 'pointed end' or actual destructive element of a system would be prohibited under a space-based weapon ban." Foreign Affairs Canada, The Non-Weaponization of Outer Space, Food for Thought Paper, 31 March 2002.

138   For a similar definition see N. Wulf, "Outer Space Arms Control: Existing Regime and Future Prospects", Proceedings from the 26th Colloquium on the Law of Outer Space, 1984, p. 367.

139   H.H. Almond, "A Public Order in Outer Space for Peaceful Purposes: The Will of the World Community and the Constitutive Process", Proceedings from the 21st Colloquium on the Law of Outer Space, 1979, p. 83; A.J. Butler, "Peaceful Use and Self Defense in Outer Space", Proceedings from the 24th Colloquium on the Law of Outer Space, 1982, p. 77; F.K. Schwetje, "Protecting Space Assets: A Legal Definition of 'Keep-out Zones'", JSL, vol. 15, 1987, p. 131.

140   United States, CD/PV.866, 15 February 2001; see also Gasparini Alves, op. cit., 1991, p. 36.

141   W.L. Spacy II, "Does the United States Need Space-Based Weapons?", College of Aerospace Doctrine, Research, and Education Air University, September 1999, <http:// research.au.af.mil>.

142   B. Jasani, op. cit., 1978, p. 2.

143   According to Stares, op. cit., 1985, p. 15. In the Gulf War the increased dependency of the US Armed Forces on communication satellites became apparent; military strategists see an increase in so-called "MILSATCOM capacity" by 2005 by a factor of 100%. See D. Gonzales, "The Changing Role of the U.S. Military in Space", Santa Monica, 1999, p. 19.

144   For instance, see the declaration of the representative of India in the plenary session of the CD, CD/PV.378, 12 August 1986; Nigeria, CD/PV.391, 24 February 1987. Brazil and a number of Latin American countries condemned the plans of active military uses of outer space as a "flagrant violation" of the Outer Space Treaty and called for the urgent negotiation of an agreement to ban space weapons. "Declaration by the Latin American Countries Members of the Legal Subcommittee of the Committee ot the Peaceful Uses of Outer Space", UN Doc. A/AC.105/C.2/L.142, 6 April 1983. Jasentuliyana, op. cit., 1999, p. 121. On 21 January 1988 the Heads of Government of Sweden, Argentina, Greece, India, Mexico and Tanzania, adopted the so-called "Stockholm Declaration", which calls for a comprehensive ban of space weapons to prevent a vertical and horizontal arms race in space. CD/807, 19 February 1988.

145   Kries, "Die militärische Nutzung des Weltraums", op. cit. 1991, p. 340.

146   The Soviet Union made such a proposal to ban reconnaissance satellites at the discussions on the outer space "Principles Declaration", UN Doc. A/AC. 105/C.2/L.6, 16 April 1963; see also M. Russel, "Military Activities in Outer Space: Soviet Legal Views", Harvard International Law Journal, vol. 25, 1984.

147   S. Cohen, "SALT Verification: The Evolution of Soviet Views and Their Meaning for the Future", Orbis, vol. 24, 1980, p. 657.

148   UNIDIR, Disarmament: Problems Related to Outer Space, Geneva, 1987, p. 31.

149   These were the temporarily deployed US Nike-Zeus and the Thor ASAT systems equipped with nuclear warheads, which the US decommissioned in 1975, and the Soviet ABM-1b/Galosh (US name) system. The ABM Treaty allows both sides two ABM locations, one for the protection of the capital and one for the protection of an intercontinental ballistic missile launch-site while prohibiting a "nationwide missile defense". The US only deployed an ABM system to protect the Grand Forks missile launch-site, which was decommissioned already in the mid-1970s; see Witzel, op. cit., 1990, p. 23; Kries, "Die militärische Nutzung des Weltraums", op. cit., 1991, p. 328; Marcoff, op. cit., 1968, p. 59; P. Lellouche (ed.), La guerre des satellites. Enjeux pour la communauté internationale, Paris, 1987, p. 50.

150   So-called "air-launched miniature vehicle system" based on F-15 combat fighter aircraft.

151   The ABM-1b/Galosh system comprises 120 land-based ABMs to protect the city of Moscow.

152   Kries, "Die militärische Nutzung des Weltraums", op. cit., 1991, p. 310; Vlasic, op. cit., 1981, p. 151.

153   R.D. Humble, The Soviet Space Programme, London, 1988, p. 50. In Art. VII, para. 2c of the "Second Common Understanding" to the SALT II Treaty the Soviet Union declared to possess eighteen rockets, which would be put out of service with the entry into force of the Treaty.

154   According to B. Jasani and D. Hafner, "The Case for a Limited ASAT Treaty" in B. Jasani (ed.), op. cit., 1991, p. 227; for a contrasting view see Kries, "Die militärische Nutzung des Weltraums", op. cit., 1991, p. 326.

155   Soviet draft treaty on the prohibition of space weapons, UN Doc. A/38/194, 23 August 1983; in parallel the Soviet Premier, Yuri Andropov declared to US Senators that the Soviet Union would undertake unilaterally not to deploy ASAT systems in outer space as long as other states would follow suit. The unilateral moratorium of the Soviet Union was welcomed at the CD. See the declaration of Czechoslovakia, CD/PV.253, 17 March 1984, p. 9 and Sweden, CD/PV.252, 22 March 1984, p. 20; Jasentuliyana, op. cit., 1999, p. 86; Gasparini Alves, op. cit., p. 100.

156   US Department of Defense, "Soviet Military Power", Washington DC, 1985, p. 43.

157   According to Jasani and Hafner, op. cit., 1991, p. 227.

158   US Department of Defense, "Space Policy", Directive 3100.10, 9 July 1999.

159   A. Carter, "BMD Applications: Performance and Limitations" in A. Carter and N. Schwartz (eds), *Ballistic Missile Defence*, Washington DC, 1984, p. 174; J. Altmann, "Laserwaffen" in R. Labusch, E. Maus and W. Send (eds), *Waffen im Weltraum*, Berlin, 1984, p. 79; J.G.G. Varni, G.M. Powers, D.S. Crawford, C.E. Jordan and D.L. Kendall, "Space Operations: Through the Looking Glass", research paper presented to the US Air Force 2025, August 1996, <http://research.au.af.mil>.

160   Heath, op. cit., 2001, p. 299; G. Neuneck and A. Rothkirch, "Space as a New Medium of Warfare? Motivations, Technology and Consequences", paper presented at the XV Amaldi Conference on Global Security, Helsinki 25-27 September 2003; G. Neuneck and A. Rothkirch, "Incentives for Space Security: Technology, Transparency and Compliance", paper presented at the Conference on Outer Space and Security, Geneva, 25-26 March 2003.

161   Heath, op. cit., 2001, p. 300; Kries, "Die militärische Nutzung des Weltraums", op. cit., 1991, p. 312; Altmann, op. cit., 1984, p. 79; R. Fischbach, "Raketenabwehrtechnologien—eine Übersicht" in Labusch, Maus, Send, op. cit., p. 62; Carter, op. cit., 1984, p. 175.

162   Varni, Powers, Crawford, Jordan and Kendall, op. cit., 1996, p. 21.

163   Beer, op. cit., 1987, p. 48; Kries, "Die militärische Nutzung des Weltraums", op. cit., 1991, p. 312; ibid., p. 21.

164   W.J. Broad, "Teller's War. The Top-Secret Story Behind the Star Wars Deception", New York, 1992, p. 291 surveys the rather modest testing results; C.A. Robinson, "Advance made on High-Energy Laser", *Aviation Week & Space Technology*, 23 February 1983, p. 25; Altmann, op. cit., 1984, p. 89.

165   Spacy II, op. cit.

166   Varni, Powers, Crawford, Jordan and Kendall, op. cit., 1996, p. 20; Beer, op. cit., 1987, p. 49; Altmann, op. cit., 1984, p. 87.

167   Beer, op. cit., 1987, p. 48.

168   Varni, Powers, Crawford, Jordan and Kendall, op. cit., 1996, p. 21; Kries, "Die militärische Nutzung des Weltraums", op. cit., 1991, p. 312; Heath, op. cit., 2001, p. 300.

169   Spacy II, op. cit.; Varni, Powers, Crawford, Jordan and Kendall, op. cit., 1996, p. 21.

170   Spacy II, op. cit., p. 22.

171   "Considering the hurdles in orbital antenna technology that must be overcome before space-based directed-energy weapons are feasible, it is unlikely that such systems can be fielded until the cost of routine access to space is reduced to the point that extensive experimentation can be undertaken". Ibid.

172   Ibid.

173   Beer, op. cit., 1987, p. 49.

174   Spacy II, op. cit.

175   K. Tsipis, "Star Wars Down to Earth: A Technical, Operational and Bureaucratic Assessment" in B. Jasani (ed.), *Space Weapons and International Security*, Oxford, 1987, p. 86; Kries, "Die militärische Nutzung des Weltraums", op. cit., 1991, p. 313.

176   Spacy II, op. cit.; United States General Accounting Office, "Strategic defense initiative estimates of Brilliant Pebbles' effectiveness are based on many unproven assumptions", Report to Chairman, Committee on Armed Services, US Senate, 1992.

177   Schneider, Press Conference of the Chairman of the US Defense Science Board, on 10 April 2002, reported "Nuclear-Tipped Interceptors Studied. Rumsfeld Revives Rejected Missile Defense Concept", *The Washington Post*, 11 April 2002; see also M. Becker, "Waffen im Orbit. USA schießen Killer-Satelliten ins All", *Spiegel Online*, 26 April 2004, <www.spiegel.de/wissenschaft/weltraum/ 0,1518,druck-295954,00.html>.

178   A.M. Sessler, "Countermeasures: A Technical Evaluation of the Operational Effectiveness of the Planned US National Missile Defense System", UCS, MIT Security Studies Program, 2000; G. Bielefeld and T. Neuneck, "Raketenabwehr-Optionen für die Bush-Administration: Die technische Dimension", *Sicherheit und Frieden*, February 2001, p. 95.

179   Declaration of US Ambassador to the Conference on Disarmament, Robert Grey, 31 August 2000.

180   B. Jasani, "US national missile defence and international security: blessing or blight?", *Space Policy*, vol. 17, 2001, p. 243.

181   Beer, op. cit., 1987, p. 46.

182   For the elaborate security and arms control literature on the development of space weapons see Witzel, op. cit., 1990, p. 23; Lupton, op. cit., 1988, p. 33; Stares, op. cit., 1985, p. 53; Kries, "Die militärische Nutzung des Weltraums", op. cit., 1991, p. 328; Jasani, op. cit., 1991, p. 46; Handberg, op. cit., 2000, pp. 63 and 189; T. Postol, "Hitting Them Where It Works", *Foreign Policy*,

Winter 1999/2000, p. 117; R.L. Garwin, "A Defense That Will Not Defend", *The Washington Quarterly*, vol. 23, 2000, p. 109; Bielefeld and Neuneck, op. cit, 2001, p. 95.

183 Kries, "Die militärische Nutzung des Weltraums", op. cit., 1991, p. 328; Lupton, op. cit., 1988, p. 33.

184 Humble, op. cit., 1988, p. 40.

185 Lt. Col. B. Deblois, "Space Sanctuary. A Viable National Strategy", 1997, <www.airpower.maxwell.af.mil/airchronicles/apj/apj98/win98/debloistxt.htm>.

186 Lt. Gen. D.O. Graham, "High Frontier: A New National Strategy", US Air Force, 1982; Lupton, op. cit., 1988, p. 91.

187 Humble, op. cit., 1988, p. 38 distinguishes between a "tactical space environment of the Earth-Moon system" considered as "gravity well zones ... that are tactically analogous to terrestrial features such as hills, promontories, and mountains, in that much effort must initially be expended to situate military forces at such locations, but once attained 'the high ground' can be used to dominate the terrain below with ease ... During the next few decades military space activities and the development of various commercial space enterprises, or the process of 'space industrialisation', will be conducted primarily within this system. Possible military missions to be eventually conducted in the space environment include ballistic missile defense, the destruction of Earth-based targets, the regulation of the flow of space traffic, the defence of military and industrial space facilities, the denial of strategic areas of space (such as choice satellite orbits at Geosynchronuous Earth Orbit—GEO—and the various Longrangian liberation points at which objects revolve with the same period as the gravitational Earth-Moon system and thus remain effectively stationary) to enemies and various surveillance, reconnaissance, navigational, data-transfer, command, control, communications and intelligence functions."

188 R.H. Zielinski, R.M. Worley II, D.S. Black, S.A. Henderson and D.C. Johnson, "Star Tek-Exploiting the Final Frontier: Counterspace Operations in 2025", research paper presented to Air Force 2025, August 1996, p. 6, <http://research.au.af.mil>.

189 US Space Command, "Long-Range Plan: Implementing USSPACECOM Vision for 2020", 1997, <www.spacecom.af.mil>.

190 J. John-Freese, "The Viability of U.S. Anti-Satellite (ASAT) Policy: Moving Toward Space Control, USAF Institute for National Security

Studies, Institute of National Security Studies", US Air Force, 2000, p. 27.

191 F. Heisbourg, Défenses antimissiles: l'analyse stratégique et l'intérêt européens", *Politique Étrangère*, July/September 2001, p. 627.

192 US Space Command, op. cit., 1997; see also G. Friedmann and M. Friedmann, *The Future of War: Power, Technology & American World Dominance in the 21st Century*, New York, 1996, p. 420.

193 Lupton, op. cit., 1988, p. 91; D.J. Johnson and S.C. Pace, "Space: Emerging Options for National Power", Santa Monica, 1998; J. Oberg, "Space Power Theory", Air University Centre for Space Studies, 1988, <http://space.au.af.mil/books/oberg>, p. 120.

194 A.T. Mahan, *The Interest of America in Sea Power, Present and Future*, Boston, 1897.

195 A.T. Mahan, *The Influence of Sea Power Upon History, 1660-1783*, Boston, 1890, p. 138.

196 See the controversial assessment of P. Lawrence and A. Hansson, "American space hegemony: Accident or design?", *Space Policy*, vol. 14, 1998.

197 Heath, op. cit., 2001, p. 298; P.-A. Salin, "Privatization and militarisation in the space business environment", *Space Policy*, vol. 17, 2001, p. 24.

198 US Space Command, op. cit., 1997.

199 P.B. Stares, "U.S. and Soviet Military Space Programs: A Comparative Assessment" in F.A. Long, D. Hafner and J. Boutwell (eds), *Weapons in Space*, Santa Monica, 1986, p. 127; Humble, op. cit., 1988, p. 48.

200 W. Mallmann, "Weltraumpolitik der Sowjetunion" in K. Kaiser and S. von Welck (eds), *Weltraum und internationale Politk*, Berlin, 1987, p. 394; V. Sevestyanow and V. Pryakhin, "Space exploration and new thinking", *International Affairs* (Moscow), 1987, p. 21.

201 Gasparini Alves, op. cit., 1991, p. 45.

202 U.S. Department of Defense, "Soviet Military Power", Washington DC, 1983, p. 68; S. Stevens, "The Soviet BMD Program" in A. Carter and N. Schwartz (eds), op. cit., 1984, p. 210; Stares, op. cit., 1985, p. 115.

203 Ibid., p. 106; S. Welck, "Erforschung und Nutzung des Weltraums" in W.Wagner (ed.), *Die Internationale Politik 1985-1986*, Munich, 1988, p. 27; Humble, op. cit., 1988, p. 52.

204 Welck, op. cit., 1988, p. 27; Humble, op. cit., 1988, p. 27; S. Schmidt, "Weltraumgestützte Raketenabwehrsysteme und

Antisatellitenwaffen. Rüstungskontrollpolitische Konzepte und Verhandlungen" in K. Kaiser and S. Welck (eds), *Weltraum und internationale Politik*, Munich, 1987, p. 231.

205 Humble, op. cit., 1988, p. 53.

206 Ibid., p. 78.

207 Welck, op. cit., 1988, p. 27; Humble, op. cit., 1988, p. 26.

208 U.S. Department of Defense, op. cit., 1983, p. 28; Humble, op. cit., 1988, p. 79; Stevens, op. cit., 1984, p. 212.

209 Stevens, op. cit., 1984, p. 217; Humble, op. cit., 1988, p. 80.

210 Humble, op. cit., 1988, p. 51.

211 Ibid., p. 77; Stevens, op. cit., 1984, p. 218; Stares, op. cit., 1985, p. 237.

212 "Let me just react to your remark that the Soviet Union is engaged in things similar to SDI. Well, it is really hard to say what the Soviet Union is not doing; the Soviet Union is practically doing everything that the United States is doing. I'd saying we are engaged in research, basic research, which relates to these aspects covered by SDI in the United States. But we will not build an SDI, we will not deploy SDI, and we call on the United States to act similarly". *Pravda*, 2 December 1987.

213 Nguyen, "Russia's Continuing Work on Space Forces", *Orbis*, vol. 37, 1993, p. 413; Tarasenko, "Transformation of the Soviet Space Program after the Cold War", *Science & Global Security*, no. 4, 1994, p. 339, however, states in contrast that "Russia is committed to maintaining military space capabilities, however, its top priority is now conversion of military space technology for civilian uses, including global environmental problems."

214 A. Flax, "Ballistic Missile Defense: Concepts and History", *Daedalus*, vol. 114, 1985, p. 48.

215 B.W. Kubbig, "Vision und Politik. SDI als Signatur Amerikas in der Ära Reaganv in B.W. Kubbig (ed.), *Die militärische Eroberung des Weltraums*, vol. I, Frankfurt, 1990, p. 7.

216 See section 2.1.3.2 of this study; and D. Schroeer, "The Present Status of the Strategic Defense Initiative" in C. Schaerf, G. Longo and D. Carlton (eds), *Space and Nuclear Weaponry in the 1990s: Studies in Disarmament and Conflict*, London, 1992, p. 1.

217 Smith, op. cit., 1985, p. 55.

218 Schroeer, op. cit., 1992, p. 1; J. Tirman, "Is Star Wars Dead?" in J. Tirman (ed.), *Empty Promise: The Growing Case Against Star Wars*, Washington DC, 1986, p. 203.

219   McG. Bundy, G. Kennan, R. McNamara and G. Smith, "The President's Choice: Star Wars or Arms Control", *Foreign Affairs*, vol. 63, 1984, p. 264.

220   York, op. cit., 1985, p. 17; R.L. Garwin, "Enforcing BMD against a determined adversary?" in Jasani (ed.), op. cit., 1987, p. 83; J. Scheffers, "Why anti-satellite warfare should be prohibited" in B. Jasani (ed.), *Space Weapons: The Arms Control Dilemma*, Oxford, 1984, p. 77; Stares, op. cit., 1985, p. 245; Handberg, op. cit., 2000, p. 82.

221   Jasani, op. cit., 1991, p. 49. According to the majority of scientific assessments, to date none of the planned space-based NMD systems are technically feasible as a "defence shield" for territories like the United States or Europe.

222   J. Pike, S. Lang and E. Stambler, "Military Use of Outer Space" in *SIPRI Yearbook 1992. World Armaments and Disarmament*, Oxford, 1992, p. 121.

223   Lt Gen. Thomas Moorman, Commander of Air Force Space Command, declared "Desert Storm will be an extraordinary learning experience for us ... Not only is it a watershed, but it is a glimpse into the future ... For the first time, we have space beginning to become fully integrated into the prosecution of hostilities." *Jane's Defense Weekly*, 9 February 1991, p. 200; Handberg, op. cit., 2000, p. 88 equally qualifies the Gulf War as a still primitive space war.

224   Secretary of Defense Dick Cheney stated in his news briefing on the FY92 defense budget, 4 February 1991, "... as Iraq has shown, modern technology can make a third-rate power a first-class military threat. By the year 2000, more than two dozen developing nations will have ballistic missiles ..."

225   United States General Accounting Office, op. cit., 1992, p. 8; Pike, Lang and Stambler, op. cit., 1992, p. 128; Grouard, "Guerre en orbite. Essai de politique et de stratégie spatiale", 1994, p. 345; Spacy II, op. cit.

226   Beer, op. cit., 1987, p. 49; according to Spacy II, op. cit. who citing Assistant Secretary of Defense Stephen Hadley writes that in the framework of GPALS only a maximum of 200 intercontinental ballistic missiles could be intercepted, and this only in boost-phase.

227   Secretary of Defense Dick Cheney, news briefing on the FY92 defense budget, 4 February 1991.

228   Congressional Record, 13 March 1991, pp. 76-89.

229 Congressional Record, 31 July 1991, pp. 437-520 and Congressional Record, 1 August 1991.

230 Pike, Lang and Stambler, op. cit., 1992, p. 128.

231 J. Kile, "Nuclear arms control and ballistic missile defence" in *SIPRI Yearbook 2001. Armaments, Disarmament and International Security*, Oxford, 2001, p. 425; Anthony, "Responses to proliferation: the North Korean ballistic missile programme" in *SIPRI Yearbook 2000. Armaments, Disarmament and International Security*, Oxford, 2000, p. 647.

232 B.W. Kubbig, "Rüstungskontrolle und Abrüstung" in B. Schoch, U. Ratsch and R. Mutz (eds), *Friedensgutachten*, 1999, p. 220.

233 National Missile Defense Act of 1999, Public Law, 22 July 1999, pp. 106-38.

234 In all BMD plans three flight phases are distinguished: boost-phase, mid-course (in outer space) and terminal phase. A nation-wide NMD needs to include interception capabilities in the mid-course phase. The BMD evaluation commission (McCarthy Commission) set up by President G.W. Bush proposes to pursue all three options with mid-course defence in space as the core option; Gasparini Alves, op. cit., 1991, p. 21.

235 Kile, op. cit., 2001, p. 428.

236 Declaration to the Press, The White House, "President Clinton Signs Missile Defense Act", 23 July 1999; J. Steinbruner, "National Missile Defense: Collision in Progress", *Arms Control Today*, November 1999, p. 3. In contrast, K. Payne, "Looming Security Threats: The Case for National Missile Defense", *Orbis*, Spring 2000, p. 187 sees the adoption of the National Missile Defense Act with the majority of both Houses and the signing by President Clinton already "a political consensus in favour of deployment".

237 Wilton Park and UNIDIR, *Missile Defence, Deterrence and Arms Control: Contradictory Aims or Compatible Goals*, Geneva, 2002, p. 8: "The crucial component in the midcourse defensive architecture—the HKV—which primarily employs on-board infrared and thermal sensors to detect, differentiate, and intercept the warhead in the exoatmosphere, did not demonstrate a capacity to effectively perform its assigned function".

238 Transcript of remarks by the President on national missile defense, 1 September 2000. President Clinton declared that "we have not enough confidence in the technology and the operational

effectiveness of the entire NMD system to move forward with deployment".

239 See the proposal by the independent US experts: Postol, op. cit., 1999/2000, p. 117 and Garwin, op. cit., 2000, p. 109 for a for a boost-phase defence based on limited sea- and land-based ABMs instead of attacking warheads in outer space. This could also give additional incentive for strengthening the Missile Technology Control Regime and for renouncing the development of launcher technologies; Garwin and Postol also suggested that a regional missile defense system against North Korea should be developed cooperatively with Russia; see also Steinbruner, op. cit., 1999, p. 6; C. Glaser and S. Fetter, "National Missile Defense and the Future of U.S. Nuclear Weapons Policy", *International Security*, vol. 26, no. 1, Summer 2001, p. 44: "Given the enormous technical and political challenges, we are sceptical of NMD. Among the alternatives, surface-based boost-phase systems are least problematic, because they are more likely to be effective against rogue missile forces and have the best prospects for reassuring Russia and China that the United States is not adopting a more competitive and threatening national security policy. The case against mid-course NMD is much more compelling—it is unlikely to work, and it would generate significant international tensions, unless the United States is successful in pursuing ambitious co-operative policies, which are most likely beyond its reach."

240 Republican Platform 2000, "Renewing America's Purpose—Together", <www.rnc.org/gopinfo/platform>.

241 President G.W. Bush, "Speech before the National Defense University", 1 May 2001; see also C. Grand, "La défense antimissile: un nouveau paradigme stratégique?", *Politique Étrangère*, 2001, p. 817.

242 Payne, op. cit., 2000, p. 187.

243 Kile, op. cit., 2001, p. 429; Bielefeld and Neuneck, op. cit., 2001, p. 94.

244 "National Missile defense considers defense against large ICBMs and SLBMs. We'll have to include cruise missiles in the future but the space segment won't have to do it all. Instead, it will be part of a worldwide, integrated system for Missile Defense based on the ground, in the air, and in space. Defenses will operate in tiers to serve all commanders and will engage missiles in all phases of flight... The Space-Based Platform (formerly the Space-Based

Interceptor) and Space Operations Vehicle will defend against missiles worldwide, responding in hours. Space-Based Lasers will reduce response time to minutes...". US Space Command, op. cit., 1997.

245   S.E. Miller, "The Flawed Case for Missile Defence", *Survival*, vol. 43, no. 3, Autumn 2001, p. 95.

246   US Air Force Advisory Board, "New World Vistas: Air and Space power for the 21st century", *Space Technology*, 1996.

247   P. Coyle, "Rhetoric or Reality? Missile Defense under Bush", *Arms Control Today*, May 2002. Coyle was director in the Pentagon in charge of the BMD tests from 1994 until 2001.

248   "Report of the Commission to Assess United States National Security Space Management and Organization", January 2001, <www.defenselink.mil/pubs/space20010111.html>.

249   Gen. Joseph Ashy, former Commander-in-Chief of the US Space Command: "It's politically sensitive, but it's going to happen. Some people don't want to hear this, and it sure isn't in vogue, but—absolutely—we're going to fight in space. We're going to fight from space and we're going to fight into space... We will engage terrestrial targets someday—ships, airlines, land targets—from space ... That's why the U.S. has development programs in directed-energy and hit-to-kill mechanisms". Quoted in A. Slater, "Star Wars and the Global War System", *Information Bulletin INESAP*, no. 18, September 2001, p. 42.

250   K. Grossman, *Weapons in Space: A Media Black-Out*, New York, 2001, p. 9.

251   US Space Command, op. cit., 1997.

252   J. Shaliskashvili, "Joint Vision 2010", Department of Defense, 1996, <www.dtic.mil/jv2010/jvpub.htm>.

253   US Space Command, op. cit., 1997.

254   Handberg, op. cit., 2000, p. 189.

255   "Report of the Commission to Assess United States National Security Space Management and Organization", op. cit., 2001, p. 13.

256   "The U.S. military... has become the most space-dependent force of any military in the world. The United States has bet a great deal of its military credibility on sustaining a major space presence in order to enhance its effectiveness". Handberg, op. cit., 2000, p. 192.

257   "... we know from history that every medium—air, land and sea— has seen conflict. Reality indicates that space will be no different. Given this virtual certainty, the U.S. must develop the means both to deter and to defend against hostile acts in and from space. This will require superior space capabilities". "Report of the Commission to Assess United States National Security Space Management and Organization", op. cit., 2001, p. 10.

258   Ibid., p. 16.

259   Handberg, op. cit., 2000, p. 192.

260   P. Grier, "The New Nuclear Theology", *Christian Science Monitor*, 8 May 2001.

261   See section 1.1.1 of this study.

262   Kries, "Die militärische Nutzung des Weltraums", op. cit., 1991, p. 349; Andem, op. cit., 1992, p. 205.

263   Speech of the Federal Chancellor before the North Atlantic Assembly, 25 May 1985, "Peace and Security in the Atlantic Alliance", *Bulletin of the Federal Government*, no. 56, 473, 21 May 1985.

264   Speech of Sir Geoffrey Howe, "Defense and Security in the Nuclear Age" presented before the Royal United Services Institute, 15 March 1985.

265   On the British reaction to SDI see T. Taylor, "SDI—The British Response" in H.G. Brauch (ed.), *Star Wars and European Defence. Implications for Europe: Perceptions and Assessments*, London, 1987; Young, op. cit., 1989, p. 220.

266   Agreement of 27 March 1986; it was preceded by a corresponding US offer to allies in a letter of Secretary of Defense Caspar Weinberger of 26 March 1986, printed in *Survival*, vol. 27, 1985, 128. Weinberger emphasizes that the SDI cooperation with allies would take place in accordance with existing international obligations of the US, in particular of the ABM Treaty and would have the character of "cooperative research short of ABM component level". According to UK Defence Minister Michael Hesseltine the cooperation rests on the premise that "any deployment of SDI-related equipment would have to be subject for further negotiations", quoted in Young, op. cit., 1989, p. 220; see also UNIDIR, op. cit., 1987, p. 96.

267   Agreement of 27 March 1986, the text was published by the *Kölner Express*, 18 April 1986; B.W. Kubbig, "Die SDI-Rahmenvereinbarung zwischen Bonn und Washington: Eine Bilanz

nach zwei Jahren", *HSFK-Report*, March 1988, p. 3; see also UNIDIR, op. cit., 1987, p. 96.

268 Agreement of May 1986; see also UNIDIR, op. cit., 1987, p. 96.

269 Agreement of 19 September 1986; see also UNIDIR, op. cit., 1987, p. 96.

270 Federal Chancellor Helmuth Kohl, "Declaration Before the German Bundestag on 18 April 1985", *Bulletin of the Federal Government*, 19 April 1985.

271 See sections 3.2.2.2 and 8.1.1 of this study.

272 Kubbig, op. cit., 1988, p. 32.

273 Ibid., p. 40.

274 On the controversy in Germany see H.G. Brauch, "SDI—The Political Debate in the Federal Republic of Germany" in Brauch (ed.), op. cit., 1987, p. 166; H.-E. Au, "Die Strategische Verteidigungsinitiative (SDI). Zur politischen Diskussion in der BR Deutschland", *HSFK-Report*, March 1988; Kubbig, op. cit., 1988, p. 18.

275 A. Carton, "French Reaction to SDI—The Debate on the Nature of Deterrence" in Brauch (ed.), op. cit., 1987, p. 150.

276 In 1969 the National Diet of Japan adopted a resolution "to the effect that the use of outer space objects and launching of rockets into outer space should be carried out exclusively for 'peaceful purposes'". The principle of the peaceful use of outer space was also included in the law establishing the National Space Development Agency of Japan. See T. Kuribayashi, "A Legal Framework for Space Station Activities" in *Commercial Use of Space Station—The Legal Framework of Transatlantic Cooperation*, DGLR Publication, 1986, p. 70; see also C. Couvalt and M.T. Foley, "Defense Decision to Use Space Station Will Delay International Negotiations", *Aviation Week & Space Technology*, vol. 22, December 1986, pp. 23 and 24.

277 Quoted in *The Disarmament Bulletin*, Autumn 1985, p. 7. Also, "It is the intent of NASA and MOSST that this MOU will, if successful, lead to cooperation in the development, operation and utilisation of the Space Station *for peaceful purposes consistent with international treaty obligations*" [emphasis added]. Agreement between NASA and the Canadian Ministry of State for Science and Technology, December 1987.

278 UNIDIR, op. cit., 1987, p. 96.

279 NASA-ESA Agreement of 29 September 1988; According to Art. II of the statute of the ESA "... purpose of the Agency shall be to provide for and promote, for exclusively peaceful purposes, cooperation among European States in space research and technology and their space applications, with a view to their being used for scientific purposes and for operational space applications systems..." See also the "Agreement between the Government of the US, the Governments of the Member States of ESA, the Government of Japan and the Government of Canada on the cooperation with regard to the space station", printed in *ZLW*, vol. 27, 1988, p. 341.

280 B.W. Kubbig, "Raketenabwehr als angemessene technologische Antwort auf das politische Proliferationsproblem?", *HSFK-Report*, September 1992, p. 28.

281 See the joint letter of 50 American Nobel laureates to the US Congress of 21 November 2001, reproduced by the Federation of American Scientists, <www.fas.org>.

282 Federal Chancellor Gerhard Schröder questioned the new threat analysis underlying NMD in an interview with the *L.A. Times*, 28 March 2001, available at <www.hsfk.de.html>.

283 Foreign Minister Joschka Fischer, Statements on NMD before the German Bundestag, 21 March 2001 and in the US on 1 May 2001, <www.hsfk.de.html>.

284 Available at <www.hsfk.de.html>; also the Swedish Foreign Minister Anna Lindh stated in a press release on 13 December 2001: "Sweden has pointed out repeatedly that a unilateral decision to go ahead with missile defence plans may potentially lead to a new arms race and have adverse effects for disarmament and non-proliferation", <www.regeringen.se>.

285 Statement by the spokesman of the French Foreign Ministry on 14 December 2001, <www.diplomatie.gouv.fr>.

286 B. Garrett, "Facing the China Factor", *Arms Control Today*, October 2000, p. 14; D. Shen, "République populaire de Chine: défense antimissile et sécurité nationale", *Politique Étrangère*, 2001, p. 895; B. Harvey, *China's Space Program: From Conception to Future Capabilities*, New York, 1998; N. Hoffmann, "L'espace, nouvel échiquier pour la rivalité sino-occidentale?", *Défense Nationale*, vol. 55, October 1999.

287 The report is named after the Chairman of the Commission set up by the US Senate to investigate the destruction of a communication

satellite of the US company Hughes, Senator Cox (Rep.) "U.S. National Security and Military/Commercial Concerns with the People's Republic of China", House of Representatives, Report 105-851, 105th Congress, May 1998, <www.access.gpo.gov/congress/house/hr105851/>; V. Niquet, "Les relations sino-américaines après la guerre du Kosovo", Défense Nationale, vol. 55, October 1999, p. 97; Hoffmann, op. cit., 1999, p. 129.

288   X. Gu, "China und die USA. Eine Partnerschaft sucht ein strategisches Element", Internationale Politik, vol. 2, 2002, p. 10.

289   Hoffmann, op. cit., 1999, p. 128.

290   Ibid., p. 124.

291   "U.S. National Security and Military/Commercial Concerns with the Peoples Republic of China", op. cit.; Garrett, op. cit., 2000, p. 14; Shen, op. cit. 2001, p. 895; Harvey, op. cit., 1998; Hoffmann, op. cit., 1999, p. 119.

292   "For the Chinese, manned space-flight would be a logical advancement for a country familiar with taking big steps: the Earth satellite in the 1960s, the recoverable cabin in the 1970s, the communications satellite in the 1980s—maybe manned flight before the end of the 1990s. One day, cosmonauts flying eastwards from Jiuquan [the most important of three Chinese space launch sites in the Gobi Desert] will orbit the Earth and watch the yellow, orange and red glow of dawn march over the skies of China; and they will be able to see, with their own eyes, that the East is Red— Dong Fang Hong!" [Dong Fang Hong is the title of the national anthem of the PR China and at the same time the name of the first Chinese satellite.] Hoffmann, op. cit., 1999, p. 125; Harvey, op. cit., 1998.

293   Hoffmann, op. cit., 1999, p. 132.

294   Harvey, op. cit., 1998, p. 154.

295   Gu, op. cit., 2002, p. 9.

296   K. Ravi, "The Military Implications of India's Space Programme: Some Observations", Defense Analysis, vol. 5, 1989. According to Gasparini Alves, India works in particular at the development of "multipurpose satellites". P. Gasparini Alves, Access to Outer Space Technologies: Implications for International Security, Geneva, 1992, p. 27.

297   "... the space and missile programmes will undoubtedly make it easier for India to exercise its nuclear option should that be its

intention". Ravi, op. cit., 1989; K. Kaiser, "Non-proliferation and nuclear deterrence", *Survival*, vol. 31, March/April 1989, p. 131.

298   Gasparini Alves, op. cit., 1992, p. 37.

299   Ibid., p. 28.

300   In 1969 the National Diet of Japan adopted a Resolution "to the effect that the use of outer space objects and launching of rockets into outer space should be carried out exclusively for 'peaceful purposes'". The principle of the peaceful use of outer space was also included in the law establishing the National Space Development Agency of Japan. See Kuribayashi, op. cit., 1986, p. 70; see also Couvalt and Foley, op. cit., 1986, pp. 23 and 24. Also, NASA-ESA Agreement of 29 September 1988.

301   Kuskuvelis, op. cit., 1988, p. 97.

302   Kile, op. cit., 2001, p. 425; Cleminson, op. cit., 1998, p. 38; Vlasic states, "To date, outer space, though heavily militarised, has been free from weapons". I.A. Vlasic, "Space Law and the Military Applications of Space Technology" in N. Jasentuliyna (ed.), *Perspectives on International Law*, London, 1995, p. 386; Gasparini Alves, op. cit., 1991, p. 18; Jasani, "Introduction" op. cit., 1991, p. 13; Kuskuvelis, op. cit., 1988, p. 97.

303   Gasparini Alves, op. cit., 1991, p. 45.

304   Handberg, op. cit., 2000, p. 58.

305   For instance, see the declaration of the representative of India at the plenary session of the CD, CD/PV.378, 12 August 1986; Nigeria CD/PV.391, 24 February 1987. Brazil and a number of Latin American States condemned the plans of active military uses of outer space as a "flagrant violation" of the Outer Space Treaty and called for the urgent negotiation of an agreement to ban space weapons; "Declaration by the Latin American Countries Members of the Legal Subcommittee of the Committee ot the Peaceful Uses of Outer Space", UN Doc. A/AC.105/C.2/L.142, 6 April 1983. Jasentuliyana, op. cit., 1999, p. 121. On 21 January 1988 the Heads of Government of Sweden, Greece, Mexico, Tanzania, Argentina and India adopted the so-called "Stockholm Declaration", which calls for a comprehensive ban of space weapons to prevent a vertical and horizontal arms race in space CD/807, 19 February 1988.

306   See section 3.5 of this study.

307   See sections 2.2.5 and 2.2.6 of this study.

308   US intervention at the plenary session of the CD, 31 August 2000; also see Andem, op. cit., 2001, p. 285.

309   "General-Secretary Regrets United States Decision to Withdraw form ABM Treaty", UN Doc. SG/SM/8080, 14 December 2001, <www.un.org/News/Press/docs/2001/sgsm8080.doc.htm>.

310   D. Deudney, "Unlocking Space", *Foreign Policy*, vol. 53, 1983/84, p. 91.

311   A good survey is given in Gasparini Alves, op. cit., 1991, p. 40; Jasani, op. cit., 1991, p. 24. On the efforts of the international community to prevent an arms race in outer space from an international legal perspective see V. Vereshschetin, *Prevention of the Arms Race in Outer Space: International Law Aspects*, Geneva, 1986; Magno, op. cit., 1984, p. 221; S.K. Agrawala, "An Approach to Arms Control in Outer Space", *ZaöRV*, vol. 45, 1985, p. 543; Vlasic, op. cit., 1981, p. 135; Menon, op. cit., 1988, p. 40; Reijnen, op. cit., 1995, p. 41; Reijnen, op. cit., 1985, p. 181; C.Q. Christol, "The Common Interest in the Exploration, Use and Exploitation of Outer Space for Peaceful Purposes: The Soviet-American Dilemma", Proceedings from the 27th Colloquium on the Law of Outer Space, 1985. In the arms control literature see C. Rousseau, "Disarmament since 1945" in N.M. Matte (ed.), *Arms Control and Disarmament in Outer Space*, Montreal, 1985, p. 149; R. Johnson, "Multilateral Approaches to Preventing the Weaponization of Space", *Disarmament Diplomacy*, no. 56, April 2001.

312   Resolution adopted (without vote) by the United Nations General Assembly on the report of the Ad hoc Committee of the Tenth Special Session, S-10/2, 30 June 1978. Cocca underlines that the General Assembly considered any measures that would transform outer space into an "arena of military confrontation" to be "contrary to the spirit of the Space treaty". A.A. Cocca, "Satellite: Warring Weapon", Proceedings from the 24th Colloquium Space Law, 1982, p. 70.

313   Predecessors were the Ten-Nation Committee on Disarmament established in September 1959 (five Western and five Eastern member states), which was transformed into the Eighteen-Nation Committee on Disarmament on 30 December 1961 under the cochairmanship of the United States and the Soviet Union (sessions from 14 March 1962 to 31 August 1978), with the later nuclear-weapon powers China and France not participating despite several membership extensions. France left its seat vacant to the end. In

addition to the nuclear-weapon states the United States, Soviet Union and Great Britain, the Committee consisted of the following members: Brazil, Bulgaria, Burma, Canada, Checkoslovakia, Ethiopia, India, Italy, Mexico, Nigeria, Poland, Romania, Sweden and the United Arab Republics. In 1969 Japan and Mongolia as well as Argentina, Hungary, Morocco, Netherlands, Pakistan and Yugoslavia joined. The Committee was renamed as Conference of the Committee on Disarmament. UN Doc. A/RES/2602 B (XXIV), 16 December 1969. In 1974 the Federal Republic of Germany, the German Democratic Republic, Iran, Peru and Zaire were admitted as members.

314 On the Geneva CD in general see Rousseau, op. cit., 1985, p. 147; N. Jasentuliyana, "The Process of Achieving Effective Arms Control" in J. Dahlitz and D. Dicke (eds), *The International Law of Arms Control and Disarmament*, New York, 1991, p. 179; J. Goldblat, *Arms Control: A Guide to Negotiations and Agreements*, Thousand Oaks, 1994, p. 9. On the role of the CD in arms control in outer space Gasparini Alves, op. cit., 1991, p. 1.

315 UN Doc. A/RES/S-10/2, para. 120, 30 June 1978.

316 UN Doc. A/A.187/97, 1 February 1978.

317 "The main objective pursued by Italy was to prohibit the development and use of Earth-based and space-based systems designed to damage, destroy or interfere with the operations of other States' satellites". CD/9, 26 March 1979; Reijnen, op. cit., 1995, p. 41; Reijnen, op. cit., 1985, p. 106; Gasparini Alves, op. cit., 1991, p. 89.

318 "We must make sure that outer space can be spared the fate of so many human discoveries of previous ages—namely, becoming a mere battle-field ... In this endeavour for peace in outer space, the Committee holds an important role". UN Doc. A/RES/33/20, p. 25.

319 Jasentuliyana, op. cit., 1999, p. 75.

320 Ibid., p. 76.

321 Gasparini Alves, op. cit., 1991, p. 5 according to whom the termination of the negotiations was due to the assessment of the United States that "an agreement involving such [ASAT] systems would pose technical and other problems of verification which were judged not to be solvable at that time". See also *United Nations Disarmament Yearbook*, vol. 6, New York, 1981, p. 267. The United States publicly justified the termination with the Soviet invasion of Afghanistan.

238

322 UN Doc. A/AC/105/PV.205, 24 June 1980, p. 27.

323 Magno, op. cit., 1984, p. 222.

324 Jasentuliyana, op. cit., 1999, p. 77.

325 UN Doc. A/AC/105/PV.204-205, 207-208, 210-213 and 215.

326 UN Doc. CD/PV.127, p. 6; Jasentuliyana, op. cit., 1999, p. 77.

327 Letter of Foreign Minister Andrei Gromykos to General-Secretary Kurt Waldheim "Consideration of a treaty on the prohibition of the stationing of weapons of any kind in outer space", UN Doc. A/RES//36/192, 20 August 1981, p. 3.

328 The draft introduced by Italy was adopted as part of the resolution on "General and complete disarmament", UN. Doc. A/36/97, 9 December 1981; the draft introduced by Mongolia on the same topic was adopted as UN. Doc. A /RES/36/99, 9 December 1981; Menon, op. cit., 1988, p. 57.

329 UN Doc. A/RES/36/97, 9 December 1981.

330 UN Doc. A/RES/36/99, 9 December 1981; Menon, op. cit., 1988, p. 57.

331 UN Doc. A/RES/36/94, 9 December 1981.

332 UN Doc. A/RES/36/99, 9 December 1981; Christol, op. cit., 1985.

333 UN Doc. A/CONF.101/10, p. 102.

334 "... the developing countries wanted it understood that they were no longer willing to regard the question of the military uses of outer space as a matter to be left up to the super powers..." Jasentuliyana, op. cit., 1999, p. 81.

335 "[A]n arms race in space would increase the areas and the potential for confrontation, adding a new dimension to the human destruction ... it would also divert urgently needed resources from programmes of social and economic development..." quoted in Jasentuliyana, op. cit., 1999, p. 67.

336 See section 2.1.1 of this study and ibid., p. 68; Menon, op. cit., 1988, p. 59; Andem, op. cit., 1992, p. 219.

337 Menon, op. cit., 1988, p. 59; Jasentuliyana, "Arms Control in Outer Space: A Review of Recent United Nations Decisions", AASL, vol. 9, 1984, p. 337.

338 UN Doc. A/36/99, para. 14, 9 December 1981; Christol, op. cit., 1985.

339 UN Doc. A/38/20, para. 77, 1983; Jasentuliyana, op. cit., 1999, p. 84.

340 UN Doc. A/38/20, para. 78, 1983.

341 Jasentuliyana, op. cit., 1999, p. 91.

342   Ibid. With regard to the CD, see Filho, op. cit., 1998, p. 358; Andem, op. cit., 1992, p. 218; Jasentuliyana, op. cit., 1999, p. 73; Rousseau, op. cit., 1985, p. 147; Jasentuliyana, op. cit., 1991, p. 179; Gasparini Alves, op. cit., 1991, p. 1; P.J. Baines, "A Variant of a Mandate for an Ad hoc Committee on Outer Space within the Conference on Disarmament: A Convention for the Non-Weaponization of Outer Space" in J.M. Beier and S. Mataila (eds), *Arms Control and the Rule of Law: A Framework for Peace and Security in Outer Space*, Proceedings of the 15th Annual Ottawa NACD Verification Symposium, Toronto, 1998, p. 65; Cleminson, op. cit., 1998, p. 35; D. Sinclair, "Outer Space: The Conference on Disarmament" in Beier and Mataila (eds), op. cit., 1998, p. 29.

343   UN Doc. A/RES/S-10/2, para. 120, 30 June 1978.

344   Jasentuliyana, op. cit., 1991, p. 179.

345   Gasparini Alves, op. cit., 1991, p. 7.

346   UN Doc. A/RES/36/97, 9 December 1981; as well as UN Doc. A/RES/37/83, 9 December 1982 (introduced by socialist and non-aligned states); and UN Doc. A/RES/37/99 D, 13 December 1982 (introduced by Western states); UN Doc. A/RES/38/80, 15 December 1983; "Prevention of an Arms Race in Outer Space", UN Doc. A/RES/39/59, 12 December 1984; UN Doc. A/RES/40/87, 12 December 1985.

347   In its resolution of 15 December 1983 the General Assembly additionally calls upon "... all States, in particular those with major space capabilities ... to undertake prompt negotiations under the auspices of the United Nations with a view to reaching agreement or agreements designed to halt the militarisation of outer space and to prevent an arms race in outer space..." [my emphasis]. UN Doc. A/RES/38/80, 15 December 1983.

348   UN Doc. A/RES/S-10/2, para. 120, 30 June 1978.

349   UN Doc. A/38/27.

350   Gasparini Alves, op. cit., 1991, p. 5; Menon, op. cit., 1988, p. 57.

351   CD/375, 14 April 1983; CD/PV.263, 12 June 1984; Gasparini Alves, op. cit., 1991, p. 5.

352   "Lack of the establishment of a working group is attributed largely to the position taken by the United States regarding its position concerning multilateral discussion of this item as well as the formulation of an appropriate mandate for the working group...". Jasentuliyana, op. cit., 1999, p. 90.

353   CD/PV.254, 29 March 1984. Also, Andem writes, "There were elaborate discussion by delegations of various issues relevant to the prevention of an arms race in outer space, such as: ... the status of outer space as the common heritage of mankind which should be used exclusively for peaceful purposes..." Andem, op. cit., 1992, p. 219.

354   Brazil and Chile proposed additional protocols on the Outer Space Treaty at the General Assembly on 2 November 1982, "with a view to preventing an arms race in outer space". UN Doc. A/SPC/37/SR.

355   Declaration by the Latin American countries members of the Legal Subcommittee of COPUS, UN Doc. A/AC.105/C.2/L.142, 6 April 1983.

356   UN Doc. A/AC.105/L. 150; CD/PV.486; Jasentuliyana, op. cit., 1999, p. 99; Gasparini Alves, op. cit., 1991, p. 101; Menon, op. cit., 1988, p. 61.

357   UN Doc. A/RES/39/59, 12 December 1984; UN Doc. A/RES/36/97, 9 December 1981; as well as UN Doc. A/RES/37/83, 9 December 1982 (introduced by socialist and non-aligned states); and UN Doc. A/RES/37/99 D, 13 December 1982 (introduced by Western States); UN Doc. A/RES/38/80, 15 December 1983; UN Doc. A/RES/39/59, 12 December 1984; UN Doc. A/RES/40/87, 12 December 1985.

358   Jasentuliyana, op. cit, 1999, p. 99; Menon, op. cit., 1988, p. 63.

359   Jasentuliyana, op. cit., 1999, p. 99; Menon, op. cit., 1988, p. 63; Andem, op. cit., 1992, p. 222.

360   UN Doc. A/RES/39/59, 12 December 1984; G. Seidel, "Die Völkerrechtsordnung an der Schwelle zum 21. Jahrhundert", AVR, vol. 38, 2000, p. 27.

361   Amendment to the Department of Defense Authorization Bill FY 1984, "Establishing Criteria Governing the Test of Antisatellite Warheads", Section 1235, Public Law 98-94, 24 September 1983, p. 695; Stares, op. cit., 1985, p. 232.

362   98th Congress, 2nd Session, 21 March 1984; Christol, op. cit., 1985. On the attitude of Congress see also B.W. Kubbig, "Die SDI-Debatte in der Reagan-Administration und im Kongreß ab 1983" in Kubbig (ed.), Die militärische Eroberung des Weltraums, vol. 1, Frankfurt, 1990, p. 94.

363   CD/PV.321, 16 July 1985 and CD/PV.542, 13 March 1990; Christol, op. cit., 1985; Gasparini Alves, op. cit., 1991, p. 52; Menon, op. cit., 1988, p. 65.

364   France, "Prevention of an Arms Race in Outer Space", CD/375, 14 April 1983 and 12 June 1984; Gasparini Alves, op. cit., 1991, p. 5; Menon, op. cit., 1988, p. 57; G. Guillaume, "France and Arms Control in Outer Space: French Proposals Respecting Space Law" in Matte (ed.), op. cit., 1985, p. 67.

365   Guillaume, op. cit., 1985, p. 84.

366   Ibid., p. 78.

367   "The main aim of France is to prevent the introduction of new weapons in space, and thus to thwart competition that might develop more rapidly than we think between the United States and the Soviet Union ... All these measures advocated by France tend to preserve the outlook of progress that mankind expects to derive from the non-military use of outer space". Ibid., p. 81.

368   Speech of Prime Minister Laurent Fabius before the Institut des Hautes Études de Défense Nationale, 17 September 1984.

369   CD/9, 26 March 1979; Reijnen, op. cit., 1995, p. 41; Reijnen, op. cit., 1985, p. 106.

370   Gasparini Alves, op. cit., 1991, p. 5; Menon, op. cit., 1988, p. 57.

371   See section 2.2.8 of this study.

372   See the draft introduced by Italy UN Doc. A/RES/36/97, 9 December 1981. The draft introduced by Mongolia on the same topic was adopted as UN Doc. A/RES/36/99, 9 December 1981.

373   Cheng, op. cit., 2000, p. 305 regards this step in particular in view of the additional proposal made by the Soviet Union for the first time in 1988 to admit "international inspectors to ensure that no object carrying weapons would be launched into outer space as a complete volte-face".

374   Draft Treaty on the Prohibition of the Stationing of Weapons of Any Kind in Outer Space of the Soviet Union, UN Doc. A/36/192, 10 August 1981.

375   Draft Treaty on the Prohibition of the Use of Force in Outer Space and from Space Against the Earth by the Soviet Union, UN Doc. A/38/194, 19 August 1983, p. 3.

376   Ibid.; Jasentuliyana, op. cit., 1999, p. 86.

377   UN Doc. A/39/243, 27 August 1984; Andem, op. cit., 1992, p. 215.

378   Premier Chernenko stated that "effective verification of compliance by the Parties with a moratorium on orbital-effect anti-satellite weapons could be assured by the means for the tracking of space objects which the Parties have at their disposal." On 16 June 1984

379 the Soviet Union presented this statement at the Geneva CD in a note to the Chairman of the Conference, CD/519, 18 June 1984. UN Doc. A/40/192, 16 August 1985.

380 E. Jaksetic, "The Peaceful Uses of Outer Space: Soviet Views", *The American University Law Review*, vol. 28, 1979, p. 483; M. Russel, "Military Activities in Outer Space. Soviet Legal Views", *Harvard International Law Journal*, vol. 25, 1984, p. 153.

381 E. Kamentskaya, "Outer Space and the term 'Militarization'", Proceedings from the 33rd Colloquium Space Law, 1991, p. 225. Further, "The principle of the use of outer space for peaceful purposes implies that states should strive actively and purposefully for the complete exclusion of space from the sphere of military activities, employing to this end both general and partial disarmament and arms limitation measures". V. Velikhov, R. Sagdeev and A. Kokoshin, *Weaponry in Space: The Dilemma of Security*, Moscow, 1986, p. 132; Kolosov, "The USSR and the 1967 Treaty on Outer Space", Proceedings from the 40th Colloquium on the Law of Outer Space, 1998, p. 17; Y. Zhukov, "On the Interpretation of the Term 'Peaceful Use of Outer Space' Contained in the Space Treaty", Proceedings from the 11th Colloquium on the Law of Outer Space, 1969, p. 38; G.P. Zhukov, "Towards the New Treaty on military Space Activity Limitation", Proceedings from the 26th Colloquium on the Law of Outer Space, 1984, p. 371.

382 Kamentskaya, op. cit., 1991, p. 225; Kolosov, op. cit., 1998, p. 17; V.M Postyshev, *The Concept of the Common Heritage of Mankind*, Moscow, 1990, p. 239.

383 Zhukov and Kolosov, op. cit., 1984, p. 58.

384 "Law of the Russian Federation on Space Activities" printed in *Rossiskaya Gazeta*, 23 October 1993.

385 CD/1271, 24 August 1994, p. 7.

386 F. Tesselkin and D. Marenkov, "Änderungen im Gesetz der Russischen Föderation über Weltraumaktivitäten vom 20. August 1993. Kurzkommentar zu der neuen Fassung vom 4. October 1996", *ZLW*, vol. 51, 2002, p. 26; Kolosov, op. cit., 1998, p. 17.

387 Filho, op. cit., 1998, p. 367 criticizes this, however, as a "high-jacking" of the original objective of the Ad Hoc Committee to negotiate a ban on space weapons.

388 See section 8.1.2 of this study.

389 CD/1271, 24 August 1994, p. 7.

390 Ibid.

391 "Draft Guidelines regarding Measures on Confidence Building and Predictability in Outer Space Activities", CD/OS/WP.69; see also section 8.1.2 of this study.

392 CD/1271, 24 August 1994, p. 7.

393 CD/PV.752, 23 January 1997.

394 CD/PV.763, 15 May 1997; Cleminson, op. cit., 1998, p. 36.

395 CD/PV.809, 21 January 1999.

396 CD/PV.782, 3 February 1998.

397 Ibid.

398 Ibid.

399 CD/PV.790, 19 March 1998.

400 CD/PV.79, 19 March 1998.

401 CD/PV.794, 28 May 1998.

402 CD/PV.802, 11 August 1998.

403 CD/PV.794, 28 May 1998.

404 Ibid.

405 CD/PV.802, 11 August 1998; See section 7.3 of this study.

406 See section 10.2.2.3 of this study.

407 Cleminson, op. cit., 1998, p. 35.

408 CD/1569, 4 February 1999.

409 CD/PV.822, 26 March 1999.

410 CD/1576, 11 March 1999.

411 CD/1584, 28 April 1999.

412 CD/PV.823, 11 May 1999.

413 Ibid.

414 Ibid.

415 CD/1571, 18 February 1999.

416 CD/1586, 19 May 1999.

417 CD/PV.824, 20 May 1999.

418 "The Conference requests the AHC, with a view to preventing the weaponization of outer space, to examine and identify, through substantive and general consideration, specific topics or proposals that might be a basis for subsequent in-depth consideration, including aspects related to possible confidence-building or transparency measures, general treaty principles or treaty commitments." CD/PV.828, 17 June 1999.

419 CD/PV.836, 7 September 1999.

420   CD/1606, 9 February 2000 and the intervention of China in the plenary session of the CD on 18 January and 20 February 2000, CD/PV.843 of 24 February 2000.

421   CD/1605, 27January 2000.

422   "A certain country, for the benefit of its own and in defiance of the requirements and appeals of the UNGA resolutions passed year after year, practices expediency and double standard towards arms control and disarmament agreements, even trying to weaken or abolish a relevant treaty to keep its hands free in research, development and proliferation of advanced missile defense system, which undermines the strategic balance and stability... are extremely worrisome ... people cannot but ask, do we prefer *common security for all states* or the absolute security enjoyed by a single state at the expense of all others [emphasis added]?" CD/PV.843, 24 February 2000.

423   CD/PV.840, 3 February 2000.

424   CD/PV.842, 17 February 2000.

425   Ibid.

426   CD/PV.843, 24 February 2000.

427   Ibid.

428   CD/PV.845, 9 March 2000.

429   Ibid.

430   CD/1609, 23 February 2000.

431   CD/PV.858, 31 August 2000.

432   CD/PV.859, 5 September 2000.

433   CD/PV.860, 14 September 2000.

434   CD/PV.861, 21 September 2000.

435   "The CD decides to establish, under agenda item 3, an Ad Hoc Committee/Ad Hoc Working Group to examine and identify specific topics or proposals that might be a basis for subsequent in-depth consideration, which could include confidence-building or transparency measures, general principles, *treaty commitments and the elaboration of a regime capable of preventing an arms race in outer space* [emphasis added]." CD/1620, 29 June 2000.

436   "... to examine and identify specific proposals ... for the elaboration of a specific regime capable of preventing an arms race in outer space"; on the negotiation of a Cut-off Treaty: "to negotiate an effectively verifiable treaty"; on complete nuclear disarmament: "to exchange information and views on practical steps for progressive

and systematic efforts to attain this objective". CD/1624, 24 August 2000.

437 "... to preserve the ABM Treaty and check the trend of weaponization of outer space. This is also indispensable for the follow-up steps as specified in the final document of the 2000 NPT Review Conference to proceed. ... Outer space is the common heritage of all humankind. It is the shared aspiration of all peoples to use outer space for peaceful purposes. That said, the missile defence systems currently under development pose the serious threat to outer space of its weaponization, which might trigger off a new arms race. We are seriously concerned by reports of a space war exercise which took place in late January this year." CD/PV.866, 15 February 2001.

438 "To put it quite simply, outer space issues are not ripe for negotiations in the CD. ... As many United States representatives have repeatedly emphasized, there is no arms race in outer space, nor any prospect of an arms race for as far down the road as anyone can see. We fully support the 1967 Outer Space Treaty and judge that it, along with a number of other international agreements, is entirely equal to the task of preventing an arms race in outer space. Ibid.

439 Ibid.

440 "... we strongly urge the Conference to explore all avenues to start substantive work ... to restore the important and central position of the Conference on Disarmament in the web of international forums upon which we all depend." Ibid.

441 "At a time when there are disturbing signs of a preference for unilateral solutions or options, it is essential for the continuation of multilateralism that this body re-engages in real work. We fully support unilateral arms reductions, but not unilateral action which might impact negatively on disarmament, arms control and non-proliferation." Ibid.

442 CD/PV.871, 22 March 2001.

443 "... an Ad Hoc Committee to negotiate with a view to reaching agreement on a regime capable of preventing an arms race in outer space. This regime could take the form of an internationally binding instrument." CD/1644, 30 May 2001.

444 CD/1606, 9 February 2000.

445 CD/PV.876, 7 June 2001.

446 CD/PV.879, 28 June 2001.

447   Ibid.

448   F. Zhigang, "The Joint Working Paper by China and Russia", *INESAP Information Bulletin*, no. 20, August 2002.

449   CD/PV.866, 15 February 2001.

450   *ICJ Reports 1996*, p. 222.

451   Ibid., para. 99, p. 264.

452   Ibid.

453   UN Doc. A/RES/39/59, 12 December 1984; UN Doc. A/RES/36/97, 9 December 1981; as well as UN Doc. A/RES/37/83, 9 December 1982 (introduced by socialist and non-aligned states); and UN Doc. A/RES/37/99 D, 13 December 1982 (introduced by Western states); UN Doc. A/RES/38/80, 15 December 1983; UN Doc. A/RES/39/59, 12 December 1984; UN Doc. A/RES/40/87, 12 December 1985.

454   See above reference as well as UN Doc. A/RES/54/53, 1 November 1999 (160 votes in favour); UN Doc. A/RES/55/32, para. 4, 3 January 2001; and UN Doc. A//RES/56/23, 21 December 2001 (156 votes in favour, 0 against, and 4 abstentions: Georgia, Israel, Micronesia, United States). For an example of the attitude of the non-aligned states, see the declaration of India at the CD, CD/PV.333, 27 August 1985, that the new weapon-systems "have been developed in utter disregard of the overwhelming body of world public opinion and ... indeed at the cost of the security and other interests of the majority of mankind."

455   Gasparini Alves, op. cit., 1991, p. 24; Stares, op. cit., 1985, p. 55; Handberg, op. cit., 2000, p. 25; Cleminson, op. cit., 1998, p. 35.

456   Jasentuliyana, op. cit., 1999, p. 115.

457   "... refrain, in their activities relating to outer space, from actions contrary to the observance of the relevant existing treaties or to the objective of preventing an arms race in outer space." UN Doc. A/RES/40/87, para. 11, 12 December 1985; also, "Emphasizing the paramount importance of strict compliance with the existing arms limitation and disarmament agreements relevant to outer space, including bilateral agreements, and with the existing legal regime concerning the use of outer space...", UN Doc. A/RES/52/37, preamble, 9 December 1997; and "Calls upon all States, in particular those with major space capabilities, to contribute actively to the objective of the peaceful use of outer space and of the prevention of an arms race in outer space and to refrain from actions contrary to that objective and to the relevant existing

treaties in the interest of maintaining international peace and security and promoting international cooperation", UN Doc. A/RES/52/37, para. 4, 9 December 1997.

458 CD/PV.871, 22 March 2001.

459 Ibid.

460 "Missed Chance", *Information Bulletin International Network of Engineers and Scientists Against Proliferation*, no. 18, September 2001.

461 R. Falk, "Nuclear Weapons, International Law and the World Court: A Historic Encounter", *AJIL*, vol. 91, 1997, p. 64.

462 "There is little likelihood in the near future that the decision will have any discernible impact on the behaviour of the nuclear-weapon states, either with respect to the roles assigned to nuclear weapons or to the duty to seek nuclear disarmament." Falk, op. cit., 1997, p. 74.

463 UN Doc. A/RES/56/23, 21 December 2001.

464 For a detailed analysis of such a legal obligation see D. Wolter, *Grundlagen "Gemeinsamer Sicherheit" nach universellem Völkerrecht. Der Grundsatz der friedlichen Nutzung des Weltraums im Lichte des völkerrechtlichen Strukturprinzips vom Gemeinsamen Erbe der Menschheit*, Berlin, 2003, p. 418.

465 Seidel, op. cit., 2000, p. l speaks of the "normative confirmation" of the demand for a universal treaty on general and complete disarmament by the declaration of principles of the United Nations General Assembly 2625 (XXV).

466 "Although the U.S. agrees with some elements of the draft resolution 'PAROS', we believe it also includes provisions that are overstated or unwise. Accordingly, the U.S. abstained, as in 1998. There is unprecedented peaceful cooperation in outer space, and we have every reason to believe that this pattern of peaceful cooperation will continue. It seems evident—indeed, almost incontestable—that there is no arms race in outer space. Military uses of outer space enhance international peace and security and have broad advantages for the international community. Practical examples include treaty compliance and monitoring, the global positioning system, refugee tracking, counter-terrorism, and sanctions enforcement. For all these reasons, the U.S. does not believe that the international community needs to undertake an active and energetic effort to prevent an arms race in outer space, nor that the task is urgent". US explanation of its vote on the draft

248

resolution on the "Prevention of an arms race in outre space" at the United Nations General Assembly. UN Doc. A/C.1/54/L.22, 1 November 1999.

467   Joint Resolution of the US House of Representatives, H.J.R. 120, 98th Congress, First Session, 2 February 1983.

468   See for instance the reasons given by Canada, CD/1569, 4 February 1999 and China, CD/1606, 9 February 2000.

469   In January 1985 a group of six countries from five continents declared that "an arms race in outer space would be enormously costly, would have grave destabilising effect and would endanger several arms limitation and disarmament agreements" ("Delhi Declaration on Space Technology Applications in Asia and the Pacific for Improved Quality of Life in the New Millennium and the Strategy and Action Plan on Space Technology Applications for Sustainable Development in Asia and the Pacific for the New Millennium"); see also Jasentuliyana, op. cit., 1999, p. 121.

470   Brazil and a number of Latin American states condemned plans for an active military use of outer space as a "flagrant violation" of the Outer Space Treaty and called for the urgent negotiation of an agreement on the prohibition of space weapons. UN Doc. A/AC.105/C.2/L.142, 6 April 1983.

471   M. Datan and R. Johnson, "UN First Committee General Debate, October 4-14, 2004", <www.acronym.org.uk/un/2004FC01.htm>.

472   K.-U. Schrogl, "Legal Aspects Related to the Application of the Principle that the Exploration and Utilization of Outer Space Should be carried out for the Benefit and in the Interest of all States Taking into Particular Account the Needs of Developing Countries" in Benkö and Schrogl, op. cit., 1993, p. 215.

473   UN Doc. A/CONF.184/6.

474   H. Feigl, "Mehr Sicherheit durch Vertrauensbildung und Verhaltenskontrolle: Zur Konzeption eines umfassenden Schutzregimes für den Weltraum" in A. Zunker (ed.), *Weltordnung oder Chaos?*, Baden-Baden, 1993, p. 511; Jasentuliyana, op. cit., 1999, p. 121; Andem, op. cit., 1992, p. 219; Menon, op. cit., 1988, p. 85.

475   *ICJ Reports 1962*, p. 26 (Temple of Preah Vihear case) and *ICJ Reports 1969*, p. 35 (North Sea-Continental Shelf case) on *estoppel*; see also G. Fitzmaurice in a separate opinion in the

	Temple of Preah Vihear case, *ICJ Reports 1962*, p. 63 on the distinction between "acquiescence" and the principle of *estoppel*.
476	See section 2.2.3 of this study.
477	According to the overwhelming majority of the literature on the topic, plans for the deployment of space weapons would lead to a new arms spiral on Earth and in outer space if not pursued in a cooperative framework. See the references in section 2.1.1 of this study.
478	A. Paulus, *Die internationale Gemeinschaft im Völkerrecht. Eine Untersuchung zur Entwicklung des Völkerrechts im Zeitalter der Globalisierung*, Munich, 2001.
479	*ICJ Reports 1996*, para. 99; see J. Burroughs, *The Legality of the Threat or Use of Nuclear Weapons: A Guide to the Historic Opinion of the International Court of Justice*, Munster, 1997.
480	Fawcett, op. cit., 1984, p. 3.
481	O'Neill Jr., op. cit., 1984, p. 169.
482	O. Schachter, "Legal Aspects of Space Travel," *Journal of the British Interplanetary Society*, January, 1952; O. Schachter, "The Prospects for a Regime in Outer Space and International Organization" in M. Cohen (ed.), *Law and Politics in Space*, Montreal, 1964, p. 95; Kroell, "Einem Weltraum entgegen", *Zeitschrift für Luftrecht*, 1952, p. 254; A. Meyer, "Legal Problems of Flight into Outer Space", Third Astronautical Congress, Stuttgart, 5 August 1952; Jenks, op. cit., 1958, p. 394; Jessup and Taubenfeld, op. cit., 1959, p. 275.
483	O. Schachter, "Who Owns the Universe?", reprinted in US Government, *Space Law—A Symposium*, Washington DC, 1959.
484	A.A. Cocca, *Teoria del Derecho Interplanetario*, Buenos Aires, 1957, p. 246.
485	A.A. Cocca, "Principles for a Declaration with Reference to the Legal Nature of the Moon", Proceedings from the 1st Colloquium on the Law of Outer Space, 1959, p. 36.
486	A.A. Cocca, "Prospective Space Law", *JSL*, vol. 26, 1998; A.A. Cocca, "Basic Statute for the Moon and Heavenly Bodies", Proceedings from the 5th Colloquium on the Law of Outer Space, 1963, p. 36; A.A. Cocca, "The Advances in International Law through the Law of Outer Space", *JSL*, vol. 9, 1981, p. 15: "... the international community ... had recognized the existence of a new subject of international law, namely mankind itself, and creates a jus humanitatis ... and endowed that new subject of international law—mankind—with the vastest common property (res communis

humanitatis) which the human mind could at present conceive of, namely outer space itself, including the Moon and the other celestial bodies"; A.A. Cocca, "Protocol to the Space Treaty on the Common Heritage of Mankind", Proceedings from the 34th Colloquium on the Law of Outer Space, 1992, p. 161.

487   UN Doc. A/RES/1962 (XVIII), 13 December 1963.

488   See section 1.1.2 of this study.

489   See section 1.1.2 of this study; de la Rochere, op. cit., 1967, p. 608.

490   UN Doc. A/AC.105/C2/SR.75, 19 June 1967.

491   On the qualification of outer space per se as CHOM see Andem, op. cit., 1992, p. 214; A.-C. Kiss, "Patrimoine commun de l'humanité, RdC, no. II, 1982; P. Reuter, Droit international public, Paris, 1976; S. Hobe, "Common Heritage of Mankind—An Outdated Concept in International Space Law?", Proceedings from the 41st Colloquium on the Law of Outer Space, 1999, p. 274; K. Baslar, The Concept of the Common Heritage of Mankind in International Law, The Hague, 1998, p. 160; Fitschen, "Gemeinsames Erbe der Menschheit" in R. Wolfrum (ed.), Handbuch der Vereinten Nationen, Munich, 1991, p. 211; Gorove, "International Space Law in Perspective", RdC, no. III, 1983; Matte, op. cit., 1987, p. 313; International Law Association, Report of the Sixty-Ninth Conference, London, 2000, p. 586; A.B. Altemir, El Patrimonio Comun de la Humanidad. Hacia un régimen juridico international para su géstion, Barcelona, 1993, pp. 124 and 245; M. Filho, "Why and How to Define 'Global Public Interest'", Proceedings from the 43rd Colloquium on the Law of Outer Space, 2001, p. 24; W. Stocker, Das Prinzip des Common Heritage of Mankind als Ausdruck des Staatengemeinschaftsinteresses im Völkerrecht, Schweizer Studien zum Internationalen Recht, Zurich, 1993, p. 102; Wolfrum, op. cit., 1984, p. 341; R. Wolfrum, "Common Heritage of Mankind", Encyclopaedia of Public International Law, vol. 11, 1989, p. 67; C.Q. Christol, "The International Law of Space Environment Resources" reprinted in C.Q. Christol, Space Law: Past, Present, and Future, New York, 1991, p. 71; Wiesner and Jung, "Das völkerrechtliche Regime der geostationären Umlaufbahn", ÖZöRVR, vol. 32, 1981/82; C.C. Okolie, "Legal Interpretation of the 1979 United Nations Treaty Concerning the Activities of Sovereign States on the Moon and other Celestial Bodies within the Meaning of the Concept of

Common Heritage of Mankind", Proceedings from the 23rd Colloquium on the Law of Outer Space, 1981, p. 216; D. Wolter, "The Peaceful Purpose Standard of the Common Heritage of Mankind Clause in Outer Space Law", *ASILS International Law Journal*, vol. IX, 1985, p. 117; Wolter, op. cit., 2002, p. 941; W. Durner, *Common Goods. Statusprinzipien von Umweltgütern im Völkerrecht*, Baden-Baden, 2000, p. 228; S.K. Agrawala, "Arms Control in Outer Space", ZaöRV, vol. 45, 1985; Reijnen, op. cit., 1995, p. 96; B. Genius-Devime, *Bedeutung und Grenzen des Erbes der Menschheit im völkerrechtlichen Kulturgüterschutz*, Baden-Baden, 1996, p. 58; W. Dettmering, *Die Rechtstellung von Menschen, Stationen und Niederlassungen auf Himmelskörpern*, Würzburg, 1971, p. 177; P. Jankowitsch, "Mond und Himmelskörper im neuen Völkerrecht des Weltraums. Das Übereinkommen vom 5. Dezember 1979", ZLW, vol. 30, 1981, p. 178; R. MacDonald, "The Common Heritage of Mankind" in U. Beyerlin, M. Bothe, R. Hofmann and E.U. Petersmann (eds), *Recht zwischen Umbruch und Bewahrung. Festschrift für Rudolf Bernhardt*, 1995, p. 153; E.E. Weeks, "Continuing Patterns of Inequality Between North and South in Outer Space", *Revue de Droit International et de Science diplomatique et politique*, vol. 79, May/August 2001, p. 170; A. Bueckling, "Weltraumrecht—auf der Schwelle in das 3. Jahrtausend" in M. Benkö and W. Kröll (eds), *Luft und Weltraumrecht im 21. Jahrhundert. Liber amicorum for Böckstiegel*, 2001, p. 291.

492 Wolfrum, op. cit., 1984, p. 277; see also Hobe, op. cit., 1992, p. 97.

493 See chapter 1 of this study.

494 UN Doc. A/3902.

495 Wolfrum, op. cit., 1984, p. 277.

496 UN Doc. A/AC.105/C.2/L.71 and Corr. 1, 1970.

497 UN Doc. A/8391 and Corr. 1 (Soviet Union); UN Doc. A/AC./115 Annex I (Bulgaria).

498 UN Doc. A/AC./115 Annex I (United States); see on these US papers in support of the CHOM concept R. Wolfrum, "Der Mondvertrag von 1979—Weiterentwicklung des Weltraumrechts", EA, vol. 35, 1980, p. 666.

499 UN Doc. AC.105/218 Annex I; Jankowitsch, op. cit., 1981, p. 173.

500 Agreement Governing the Activities of States on the Moon and Other Celestial Bodies (Moon Treaty), entered into force on 12 July

1984; UN Doc. A/RES/34/68 Annex, 5 December 1979; Welck and Platzöder, op. cit., p. 30 (as of 1 February 2001: 9 ratifications plus 5 signatures).

[501] W. Kewenig, "Menschheitserbe, Konsens und Völkerrechtsordnung", EA, vol. 36, 1981, p. 3; Hobe, op. cit., 1992, p. 260; K.U. Pritzsche, Natürliche Ressourcen im Weltraum—das Recht ihrer wirtschaftlichen Nutzung, Fankfurt, 1989; K.U. Pritzsche, "Die Nutzung der natürlichen Ressourcen" in Böckstiegel (ed.), op. cit., 1991, p. 574.

[502] Christol, op. cit., 1991, p. 71.

[503] W. Kewenig, "Menschheiterbe: politischer Slogan oder Schlüsselbegriff des Völkerrechts?" in I. von Münch (ed.) Staatsrecht, Völkerrecht, Europarecht. Festschrift für Hans-Jürgen Schlochauer, Berlin, 1981, p. 400; Kewenig, op. cit., 1981, p. 3; similarly on the five elements D.E. Riedel, "International Environmental Law: A Law to Serve the Public Interest? An Analysis of the Scope of the Binding Effect of Basic Principles (Public Interest Norms)" in J. Delbrück (ed.), New Trends in International Lawmaking—International 'Legislation' in the Public Interest, Kiel, 1997, p. 81; Kiss, op. cit., 1982; Reuter, op. cit., 1976, p. 155; Hobe, op. cit., 1992, p. 274.

[504] Kries, "Die militärische Nutzung des Weltraums", op. cit., 1991, p. 349.

[505] N. Jasentuliyana, "A United Nations Perspective of the Moon Agreement", Proceedings from the 23rd Colloquium on the Law of Outer Space, 1981, p. 176 emphasizes that the Treaty, hence, also "... covers some of the legal lacuna left in the Outer Space Treaty concerning military activities on the moon and other celestial bodies This alone makes the Moon Treaty a worthy and timely document to be adopted by the international community."

[506] For a detailed analysis of all elements of the CHOM principle and their legal nature see Wolter, op. cit., 2003, p. 177; Kewenig, op. cit., 1981; Hobe, op. cit., 1992, p. 114; Altemir, op. cit., 1993, p. 75; Matte, op. cit., 1987, p. 313; Virally, op. cit., 1984, p. 5; J. Kish, The Law of International Spaces, Leyden, 1973, p. 43; Wolfrum, op. cit., 1984; D. Shraga, "The Common Heritage of Mankind: The Concept and its Application", Annales d'études internationales, vol. 15, 1986, p. 60; M.V. White, "The Common Heritage of Mankind: An Assessment", Case Western Journal of International Law, vol. 14, 1982, p. 535; P. Jankowitsch, "Legal

Aspects of Military Space Activities" in N. Jasentuliyana (ed.), *Space Law: Development and Scope*, 1992, p. 146; Payoyo, op. cit., 1997, p. 314.

507 The preamble of the Antarctic Treaty reads: "... Antarctica shall continue forever to be used exclusively for peaceful purposes"; Payoyo, op. cit., 1997, p. 314.

508 Hobe, op. cit., 1992, p. 97; P. Dekanosov, "Principle of Peaceful Use in International Outer Space and Maritime Law", Proceedings from the 29th Colloquium on the Law of Outer Space, 1987, p. 29.

509 This is also evident from the title of the note of Malta addressed to the United Nations General-Secretary, "Declaration and Treaty Concerning the Reservation Exclusively for Peaceful Purposes of the Seabed and of the Ocean Floor, Underlying the Seas Beyond the Limits of National Jurisdiction, and the Use of their Resources in the Interests of Mankind", UN Doc. A/AC.105/C.2/SR.75, 12 August 1967; statement of Arvid Pardo in UN Doc. A/C.1/PV.1515, 1 November 1967.

510 Paulus, op. cit., 2001, p. 298. With regard to environmental protection see J. Delbrück, "Wirksameres Völkerrecht oder neues 'Weltinnenrecht'? Perspektiven der Völkerrechtsentwicklung in einem sich wandelnden internationalen System" in J. Delbrück (ed.), *Delbrück: Die Konstituierung des Friedens als Rechtsordnung. Zum Verständnis rechtlicher und politischer Bedingungen der Friedenssicherung im internationalen System der Gegenwart*, Berlin, 1996, p. 348; Simma, op. cit., 1994, p. 236; J.A. Frowein, "Das Staatengemeinschaftsinteresse—Probleme bei Formulierung und Durchsetzung" in K. Hailbronner, G. Ress and T. Stein (eds), *Staat und Völkerrechtsordnung, Festschrift für Doehring*, Berlin, 1989; J.A. Frowein, "Die Staatengemeinschaft als Rechtsbegriff der Völkerrechtsordnung", *Liechtensteinische Juristenzeitung*, vol. 12, 1991.

511 Baslar, op. cit., 1998, p. 105.

512 Ibid., p. 106. Baslar, in his disagreement with my article Wolter, op. cit., 1985, p. 117, blends out the fact that both in the law of the sea as well as in outer space law the CHOM principle was from the outset connected with the peaceful use principle.

513 S. Bhatt, "Legal Controls for Outer Space", Proceedings from the 40th Colloquium on the Law of Outer Space, 1973, p. 273; Goedhuis, op. cit., 1968, p. 18.

514   R. Dolzer, "International Cooperation in Outer Space", ZaöRV, vol. 45, 1985, p. 527.

515   Wolfrum, op. cit., 1984, p. 290; Ibid., p. 541; Focke, "Internationale Zusammenarbeit im Weltraum" in Böckstiegel (ed.), op. cit., 1991, p. 642; V.S. Vereshchetin and E. Kamenetskaya, "On the Way to a World Space Organization", AASL, vol. 12, 1987, p. 338; Seidel, op. cit., 2000, p. 44.

516   Wolfrum, op. cit., 1984, p. 292.

517   C.Q. Christol, "The 1966-67 Treaty: A Manifestation of the World Social Complex" in World Peace Through Law Centre (ed.), World Peace Through Law, The Geneva World Conference, 1969, p. 155.

518   W. de Vries, "The Creation of a Concept of the Law of Outer Space" in Zwaan, Vries, Tuinder and Kuskuvelis (eds), op. cit., 1988, p. 28.

519   K.-H. Böckstiegel, "Perspektiven der Entwicklung des Weltraumrechts bis zum Jahr 2000" in B. Bröner (ed.), Einigkeit und Recht und Freiheit: Festschrift für Karl Carstens zum 70 Geburtstag, Cologne, 1994, p. 320.

520   Focke, op. cit., 1991, p. 642; D. Goedhuis, "Some Substantive and Procedural Issues Presently at Stake in Space Legislation", ZLW, vol. 25, 1976, p. 198.

521   Dolzer, op. cit., 1985, p. 539; "... international cooperation has become a legal obligation which dictates the lawfulness of space activities..."; Wolfrum, op. cit., 1984, p. 335.

522   International Law Association, Report of the Sixty-Fifth Conference, London, 1992, p. 149.

523   Dolzer, op. cit., 1985, p. 54; C. Horsford, "Is I.C.A.O. the Model for an International Space Agency?", Proceedings from the 38th Colloquium on the Law of Outer Space, 1996, p. 201.

524   Wolfrum, op. cit., 1984, p. 335.

525   N. Jasentuliyana, "Article I of the Outer Space Treaty Revisited", JSL, vol. 17, 1989, p. 138.

526   T.M. Franck, Fairness in International Law and Institutions, Oxford, 1995, p. 75.

527   Verdross and Simma, op. cit., 1984, p. 311.

528   C. Tomuschat, "International Law as the Constitution of Mankind" in United Nations (ed.), International Law on the Eve of the Twenty-First Century: Views from the International Law Commission, New York, 1997, p. 43; ibid., p. 310.

529 United Nations General Assembly resolutions: 1148 (XII), 14 November 1957; 1472, 12 December 1959; 1721, 13 December 1961; and 1962, 13 December 1963.

530 K.-H. Böckstiegel, "Allgemeine Grundsätze" in Böckstiegel (ed.), op. cit., 1991, p. 271; Bueckling, op. cit., 2001, p. 291; B. Cheng, "Nineteen Hundred and Sixty Seven Space Treaty", *Journal du Droit International*, vol. 95, 1968, p. 523; D. Goedhuis, "Some Legal Problems Arising from the Utilization of Outer Space" in International Law Association, *Report of the Fifty-Third Conference*, London, 1971, p. 434; A.D. Roth, *La prohibition de l'appropriation et les régimes d'accès aux espaces extra-terrestres*, Paris, 1992, p. 65.

531 Roth, op. cit., 1992, p. 59.

532 "Although Article 1 (1) does not obligate a state to share specific space acquisitions, it may serve an even more important general interestthe... guidance offered by Article 1 (1) clearly conditions the meaning to be given to all other treaty terms." Christol, op. cit., 1991, p. 70; Hobe, op. cit., 1992, p. 104; Reijnen, op. cit., 1985, p. 178; M.G. Marcoff, *Traité de droit international de l'espace*, New York, 1973, p. 388; I.A. Vlasic, "A Survey of the space law treaties and principles developed through the United Nations", Proceedings from the 38th Colloquium on the Law of Outer Space, 1996, p. 324; Vlasic, op. cit., 1981, p. 135; Vlasic, op. cit., 1995, p. 385; Zhukov and Kolosov, op. cit., 1984, p. 41; P.-A. Salin, *Satellite Communications Regulations in the Early 21st Century: Changes for a New Era*, The Hague, 2000, p. 17.

533 C.-A. Colliard, "Espace extra-atmosphérique et grands fonds marins" in R.-J. Dupuy (ed.) *Humanité et Droit international*, Paris, 1991; Christol, op. cit., 1991; Andem, op. cit., 1992 p. 205; Gorove, op. cit., 1983, p. 372; Jenks, op. cit., 1958, p. 394; Jessup and Taubenfeld, op. cit., 1959.

534 "The fact that these clauses could not be interpreted as imposing on the Parties of the Treaty the obligation to carry out their activities in outer space exclusively for the benefit of all countries did not mean that States would be entitled to ignore them. The common and real intention of the Parties at the time of the conclusion of the Treaty was to acknowledge that, apart from the specific national interests in the utilization of outer space, there were wider interests which States in their exploitation of outer space are obliged to take into account. It was realized that a sole concentration on purely national

interests, thus nullifying the common interest, would lead to serious conflicts tensions." International Law Association, *Report of the Fifty-Fouth Conference*, London, 1971, p. 427.

535   "Article I is supported by the remainder of the Outer Space Treaty, among which: the denial of appropriation (Art. II), the compliance with international law and the UN Charter (Art. III), the prohibition of weapons of mass destruction (Art. IV), the prohibition of military installation or manoeuvres (Art. V), the States Parties international responsibility for national activities (Art. VI), the prevention of environmental contamination (Art. IX) and the disclosure of space activities (Art. XI)." Salin, op. cit., 2000, p. 17.

536   Vlasic, op. cit., 1995, p. 385.

537   Böckstiegel, op. cit., 1991, p. 271.

538   M. Nakamura, "Community-Interests of International Law, Especially in the Field of Space Law", Proceedings from the 33rd Colloquium on the Law of Outer Space, 1991, p. 231; H. Quizhi, "Basic Principles of International Law in the Peaceful Uses of Outer Space", Proceedings from the 26th Colloquium on the Law of Outer Space, 1984, p. 251.

539   Jessup and Taubenfeld, op. cit., 1959, p. 275; S. Wiessner, "Human Activities in Outer Space: A Framework for Decision-Making" in Zwaan, Vries, Tuinder and Kuskuvelis (eds), op. cit., 1988, p. 12.

540   United Nations General Assembly resolutions: 1148 (XII), 14 November 1957; 1472, 12 December 1959; 1721, 13 December 1961; and 1962, 13 December 1963.

541   Declaration by Brazil, UN Doc. A/AC.105/C.2/SR.63, 1966 and UN Doc. A/AC.105/C.2/SR.64, 1966.

542   Soviet draft treaty of A/6352 of 16 June 1966 containing the mankind clause in Art. I, para. 1 and the statement by the Soviet delegate, UN Doc. A/AC.105/C.2/SR.64, 1966.

543   "... a solemn treaty obligation should be created, confirming with legal force..." UN Doc. A/AC.105/C.2/SR.70, 1966.

544   Treaty on Outer Space, Hearing on Executive D Before the Committee on Foreign Relations, US Senate, 90th Congress, First Session, 7 March-12 April, 1967, p. 59.

545   Ibid., p. 69. Goldberg called Art. I a norm stipulating "general goals", that needed to be implemented by further specialized treaties.

546   Ibid., p. 4.

547 "... the principle of international cooperation in exploring and using outer space for peaceful purposes is given body through the conclusion of specialised treaties by States and international organizations." UN Doc. A/AC.105/C.2/SR.74; Zhukov and Kolosov, op. cit., p. 186.

548 "Even when further legislative or executive implementing acts are needed in order to permit national courts or administrative authorities to apply a non-self-executing provision, it remains subject to compulsory execution or application in the municipal legal order. By virtue of the contractual nature of the treaty provision, which is legally binding on all contracting parties, a non-self-executing treaty rule is as operable as the self-executing ones; only its application is subject to different executory procedures, involving the legislative and the executive, rather than the judicial department. The efficacy, not the validity of the norm or its binding force, is affected by its non-self-executing nature." Marcoff, op. cit., 1973, p. 13.

549 UN Doc. A/AC.105/C.2/SR.74; Zhukov and Kolosov, op. cit., 1984, p. 186.

550 A. Pardo and C.Q. Christol, "The Common Interest: Tension Between the Whole and the Parts" in R. D.M. MacDonald and Johnston (eds), *The Structure and Process of International Law: Essays in Legal Philosophy, Doctrine and Theory*, The Hague, 1983, p. 643.

551 China, CD/PV.866, 15 February 2001; Egypt, CD/PV.752, 23 January 1997; Egypt, CD/PV.254, 29 March 1984.

552 Friedmann, op. cit., 1964 offers an elaborate characterisation of the structural elements of the new international law of the post-war era.

553 A. Bleckmann, *Grundprobleme und Methoden des Völkerrechts*, Augsburg, 1982, p. 217; A. Bleckmann, "Zur Strukturanalyse im Völkerrecht", *Rechtstheorie*, vol. 9, 1978, p. 143.

554 Bleckmann, op. cit., 1978, p. 143.

555 Dahm, Delbrück and Wolfrum, op.cit., 1989, p. 28.

556 G. Abi-Saab, "La reformulation des principes de la Charte et la transformation des structures juridiques", M. Virally (ed.), *Le droit international au service de la paix, de la justice et du développement*, Paris, 1991, p. 7; G. Abi-Saab, "Whither the International Community?", *EJIL*, vol. 9, 1998, p. 265; O. Kimminich and S. Hobe, *Einführung in das Völkerrecht*, Tubingen, 2000, p. 65.

557   Bleckmann, op. cit., 1982, p. 217.

558   Ibid.

559   A. Bleckmann, *Vom Kompetenzrecht zum Kooperationsrecht*, Berlin, 1985; A. Bleckman, "Zur Wandlung der Strukturen der Völkerrechtsverträge—Theorie des multipolen Vertrages", *AVR*, vol. 34, 1996, p. 218; Paulus, op. cit., 2001, p. 186.

560   E. Menzel, "Das Völkerrecht und die politisch-sozialen Grundstrukturen der modernen Welt" in G. Picht and C. Eisenbart (ed.), *Frieden und Völkerrecht*, Stuttgart, 1973, p. 401.

561   Ibid., p. 407.

562   Ibid., p. 408.

563   R.-J. Dupuy, *Le droit international*, Paris, 1963. For a comparison of Friedmann and Dupuy see C. Leben, "The Changing Structure of International Law Revisited: By Way of Introduction", *EJIL*, vol. 8, 1997, p. 401.

564   Abi-Saab, op. cit., 1991.

565   Ibid.; Abi-Saab, op. cit., 1998, p. 265.

566   Abi-Saab, op. cit., 1991; p. 6; Abi-Saab, op. cit., 1998, p. 265.

567   *ICJ Reports 1970*, p. 32 (Barcelona Traction case); *ICJ Reports 1993*, p. 3 (Genocide case); *ICJ Reports 1995*, p. 90 (East Timor case).

568   Paulus, op. cit., 2001, p. 377.

569   F.S. Northedge, "Order and Change in International Society" in A. James (ed.), *The Bases of International Order*, London, 1973, p."1; Kimminich and Hobe, op. cit., 2000, p. 17.

570   V. van Themaat, *The Changing Structure of International Economic Law*, The Hague, 1972; C. Tomuschat, "Tyrannei der Minderheit? Betrachtungen zur Verfasssungsstruktur der Vereinten Nationen", *GYIL*, vol. 19, 1976, p. 278.

571   A. Epiney and M. Scheyli, *Statusprinzipien des Umweltvölkerrechts*, Baden-Baden, 1998; E. Lorenz, *Zur Struktur des internationalen Privatrechts. Ein Beitrag zur Reformdiskussion*, Berlin, 1977.

572   K.-H. Ziegler, *Völkerrechtsgeschichte*, Munich, 1998; Verdross and Simma, op. cit., 1984; T. Serra, "Genèse et structure de la société internationale", *RCADI*, no. I, 1959 and recently H. Steiger, "Rechtliche Strukturen der Europäischen Staatenordnung 1648-1792", *ZaöRV*, vol. 59, 1999.

573   K. Dicke, *Erscheinungsformen und Wirkungen von Globalisierung in Struktur und Recht des internationalen Systems auf universaler und regionaler Ebene sowie gegenläufige Renationalisierungstendenzen*,

Bericht der Deutschen Gesellschaft für Völkerrecht, vol. 39, Keil, 2000, p. 13; E. Galloway, "Globalization, Sovereignty and the Common Heritage", Proceedings from the 42nd Colloquium on the Law of Outer Space, 2000, p. 340 assumes that the globalization will strengthen the CHOM principle in relation to the classic sovereignty principle. He views "Nationalism and Realism as sources of the concept of sovereignty in international law. Idealism and Liberalism are sources of the CHM principle... liberal meanings of globalization—rather than mercantilist and radical—will predominate over the long term with the consequence that this process will reinforce Article II Outer Space Treaty and the promotion of collective goods notions of the Common Heritage of Mankind principle."

574 U. Scheuner, "Friedensordnung und Struktur der Staatengemeinschaft" in *Der Beitrag des Völkerrechts zur Überwindung des Krieges, Protocols of Loccum*, June 1968, p. 10; U. Scheuner, "Solidarität unter den Nationen als Grundsatz in der gegenwärtigen internationalen Gemeinschaft" in J. Delbrück, K. Ipsen and D. Rauschning (eds), *Recht und Dienst des Friedens. Festschrift Eberhard Menzel zum 65 Geburtstag*, Berlin, 1975, p. 252.

575 Fischer, op. cit., 1986, p. 55; Fischer, op. cit., 1987, p. 46.

576 See section 7.1 of this study.

577 P. Sontag, op. cit., 1966, p. 168.

578 W. Friedmann, "General Course in Public International Law", *RdC*, no. III, 1969, p. 3.

579 Kewenig, op. cit., 1981, p. 2; Kewenig, op. cit., 1981, p. 405.

580 Hobe, op. cit., 1992, p. 97; Wolfrum, op. cit., 1984, p. 292; A.-C. Kiss, "The common heritage of mankind: utopia or reality?", *International Journal*, vol. 15, 1985, p. 440; Baslar, op. cit., 1998; and according to W. Stocker, op. cit., 1993, p. 223: "... the principle of the Common Heritage of Mankind could be the starting point of a fundamental structural change of international law..."

581 Almond, op. cit., 1980, p. 83.

582 "Law should adhere to the most fundamental principles of international (space) law which have so far weathered all storms. Precisely because of the flexibility needed, moreover, when it comes to envisaging what particular activities might take place in the future and the substantive rules needed as a consequence, these principles relate to the structure of applying law, and not to

its actual contents. These fundamental principles boil down to the fact that all space activities are undertaken in the sovereignty-free, truly internationalized *res communis* which is outer space, including its celestial bodies." F.G. von der Dunk, "The role of law with respect to future space activities", *Space Policy*, vol. 12, 1996, pp. 5 and 6.

583   Durner, op. cit., 2000.

584   Friedmann, op. cit., 1964, p. 57.

585   R.-J. Dupuy, *La Communauté internationale entre le mythe et l'histoire*, Paris, 1986, p. 159.

586   Bleckmann, op. cit., 1982, p. 155.

587   Abi-Saab, op. cit., 1991, p. 6.

588   Dicke, op. cit., 2000, p. 34.

589   Northedge, op. cit., 1973, p. 1.

590   Edmund Burke quoted in ibid., p. 1.

591   A. Truyoly y Serra, *Die Entstehung der Weltstaatengesellschaft unserer Zeit*, Berlin, 1963; B.V.A. Röling, *International Law in an Expanded World*, Amsterdam, 1960; Friedmann, op. cit., 1964, p. 11; P. Allot, *Eunomia: New Order for a New World*, New York, 1990, p. 355; Kimminich and Hobe, op. cit., 2000, p. 63; G. Schwarzenberger, *Civitas Maxima?*, Tubingen, 1973; M. Reisman, "Designing and Managing the Future of the State", *EJIL*, vol. 8, 1997, p. 415; Tomuschat, op. cit., 1999, p. 88; C. Tomuschat, "Obligations Arising for States without or against Their Will", *RdC*, no. IV, 1993, p. 232; Simma, op. cit., 1994, p. 245; Leben, op. cit., 1997, p. 399; Paulus, op. cit., 2001, pp. 250 and 425; P.-M. Dupuy, "International Law: Torn between Coexistence, Cooperation and Globalization. General Conclusions", *EJIL*, vol. 9, 1998, p. 287; S. Hobe, "Zur Zukunft des Völkerrechts im Zeitalter der Globalisierung", *AVR*, vol. 37, 1999, p. 253; B. Fassbender, "The United Nations Charter as Constitution of the International Community", *Columbia Journal of Transnational Law*, vol. 36, 1998, p. 529; P. Allot, "The Concept of International Law", *EJIL*, vol. 10, 1999, p. 31; M. Scheyli, "Der Schutz des Klimas als Prüfstein völkerrechtlicher Konstitutionalisierung?", *AVR*, vol. 40, 2002, p. 273.

592   Allot, op. cit., 1990, p. 355.

593   Reisman, op. cit., 1997, p. 415.

594   Friedmann, op. cit., 1969, p. 47.

595   Scheuner, op. cit., 1975, p. 379.

596   Friedmann, op. cit., 1964, pp. 60, 64 and 367.
597   Friedmann, op. cit., 1969, p. 48: "The need to create an institutional structure that *substitutes international for national authority* in the enforcement of rules of conduct remains the most urgent task in the development of international law" [emphasis in the original].
598   See section 6.2 of this study.
599   Friedmann, op. cit., 1964, p. 297; Paulus, op. cit., 2001. For a contrasting view see S.P. Huntington, "The Clash of Civilizations", *Foreign Affairs*, vol. 72, 1993, p. 22.
600   P. Lyon, "New States and International Order" in A. James (ed.), op. cit., 1973, p. 24; T.O. Elias and F.M. Ssekandi, *New Horizons in International Law*, Dordrecht, 1992, p. 383; N.S. Rembe, *Africa and the International Law of the Sea: A Study of the Contribution of the African States to the Third United Nations Conference on the Law of the Sea*, Alphen aan den Rijn, 1980.
601   United Nations General Assembly resolutions: 1148 (XII), 14 November 1957; 1472, 12 December 1959; 1721, 13 December 1961; and 1962, 13 December 1963.
602   Deudney, op. cit., 1983/84, p.91
603   Bleckmann, op. cit., 1982, p. 219.
604   Seidel, op. cit., p. 44.
605   Paulus, op. cit., 2001, p. 425.
606   C. Tomuschat, "Die internationale Gemeinschaft", *AVR*, vol. 33, 1995, p. 20.
607   Paulus, op. cit., 2001, p. 425.
608   Schrijver, "The Changing Nature of State Sovereignty", *BYIL*, 2000, p. 71; Dicke, op. cit., 2000, pp. 22 and 27.
609   Tomuschat, op. cit., 1988, p. 73; Tomuschat, op. cit., 1995, p. 6; Tomuschat, op. cit., 1999, p. 88; Simma and Paulus, op. cit., 1998, p. 276; Paulus, op. cit., 2001, p. 225; ICJ President Mohammed Bedjaoui in his declaration in the Advisory Opinion on the Legality of the Threat or Use of Nuclear Weapons, *ICJ Reports 1996*, para. 13, p. 270 expressly refers to the CHOM principle as an element of the concept of a "legal international community".
610   Tomuschat, op. cit., 1999; Tomuschat, op. cit., 1993; Simma, op. cit., 1994, p. 248.
611   Lyon, op. cit., 1973, p. 24; Elias and Ssekandi, op. cit., 1992, p. 24.
612   Scheuner, op. cit., 1975, p. 252.

[613] Kimminich and Hobe, op. cit., 2000, p. 61; S. Verosta, "Der Begriff 'internationale Sicherheit' in der Satzung der Vereinten Nationen" in Marcic and H. Mosler et al. (eds), *Festschrift für Alfred Verdross*, Berlin, 1960, p. 534.

[614] Dicke, op. cit., 2000, p. 32.

[615] Paulus, op. cit., 2001, p. 425.

[616] B.H. Oxman, "The International Commons, the International Public Interest and New Modes of International Lawmaking" in Delbrück (ed.), op. cit., 1996, p. 21; for enhanced community interests in international environmental law see J. Brunne, "'Common Interest'—Echoes from an Empty Shell? Some Thoughts on Common Interest and International Environmental Law", *ZaöRV*, vol. 49, 1989, p. 791; F. Biermann, "'Common Concern of Humankind': The Emergence of a New Concept of International Environmental Law", *AVR*, vol. 34, 1996, p. 428; U. Beyerlin, "State Community Interests and Institution-Building", *International Environmental Law*, vol. 56, 1996, p. 602; A. Cranston, "The Sovereignty Revolution" in K. Cranston (ed.), *The Sovereignty Revolution*, Stanford, 2004, p. 27.

[617] Dicke, op. cit., 2000, p. 41.

[618] Schrijver, op. cit., 2000, p. 71; Reisman, op. cit., 1997, p. 410; Galloway, op. cit., 1999, p. 84, however, states: "Paradoxically it is sovereign states which are limiting themselves but the consequences of each self-limitation may add over time into an irreversible force of history"; Dupuy, op. cit., 1998, p. 283.

[619] Friedmann, op. cit., 1964, p. 365.

[620] Hobe, op. cit., 1992, p. 253; Dicke, op. cit., 2000, p. 14.

[621] Dupuy, op. cit., 1998, p. 287.

[622] Bleckmann, op. cit., 1982, p. 219.

[623] Paulus, op. cit., 2001, p. 425; Simma, op. cit., 1994, p. 245.623

[624] C. Tomuschat, "Völkerrechtlicher Vertrag und Drittstaaten", *Berichte der Deutschen Gesellschaft für Völkerrecht*, vol. 28, 1988, p. 63; Tomuschat, op. cit., 1999, p. 76; Simma, op. cit., 1994, p. 237.

[625] Tomuschat, op. cit., 1999, p. 63; Simma, op. cit., 1994, p. 237; Reisman, op. cit., 1997, p. 409; J. Granoff, "Sovereignty and Duty" in Cranston (ed.), op. cit., p. 92.

[626] Scheuner, op. cit., 1975, p. 379.

[627] "With regard to territory and the use of natural resources, community interest has recently found a particularly well-known

expression in the concept of the 'common heritage of mankind'".
Simma, op. cit., 1994, p. 240; specifically with regard to the
CHOM principle as representing the community interests see
Stocker, op. cit., 1993, p. 179.

628   *ICJ Reports 1970*, para. 32, p. 3 (Barcelona Traction case); *ICJ
Reports 1986*, para. 188 (Nicaragua case); *ICJ Reports 1996*
(Advisory Opinion on the Legality of the Threat or Use of Nuclear
Weapons); Paulus, op. cit., 2001, p. 363.

629   *YILC 1980*, vol. II, p. 30.

630   Simma, op. cit., 1994, p. 248; *ICJ Reports 1996*, para. 95, p. 40.

631   *ICJ Reports 1996*, para. 93 and 63, pp. 31 and 40.

632   C. Tomuschat, op. cit., 1995, p. 6.

633   Wolfrum, op. cit., 1984, pp. 705 and 706.

634   Friedmann, op. cit., 1969, p. 63; also C.D. Classen,
"Fernerkundung und Völkerrecht. Völkerrechtliche Probleme der
Fernerkundung der Erde aus dem Weltraum", dissertation, 1987,
p. 23.

635   D. de la Rochere, "La Convention sur l'internationalisation de
l'espace", *Annuaire Français de Droit International*, 1967, p. 625.

636   C. Chaumont, "Orientation actuelle du droit de l'espace", *RGAE*,
1965.

637   Seidel, op. cit., 2000, p. 44.

638   P. Saladin and C.A. Zenger, *Rechte künftiger Generationen*, Basel,
1988, p. 67; A. D'Ammato, E.B. Weiss and L. Gündling, "Agora:
What Obligation Does our Generation Owe to the Next? An
approach to Global Environmental Responsibility", *AJIL*, vol. 84,
1990, p. 190; B. Nagy, "Common Heritage of Mankind: The Status
of Future Generations", Proceedings from the 31st Colloquium on
the Law of Outer Space, 1989, p. 319; Wolfrum, op. cit., 1984,
p. 340.

639   Christol, op. cit., 1969, p. 153.

640   "Another important feature in the Treaty, which reflects the
gradually changing structure of international relations, is the
recognition of the necessity of international cooperation in the field
of outer space." D. Goedhuis, "Suggestions Regarding the
Interpretation and the Implementation of the United Nations Outer
Space Treaty 19 December 1966" in World Peace through Law
Center (ed.), op. cit., 1969, p. 139.

641 M. Benkö and K.-U.Schrogl, "The UN Committee on the Peaceful Uses of Outer Space: Progress on 'Space Benefits' and other Recent Developments", *ZLW*, vol. 44, 1995, p. 291.

642 Hobe, op. cit., 1992, p. 288.

643 Ibid., p. 293.

644 Verosta, op. cit., 1960, p. 537.

645 M. Mateesco-Matte, *Le droit extra-atmosphérique et la course aux armements. Droit spatial ou droit aéro-orbital?*, Paris, 1984, p. 316.

646 K. Hailbronner, "Principles of New International Law and the Emerging Space Law", Proceedings from the 17th Colloquium on the Law of Outer Space, 1975, p. 118.

647 D. Adams, "The Outer Space Treaty: An Interpretation in Light of the No-Sovereignty Provision", *Harvard International Law Journal*, vol. 9, 1968, p. 143.

648 A. Pardo, "Ocean Space and Mankind", *Third World Quarterly*, vol. 6, 1984, p. 568; Stocker, op. cit, 1993, p. 5.

649 A. Cassese, *International Law in a Divided World*, Oxford, 1986, p. 379.

650 E. Riedel, "Menschenrechte der dritten Dimension", *EuGRZ*, 1989, p. 19; Wolter, op. cit., 1985, p. 137.

651 A. Bueckling, "The Strategy of Semantics and the 'Mankind Provisions' of the Space Treaty", *JSL*, vol. 7, 1979.

652 Jenks, op. cit., 1958, p. 192.

653 Ibid.

654 Ibid.

655 Bleckmann, op. cit., 1978, p. 155.

656 C.W. Jenks, *Law, Freedom and Welfare*, New York, 1963.

657 Tomuschat, op. cit., 1999, p. 88; Tomuschat, op. cit., 1995; C.W. Jenks, *A New Law for a New World Order*, London, 1969; Dupuy, op. cit., 1986, p. 154; Simma, op. cit., 1994, p. 243.

658 Tomuschat, op. cit., 1999, pp. 88 and 262; Reisman, op. cit., 1997, p. 409; Granoff, op. cit., 2004, p. 92; D. Roche, *The Right to Peace*, Ottawa, 2003.

659 *ICJ Reports 1996*, para. 63, p. 31.

660 Falk, op. cit., 1997, p. 72.

661 Friedmann, op. cit., 1964, p. 13.

662 E. Stein, "Impact of New Weapons Technology on International Law: Selected Aspects", *RdC*, no. II, 1971, p. 248.

663 Reproduced in Bundespresseamt (ed.), *Stichworte zur Sicherheitspolitik*, Bonn, 1978, p. 7.

664   Independent Commission on Disarmament and Security Issues, *Common Security: A Blueprint for Survival*, New York, 1982, p. 22.

665   UN Doc. A/RES/37/99 resolution B on the "Report of the Independent Commission on Disarmament and Security Issues", 13 December 1982.

666   E. Bahr, "Gemeinsame Sicherheit: Einführende Überlegungen" in E. Bahr and H.-D. Lutz (eds), *Gemeinsame Sicherheit*, vol. 2, 1987, p. 18; Lutz, "Gemeinsame Sicherheit—das Konzept. Definitionsmerkmale und Strukturelemente im Vergleich mit anderen sicherheitspolitischen Modellen und Strategien" in Bahr and Lutz (eds), op. cit., 1987, p. 54.

667   J. Nolan, "The Concept of Cooperative Security" in J. Nolan (ed.), *Global Engagement: Cooperation and Security in the 21st Century*, Washington DC, 1994, p. 9.

668   Speech of the German Foreign Minister, Joschka Fischer, before the General Assembly of the United Nations on 14 September 2002, "In Favour of a System of global cooperative security", printed in IP 11/2002, Doc., 129.

669   Fischer, op. cit., 1987, p. 46; G. Seidel, "Das Völkerrecht als Instrument zur Stärkung der internationalen Sicherheit" in P. Fischer-Appelt and D.S. Lutz (eds), "Universitäten im Friedensdialog", Baden-Baden, 1990, p. 129.

670   Fischer, op. cit., p. 94.

671   Ibid., p. 46.

672   Kewenig, op. cit., 1981, p. 3; Andem, op. cit., 1992, p. 214; Vlasic, op. cit., 1981, p. 135; G. Bunn and J. Rhinelander, "Outer Space Treaty May Ban Strike Weapons", *Arms Control Today*, vol. 32, No. 5, June 2002, p. 24; D. Wolter, "Völkerrechtliche Grundlagen 'Gemeinsamer Sicherheit' im Weltraum", *ZaöRV*, vol. 62, 2002, p. 941.

673   Deudney, op. cit., 1983/84, p. 93.

674   Feigl, op. cit., 1993, p. 509.

675   Bundesakademie für Sicherheitspolitik, *Sicherheitspolitik in neuen Dimensionen. Ein Kompendium zum erweiterten Sicherheitsbegriff*, Hamburg, 2001.

676   Bahr, op. cit, 1987, p. 18.

677   J.E. Nolan et al., "The Imperatives for Cooperation" in J.E. Nolan (ed.), *Global Engagement: Cooperation and Security in the 21st Century*, Washington DC, 1994, p. 33; Granoff, op. cit., 2004, p. 92.

678 "The internationalization of the global economy is by far the most obvious driving force helping to break down national and ideological barriers and forcing a high degree of conformity among governments and private actors to a common set of operating rules. An integrated international economy is well along in formation, although its evolution has been largely spontaneous. Its logic and policy requirements have yet to be fully mastered, but almost certainly its management challenges will transcend the capacity of national governments. It is safe to say that the condition of the emerging economy already compels more pervasive international coordination than that to which nations have ordinarily been accustomed." Ibid., pp. 35 and 38.

679 C.W. Jenks, "Seven Stages in the Development of Space Law", Proceedings from the 11th Colloquium on the Law of Outer Space, 1969, p. 260.

680 Bahr, op. cit., 1987, p. 25; E. Bahr and H.-D. Lutz, "Gemeinsame Sicherheit: Einführende Überlegungen" in E. Bahr and H.D. Lutz (eds), Gemeinsame Sicherheit – Idee und Konzept. Zu den Ausgangsüberlegungen, Grundlagen und Strukturmerkmalen Gemeinsamer Sicherheit, vol. 1, 1986, p. 26.

681 Nolan et al., 1994, p. 11; A.B. Carter, W.J. Perry and J.D. Steinbruner, "A New Concept of Cooperative Security", Washington DC, 1992, p. 7.

682 Nolan et al., 1994, p. 10.

683 Ibid., p. 10; Carter, Perry and Steinbruner, op. cit., 1992, p. 20.

684 Bahr, op. cit., 1987, p. 25; Carter, Perry and Steinbruner, op. cit., 1992, p. 20.

685 Carter, op. cit., 1992, p. 24.

686 "Cooperative security differs from the traditional idea of collective security much as preventive medicine differs from acute care. Cooperative security is designed to ensure that organized aggression cannot start or be prosecuted on any large scale. By contrast, collective security is an arrangement for deterring aggression through military preparation and defeating it if it occurs ... A fully developed cooperative security framework would include provisions for collective security as a residual guarantee to its members in the event of aggression...", Nolan et al., 1994, p. 5.

687 Carter, Perry and Steinbruner, op. cit., 1992, p. 10.

688 F.R. Cleminson, "Confidence-Building Measures and Outer Space" in P. Gasparini Alves (ed.), Building Confidence in Outer Space

Activities: CSBMs and Earth-to-Space Monitoring, Geneva, 1995, p. 29.

689   "A cooperative security order need not take the form of a single, all-encompassing legal regime or arms control agreement, but would probably begin with a set of overlapping, mutually reinforcing arrangement derived from agreements already in force. In fact, ... existing ingredients of cooperative security are not hard to find on the international landscape." Nolan et al., 1994, p. 7.

690   A. Chayes and A.H. Chayes, "Regime Architecture: Elements and Principles" in J.E. Nolan (ed.), *Global Engagement: Cooperation and Security in the 21st Century*, Washington DC, 1994, p. 68.

691   A. Chayes and A.H. Chayes, *The New Sovereignty: Compliance with International Regulatory Regimes*, Cambridge, 1995, p. 2; Seidel, op. cit., 1990, p. 44; Granoff, op. cit., 2004, p. 92.

692   Chayes and Chayes, op. cit., 1995, p. 2.

693   "Talks on Missiles and Arms" in Space, *New York Times*, 9 October 1985, A 10; Christol, op. cit., 1985.

694   CD/PV.553; CD/1087; D.J. Smith, "The Defence and Space Talks: Moving towards Non-nuclear Strategic Defences", *NATO Review*, no. 5, 1990, p. 17.

695   A.B. Carter and W.J. Perry, *Preventive Defense: A New Security Strategy for America*, Washington DC, 1999, p. 65; K.N. Luongo, "The Uncertain Future of US-Russian Cooperative Nuclear Security", *Arms Control Today*, January/February, 2001, p. 6; M. Fortmann and F. Chinchilla, "Les mesures coopérative de lutte contre la prolifération dans l'ancien espace soviétique: bilan et perspective", January 2002, <www.hsfk.de/abm/forum/fortman1.htm>.

696   Senator R. Lugar, "NATO After 9/11: Crisis or Opportunity?", speech before the Council on Foreign Relations, 4 March 2002, <www.cfr.org/publication.html?id=4379>. The EU also adopted a broad concept of cooperative security in its Common Strategy towards Russia proclaimed at the European Summit in Cologne in 1999, see D. Wolter, "Gemeinsame Strategie gegenüber Rußland. Ein neues Instrument europäischer Politik", *Internationale Politik*, vol. 9, 1999, p. 57.

697   "Joint Statement on Common Security Challenges at the Threshold of the Twenty-First Century", 2 August 1998, <www.ceip.org/files/projects/npp/resources/summits7.htm#security >.

698   "Joint Statement of the Presidenta of the Unites States of America and the President of the Russian Federation on the Principles of Strategic Stability", 5 June 2000, <www.ceip.org/files/projects/npp/resources/Summit8.htm>.

699   L. David, "U.S.-Russia Working on Satellite Missile Watching System", 24 October 2001, <www.space.com.html>.

700   "Memorandum of Agreement Between the United States of America and the Russian Federation on the Establishment of a Joint Center for the Exchange of Data from Early Warning Systems and Notifications of Missile Launches", 5 August 2000, <www.ceip.org/files/projects/npp/resources/Summit8.htm>. The planned JDEC with headquarters in Moscow is, however, not as yet operational because of unsolved questions relating to tax exemption of equipment imports.

701   "Boris Yeltsin's Statement on Arms Control", *ITAR-TASS*, 29 January 1992; K.B. Payne, L.H. Vlahos and W.A. Stanley, "Evolving Russian Views on Defense: An Opportunity for Cooperation", *Strategic Review*, Winter 1993, p. 61.

702   UN Doc. S/PV.3046, 31 January 1992.

703   See point 5 of the Missile Defense Papers, 11 July 2001, <www.ceip.org/files/projects/npp/resources/Embassy/CableNMD.htm>.

704   Luongo, op. cit., 2001, p. 8.

705   "We are achieving a new strategic relationship ... We are partners and we will cooperate to advance stability, security, ... and to jointly counter global challenges and to help resolve regional conflicts ... We recognize that the security, prosperity, and future hopes of our peoples rest on a benign security environment, the advancement of political and economic freedoms, and international cooperation... The United States and Russia agree that a new strategic relationship between the two countries, based on *the principles of mutual security, trust, openness, cooperation, and predictability* requires substantive consultation across a broad range of international security issues..." [emphasis added]. US-Russia "Joint Declaration on the New Strategic Partnership", 24 May 2002, <www.whitehouse.gov/news/releases/2002/05/20020524-2.html>.

706   President G.W. Bush, "Remarks to a Special Session of the German Bundestag", 23 May 2002, <www.whitehouse.gov/news/releases/2002/05/20020523-2.html>.

707   Tesselkin and Marenkov, op. cit., 2002, p. 25.

708   Carter and W.J. Perry, op. cit., 1999, p. 46.

709   Joint Chinese-Russian statement adopted on 10 December 1999; CD/PV.822, 26 March 1999.

710   CD/PV.822, 26 March 1999.

711   Bahr and Lutz, op. cit., 1986, p. 26; Lutz, op. cit., 1987, p. 54.

712   Speech of President G.W. Bush before the National Defense University, 1 May 2001; M. Krepon, "Moving Away from MAD", *Survival*, vol. 43, 2001, p. 81; Grand, op. cit., 2001, p. 817; G. Neuneck, "The United States, Europe and Arms Control", *INESAP Information Bulletin*, no. 18, September 2001, p. 52.

713   See section 2.1.1 of this study.

714   S.F. March, "The Strategic Defense Initiative Debate: An Interdisciplinary Approach", Proceedings from the 28th Colloquium on the Law of Outer Space, 1986, p. 89; E.R. Finch, "Magna Charta of Outer Space and SDI", Proceedings from the 30th Colloquium on the Law of Outer Space, 1987, p. 310.

715   Bahr and Lutz, op. cit., 1986, p. 19.

716   Lutz, op. cit., 1987, p. 54.

717   See section 3.2.2.1 of this study.

718   E. Fujita, "CSBMs in Outer Space: Some Political Considerations" in Gasparini Alves (ed.), op. cit., 1995, p. 73.

719   The document provides for joint research with regard to defensive systems.

720   Krepon, op. cit., 2001, p. 81.

721   B. Garrett, "The Need for Strategic Reassurance in the 21st Century", *Arms Control Today*, vol. 31, March 2001, p. 9.

722   S. Pullinger, "Missile Defence in Perspective", *ISIS Briefing on Ballistic Missile Defence*, no. 7, 2001, p. 102.

723   See the proposal by representatives of the Union of German Scientists in "Memorandum. Warnung vor den Raketenabwehrplänen der USA. Plädoyer für ein europäisches 'Diplomatie-Zuerst!'-Konzept", *Wissenschaft und Frieden*, vol. 1, 2001, p. 40.

724   See K. Holmes, "Par-delà de la destruction mutuelle assurée: le rôle d'une défense antimissile pour assurer la paix et la stabilité", *Politique Étrangère*, no. 4, 2001, p. 867.

725   Krepon, op. cit., 2001, p. 81; Grand, op. cit., 2001, p. 817; Neuneck, op. cit., 2001, p. 52.

726   Senator Richard Lugar urges to adopt an active global non-proliferation policy proposing the globalization of the "Nunn-Lugar" programme of 1991, which so far has been limited to reducing threat coming from of the former Soviet Union. The objective would be to identify, control and finally destroy all WMD worldwide by achieving a "satisfactory level of accountability, transparency, and safety ... in every nation with a WMD program". He announced a draft bill for this purpose, which should authorize the Administration to globalize the "Nunn-Lugar" programme by approaching all relevant states. Speech by Senator R. Lugar, op. cit., 2002.

727   P. Jankowitsch, "Arms Control in Outer Space: the need for new legal action" in B. Jasani (ed.), *Space Weapons—The Arms Control Dilemma*, Oxford, 1984, p. 180.

728   See Gasparini Alves, op. cit., 1992; Baines, op. cit., 1998, p. 65.

729   York, op. cit., 1985, p. 30.

730   Baines, op. cit., 1998, p. 65.

731   Arms control literature on PAROS: Gasparini Alves, op. cit., 1991; Beier and Mataila (eds), op. cit., 1998, p. 65; Cleminson, op. cit., 1998, p. 65; B. Jasani, "The Arms Control Dilemma—An Overview" in Jasani (ed.), op. cit., 1984; Feigl, op. cit., 1993, p. 513; Legal literature: P. Jankowitsch, "Arms control in space: the need for new legal action" in Jasani (ed.), op. cit., 1984, p. 173; Jasentuliyana, op. cit., 1999; W. von Kries, "Space-Based Defences and the Law of Outer Space", Proceedings from the 30th Colloquium on the Law of Outer Space, 1988; A. Chayes, A.H. Chayes and E. Spitzer, "Space Weapons: The Legal Context" in F.A. Long, D. Hafner and J. Boutwell (eds), *Weapons in Space*, New York, 1986; B. Hurwitz, *The Legality of Space Militarization*, Jerusalem, 1986; H. Fischer, "Völkerrechtliche Schranken der Weltraumrüstung" in R. Labusch, E. Maus and W. Send (eds), *Weltraum ohne Waffen. Naturwissenschaftler warnen vor der Militarisierung des Weltraums*, Munich, 1984; S. Gorove, *Developments in Space Law: Issues and Policies*, Utrecht, 1991; S. Gorove, "Arms Control in Space: Issues and Alternatives", *ZLW*, vol. 33, 1984; S. Gorove, "Arms Control Provisions in the Outer Space Treaty: A scrutinising reappraisal", *Georgia Journal of International and Comparative Law*, no. 3, 1973; Markoff, op. cit., 1976, p. 11; S.K. Agrawala, "Arms Control in Outer Space", *ZaöRV*, vol. 45, 1985; Reijnen, op. cit., 1995, p. 103; G.C.M. Reijnen,

"The Prevention of an Arms Race in Outer Space" in Benkö, Graaff and Reijnen (eds), op. cit., 1985; Vlasic, op. cit., 1995, p. 385; Vlasic, op. cit., 1991, p. 37; Vlasic, op. cit., 1981, p. 135; Christol, op. cit., 1985; C.Q. Christol, "The Use of Outer Space for Peaceful Purposes: Legal and Political Implications", Proceedings from the 28th Colloquium on the Law of Outer Space, 1986; Magno, op. cit., 1984, p. 221.

732 On the US position to reject multilateral negotiations on a space weapons ban see US explanation of vote UN Doc. A/C.1/54/l.22, 1 November 1999; see also section 3.2.3.1 of this study.

733 Feigl, op. cit., 1993, p. 513.

734 UN Doc. A/7221, 9 September 1968; see also section 3.1.1 of this study.

735 UN Doc. A/AC.187/97, 1 February 1978.

736 CD/9, 26 March 1979.

737 See section 10.1.5.1 of this study.

738 CD/PV.398, S. 9, 19 March 1987.

739 CD/PV.939, 28 July 1989, p. 2.

740 UN Doc. A/36/192, 20 August 1981; on the Soviet proposals see Kolosov, op. cit., 1998, p. 14; Y. Kolosov, "Non-Use of Force in Outer Space", Proceedings from the 25th Colloquium on the Law of Outer Space, 1983, p. 205; Zhukov, op. cit., 1984, p. 371; Christol, op. cit., 1986, p. 4.

741 CD 274, 7 April 1982.

742 Italy, CD/9, 26 March 1979.

743 Gasparini Alves, op. cit., 1991, p. 97.

744 The formulation "would have the effect of authorising states to take the law into their own hands in Outer Space on the basis of their suspicions, thus creating mistrust and insecurity for all", France, CD/375, 14 April 1983; Jankowitsch, op. cit., 1984, p. 182; see also section 8.1.2 of this study.

745 UN Doc. A/38/194, 23 August 1983; CD/476, 20 March 1984.

746 Germany, CD/PV.171, p. 10, Netherlands, CD/PV.170, p. 12, and France, CD/PV.172, p. 17 criticized the limitation of "national means of verification" of the first draft.

747 Gasparini Alves, op. cit., 1991, p. 100.

748 Ibid.

749 Sweden, CD/PV.252, p. 20; Italy, CD/PV.253, p. 17.

750 China, CD/579, 19 March 1985, p. 1; H. Quizhi, "Towards Legal Control of Space Arms: A Difficult Process" in Matte, (ed.), op. cit.,

1985, p. 125; H. Quizhi, "On Strengthening Legal Measures for the Prevention of an Arms Race in Outer Space", Proceedings from the 27th Colloquium on the Law of Outer Space, 1985, p. 354; see also section 3.2.2.1 of this study.

751 "China has all along maintained that the exploration and use of outer space should only serve to promote the economic, scientific and cultural development of all countries in the world and benefit all mankind. China has always opposed arms race of any kind, including arms race in outer space. This basic position remains unchanged", CD/1606, 9 February 2000; see also section 3.2.3 of this study.

752 Canada, CD/320, 26 August 1982; CD/PV.252, 22 March 1984, p. 15; CD/301, 21 March 1985, p. 16; on the active role of Canada at the CD and in particular on the agenda topic PAROS see Cleminson, op. cit., 1998, p. 35; Baines, op. cit., 1998, p. 65.

753 See section 10.1.5.2 of this study.

754 Canada, CD/410, 30 April 1987, p. 12.

755 India, CD/PV.486, p. 6; CD/PV.484, 7 February 1989, p. 15; S.R. Chowdhury, "Legal Aspects of Maintaining Outer Space for Peaceful Purposes", Proceedings from the 31st Colloquium on the Law of Outer Space, 1989, p. 14; see also section 3.2.2.1 of this study.

756 Pakistan, CD/708, 26 June 1986, p. 1.

757 Sri Lanka, CD/PV.325, 30 July 1985, p. 12.

758 India, CD/PV.423, p. 11.

759 Sweden, CD/PV.516, p. 18; CD/PV.484, 7 February 1989, p. 15; S. Danielsson, "The ABM Treaty: To be or not to be" in Jasani (ed.), op. cit., 1987, p. 163; Danielsson, "Approaches to prevent an arms race in outer space" in Jasani (ed.), op. cit., 1984, p. 157.

760 CD/807, 19 February 1988.

761 CD/PV.263, 12 June 1984, p. 19; UN Doc. A/S-10/AC.1/7, 1 June 1978; see also Guillaume, op. cit., 1985, p. 67.

762 Germany, CD/PV.35, 6 March 1986, p. 9.

763 France, CD/PV.390, 6 February 1987, p. 6.

764 See section 10.1.2 of this study.

765 UNIDIR, op. cit., 1987, p. 166.

766 Ibid., p. 178 and section 3.2.2.1 of this study.

767 Germany, CD/PV.289, 7 February 1985, p. 9; CD/318, 4 July 1985, p. 13 and CD/PV.345, 6 March 1989; UNIDIR, op. cit.,

1987, p. 173; Gasparini Alves, op. cit., 1991, p. 110; see also Feigl, op. cit., 1993, p. 509.

768   Senate Joint Resolution, S.J.R. 28, 98th Congress, First Session, 3 February 1983 and Senate Joint Resolution, S.J.R. 129, 98th Congress, First Session, 14 November 1983 as well as House Joint Resolution, H.J. R. 523, 98th Congress, Second Session, 21 March 1984. For the role of Congress on the ABM/ASAT issue, see Christol, op. cit., 1985.

769   House Joint Resolution, H.J.R. 120, 98th Congress, First Session, 2 February 1983.

770   See section 3.2.3.1 of this study.

771   CD/1606, 9 February 2000; section 3.2.3.1 of this study.

772   CD/PV.843, 24 February 2000; section 3.2.3.1 of this study.

773   CD/PV.871, 22 March 2001, p. 3.

774   UN Doc. A/56/PV.7, 24 September 2001.

775   CD/1569, 4 February 1999.

776   Space Preservation Act, House Resolution, H.R. 2977, 107th Congress, First Session, 2 October 2001.

777   Ibid., (preamble).

778   Ibid.

779   See sections 3.2.2.2 and 2.3.1 of this study.

780   International Law Association, op. cit., 1988, p. 16.

781   Reproduced in Welck and Platzöder, op. cit., 1987, p. 125; see also K. Gottfried, "An ASAT Test Ban Treaty" in Jasani (ed.), op. cit., 1984, p. 132.

782   Spacey II, op. cit.

783   L.J. Korb and A. Tiersky, "The end of Unilaterlism?—Arms Control After September 11", Arms Control Today, vol. 31, October 2001, p. 3.

784   H. Fischer, R. Labusch, E. Maus and J. Scheffran, "Entwurf eines Vertrages zur Begrenzung der militärischen Nutzung des Weltraums" in Labusch, Maus and Send (eds), op. cit., 1984, p. 175; Welck and Platzöder, op. cit., 1987, p. 129.

785   Protocol of the German Bundestag, 10th Legislature, 166th Session, 18 October 1984, p. 57.

786   E. Maus, "Prinzipien des Göttinger Vertragsentwurfs" in Labusch, Maus and Send (eds), p. 171.

787   Ibid.

788 The Federation of American Scientists has proposed a general security distance of 250 km; see commentary of the draft in Fischer, Labusch, Maus and Scheffran, op. cit., 1984, p. 178.

789 E. Maus, op. cit., 1984.

790 S. Gorove, *Studies in Space Law: Its Challenges and Prospects*, Leyden, 1977, p. 171.

791 S. Gorove, in "Arms Control in Outer Space", Panel Proceedings from the ASIL 76th Annual Meeting, 1982, p. 295.

792 S. Sanders, "Arms Control in Outer Space", Panel in Proceedings from the ASIL 76th Annual Meeting, 1982, p. 289.

793 R. Johnson, "Multilateral Approaches to Preventing the Weaponisation of Space", *Disarmament Diplomacy*, no. 56, 2001.

794 E. Galloway, "Expanding Article IV of the Outer Space Treaty: A Proposal", Proceedings from the 25th Colloquium on the Law of Outer Space, 1983, p. 89; E. Galloway, "Guidelines for the Review and Formulation of Outer Space Treaties", Proceedings from the 41st Colloquium on the Law of Outer Space, 1999, p. 251.

795 On the definition and concept of confidence-building measure in general see chapter 7 of this study; see also UN Doc. A/48/305, 15 October 1993 and Cleminson, op. cit., 1995, p. 29.

796 UN Doc. A/48/305, 15 October 1993.

797 For terminology see Gasparini Alves, op. cit., 1991, p. 107; L. Beau, "CSBMs and Earth-to-Space Tracking: A General Overview of Existing Proposals" in Gasparini Alves (ed.), op. cit, 1995, p. 63; R. DalBello, "'Rules of the Road': Legal Measures to Strengthen the Peaceful Uses of Outer Space", Proceedings from the 28th Colloquium on the Law of Outer Space, 1986, p. 8; France, CD/937.

798 CD/905, 2 August 1988; CD/OS/WP.28, 21 March 1989: "... international legal instruments already exist intended to ensure the immunity of satellites. These instruments prohibit the use of force against satellites except in cases of self-defence. Indeed, these international agreements go further than the proposals because they also prohibit the threat of the use of force against satellites..."; see also section 9.3.5 of this study.

799 Germany, CD/OS/WP.62, 12 August 1991 and CD/PV.318, 4 July 1985; CD/PV.345, 6 March 1986; CD/PV.516, 11 July 1989.

800 France, CD/OS/WP.59; CD/OS/WP.58; CD/1092, 1 August 1991.

801 CD/OS/WP.72; CD/OS/WP.74.

802 CD/OS/WP.69.

803   CD/PV.300, 19 March 1985, p. 22; CD/PV.349, 20 March 1985. See also the US reaction to UN Doc. A/48/305, 15 October 1993. The US representative did not object to the results of the study, however, and only attached some reservations that were circulated as a separate document (UN Doc. A/48/553, 26 October 1993). Therein, the US reaffirmed its position that "the existing legal regimes for outer space are adequate and that no changes are needed at this time". At the same time, thus recognizing the objective of common security, the US was "not opposed to cooperative efforts in outer space including confidence-building measures", but reserved the right to choose whether to agree to such measures bilaterally or multilaterally; see also Gasparini Alves, op. cit., 1991, p. 103.

804   CD/PV.345, 6 March 1986.

805   Beau, op. cit., 1996, p. 64.

806   CD/OS/WP.62; CD/OS/WP.62, 12 August 1991 and CD/PV.318, 4 July 1985; ibid., p. 61.

807   CD/PV.345, 6 March 1986; CD/PV.318, 4 July 1985; CD/516, p. 8; CD/1092, 1 July 1991.

808   CD/1092, 1 August 1991.

809   "... la création de zones d'exclusion ... ne sont sans doute pas conformes à l'esprit sinon à la lettre de l'article II du Traité de 1967" quoted in Roth, op. cit., 1992, p. 71; W. von Kries, "Weltraumrechtliche Aspekte der amerikanischen SDI-und ASAT-Programme", ZLW, vol. 34, 1985, p. 279; W. Kries, "International Space Law Implications of the U.S. SDI and ASAT Programs: The Current Legal Debate", ZLW, vol. 35, 1986, p. 314; Kries, op. cit., 1988, p. 106; W. von Kries, "'Keep-out Zones' and the Non-Appropriation Principle of International Space Law", Proceedings from the 31st Colloquium on the Law of Outer Space, 1989, p. 6; DalBello, op. cit., 1986, p. 9.

810   CD/937, 21 July 1989; CD/1092, 1 August 1991.

811   CD/OS/WP.62, 12 August 1991 and CD/PV.318, 4 July 1985.

812   Beau, op. cit., 1996, p. 63; Gasparini Alves, op. cit., 1991, p. 111, speaks of a "general consensus ... that the elaboration of a Space Code of Conduct and Rules of the Road would constitute a concrete step towards the development of a space order."

813   CD/937, 21 July 1989; Beau, op. cit., 1991, p. 111.

814   CD/937, 21 July 1989 and French intervention before the 47th United Nations General Assembly on 23 September 1992; Beau, op. cit., 1996, p. 69; Gasparini Alves, op. cit., 1991, p. 112.

815   Beau, op. cit., 1991, p. 112; Alves, op. cit., 1992, p. 102.

816   P. Gasparini Alves, "General Introduction" in Gasparini Alves (ed.), op. cit., 1995, p. 9; Fujita, op. cit., 1995, p. 73; Beau, op. cit., 1996, p. 63; DalBello, op. cit., 1986, p. 8; J. Macintosh, "Confidence Building and Outer Space" in Beier and Mataila (eds), op. cit., 1998, p. 85; P.H. Tuinder, "CBM's For Outer Space", Proceedings from the 31st Colloquium on the Law of Outer Space, 1989, p. 84; Ondrej, "Some Legal Aspects of Confidence-Building Measures Concerning Outer Space", Proceedings from the 37th Colloquium on the Law of Outer Space, 1995, p. 257; Doyle, "Confidence Building Measures Using Space Resources", Proceedings from the 41st Colloquium on the Law of Outer Space, 1999, p.108; R. Chadbourne, "Confidence Building Measures and the Fourth Medium", Proceedings from the 41st Colloquium on the Law of Outer Space, 1999, p. 97; G. Neuneck and A. Rothkirch, "Incentives for Space Security: Technology, Transparency and Compliance", Conference on Outer Space and Security, Geneva, 25-26 March 2003.

817   Feigl, op. cit., 1993, p. 517; CD/OS/WP 48, 12 August 1991.

818   Feigl assumes—in the year 1993—that an arms race in outer space is no longer imminent, given that the Clinton Administration scaled back the SDI project. Feigl, op. cit., 1993, p. 509.

819   Ibid., p. 515.

820   DalBello, op. cit, 1986, p. 9.

821   See section 2.2.3 of this study.

822   CD/PV.349, 20 March 1986; UN Doc. A/41/422, 11 July 1986.

823   See section 2.2.4 of this study.

824   Vladimir Lukin on Radio Rossii, printed in "Daily Report: Soviet Union", *FBIS*, 1 October 1991, p. 50.

825   E. Velikhov and G. Chernyavskiy, "From 'Star Wars' to a Global System for the Protection of the World Community: Boris Yeltsin Will Discuss that Topic With George Bush", *Nezavissimaya Gazeta*, 10 June 1992; Payne, Vlahos and Stanley, op. cit., 1993, p. 65; Also, the joint early warning system agreed in 2000 between the United States and Russia is a concrete result of this concept. See section 7.3 of this study.

826   Vladimir Kozin from the Disarmament Department of the Russian Foreign Ministry stated: "As in the case of SDI, we would not like to see 'space-earth' strike arms deployed in space, space saturated with anti-satellite systems or a refusal encountered to conclude an international agreement on immunity for civil and non-combat (photographic reconnaissance, communications, etc.) military satellites and orbital stations" quoted in Payne, Vlahos, Stanley, op. cit., 1993, p. 65.

827   CD/PV.843, 24 February 2000.

828   "The United States and Russia have also agreed to study possible areas for missile defense cooperation, including the expansion of joint exercises related to missile defense, and the exploration of potential programs for the joint research and development of missile defense technologies... The United States and Russia will, in the framework of the NATO-Russia Council, explore opportunities for intensified practical cooperation on missile defense for Europe." US-Russia "Joint Declaration on the New Strategic Partnership", 24 May 2002, <www.whitehouse.gov/news/releases/2002/05/20020524-2.html>.

829   March, op. cit., 1986, p. 89; Finch, op. cit., 1988, p. 310.

830   Finch, op. cit., 1988, p. 310.

831   March, op. cit., 1986, p. 89.

832   "Using either its own resources or—preferably—those placed at its disposal—for example, military reconnaissance images, a world space organization could furthermore help reduce the risks inherent in the militarisation of space, reduce worldwide arms proliferation, and uphold collective security. This project is not, of course, in itself a priority. Nevertheless, it could be an important aspect of another, altogether burning and top-priority issue: the control of sensitive technologies, and in particular of the proliferation of missile technology." O. de Saint Lager, "Should there be a World Space Organisation?", Proceedings from the 34th Colloquium on the Law of Outer Space, 1992, p. 163.

833   G.P. Sloup, "United Nations Peacekeeping in the Age of Ballistic Missile Defense", Proceedings from the 34th Colloquium on the Law of Outer Space, 1992, p. 339.

834   UN Doc. A/RES/45/55 B, 4 December 1990.

835   UN Doc. A/48/305, 15 October 1993; on the US position in relation to the study, see CD/PV.300, 19 March 1985; CD/PV.349, 20 March 1985.

836   UN Doc. A/48/305, para. 317, 15 October 1993.

837   Ibid., para. 326.

838   Ibid., para. 304 and 316.

839   Ibid., para. 310.

840   Ibid., para. 322.

841   Ibid., para. 325.

842   Ibid., para. 324.

843   Ibid., para. 326.

844   UN Doc. A/48/305, para. 318, 15 October 1993.

845   Ibid., para. 323.

846   Ibid., para. 327 and 328.

847   Jankowitsch, op. cit., 1984, p. 184; Jankowitsch, op. cit., 1992, p. 143.

848   Jankowitsch, op. cit., 1984, p. 184.

849   Union of German Scientists, op. cit., 2001, p. 40.

850   T. Hitchens, *Future Security in Space: Charting a Cooperative Course*, Washington DC, 2004.

851   Krepon, op. cit., 2001, p. 81.

852   "Strategic mistrust in the post-Cold War era creates the need for measures to reduce suspicions between and among states about their long-term political, military, and economic objectives—that is, their strategic intentions. Broadly speaking, strategic reassurance measures are steps that one nation takes to address the concerns of other nations that are suspicious of its broad, long-run intentions." Garrett, op. cit., 2001, p. 9.

853   Vlasic, op. cit., 1995, p. 409.

854   "A growing consciousness is emerging on the importance of devising a new approach to collective security to replace concepts of selective security sought at a cost of collective insecurity." Fujita, op. cit., 1995, p. 74.

855   A. Kelle, "Das Chemiewaffen-Übereinkommen und seine Umsetzung—einführende Darstellung und Stand der Diskussion", *HSFK-Report*, vol. 12, 1996; and for a comprehensive legal analysis of the various multilateral verification and implementation regimes of multilateral arms control and disarmament agreements, see G. Dekker, *The Law of Arms Control: International Supervision and Enforcement*, The Hague, 2001.

856   "In a different context but in the same trend, the conclusion of the Chemical Weapons Convention in 1992 marked an important conceptual breakthrough in the field of multilateral disarmament,

as a possible harbinger of new mentalities. For the first time, a whole category of weapons is to be totally eliminated, on a non-discriminatory basis, under strict international verification, and without hampering the development of the chemical industry for peaceful purposes. The complex but basically equitable architecture of the Convention, as well as of the Organization for the Prohibition of Chemical Weapons, which is charged with its implementation, should encourage a wide-ranging participation of states, large and small, thus underscoring its universality. This would constitute an important model for future agreements concerning other categories of weapons." Fujita, op. cit., 1995, p. 74.

857 Agreement between the United States of America and the Union of Soviet Socialist Republics on Destruction and Non-Production of Chemical Weapons and on Measures to Facilitate the Multilateral Convention on Banning Chemical Weapons, 1 June 1990.

858 See section 3.2.2.1 of this study.

859 The CWC contains in Art. VI, para. 10 and in the annexe on the protection of confidentiality ("Confidentiality Annex") explicit provisions on the protection of industrial confidentiality including the institutional safeguard by the "Confidentiality Commission", an assistant body of the state conference; see Dekker, op. cit., 2001, p. 225.

860 "Report of the Independent Commission on Disarmament and Security Issues", UN Doc. A/RES/ 37/99, 13 December 1982, p. 22; See section 7.1 of this study.

861 See section 8.1.2 of this study.

862 Bahr and Lutz, op. cit., 1986, p. 26; Bahr, op. cit., 1987, p. 18; Lutz, op. cit., 1987, p. 54.

863 Bahr, op. cit., 1987, p. 19; Lutz, op. cit., 1987, p. 50.

864 "By restricting missile defence to a system that specifically targets only those that flagrantly disregard the obligations of the non-proliferation regime the validity of that regime would be upheld." Pullinger, op. cit., 2001, p. 11; Neuneck, op. cit., 2001, p. 52.

865 "So long as such [BMD] defences are subject to quantitative limits that prevent them from negating the strategic arsenals of both these countries [Russia and China] they should be acceptable." Pullinger, op. cit., 2001, p. 11.

866 "A good way of cutting the risk of unauthorised use is to further dramatically reduce the number of ballistic missiles held by each side." Ibid., p. 10.

867   T. Petermann, M. Socher and C. Wennrich, "Präventive Rüstungskontrolle bei Neuen Technologien. Utopie oder Notwendigkeit?", Büro für Technikfolgen-Abschätzung beim Deutschen Bundestag, Berlin, 1997, p. 137.

868   Ibid., p. 70.

869   For the distinction between a vertical and horizontal arms race see CD/PV.541, 28 March 1990, 4; Gasparini Alves, op. cit., 1991, p. 14.

870   Petermann, Socher and Wennrich, op. cit., 1997, p. 137.

871   See section 2.1.3.2 of this study.

872   The principle of equal security was recently reaffirmed in the US-Russia "Joint Declaration on the New Strategic Partnership" of 24 May 2002, available at the US State Department website US-Russia "Joint Declaration on the New Strategic Partnership", 24 May 2002, <www.whitehouse.gov/news/releases/2002/05/20020524-2.html>. For the criteria for arms control agreements posed by the United States, see CD/PV.349, 20 March 1986.

873   See section 9.3.6 of this study.

874   In the following, this will be exemplified in drawing mainly on the analysis of C. Glaser and S. Fetter, "National Missile Defence and the Future of U.S. Nuclear Weapons Policy", International Security, no.26, Summer 2001, p. 40, which represents the prevailing arms control assessment of the NMD plans; Korb and Tiersky, op. cit., 2001, p. 3; Mendelsohn, "America, Russia and the Future of Arms Control", Current History No. 31, October 2001, p. 323; UNIDIR and Wilton Park, op. cit., 2002; Miller, op. cit., 2001, p. 107; Krepon, op. cit., 2001, p. 85; Cleminson, op. cit., 1995, p. 35; Garrett, op. cit., 2001, p. 9; Pullinger, op. cit., 2001, p. 9; Neuneck, op. cit., 2001, p. 52;Union of German Scientists, op. cit., 2001, p. 40.

875   The numerous principled objections against the justification of an NMD system as a defence against "states of concern" are at this stage left aside; section 2.2.8 of this study.

876   R.L. Garwin, "A Defence That Will Not Defend", The Washington Quarterly, vol. 23, Summer 2000, p. 109; R.L. Garwin, "The Wrong Plan", The Bulletin of the Atomic Scientists, vol. 56, March/April 2000, p. 36; Postol, op. cit., 1999/2000, p. 117; Bielefeld and Neuneck, op. cit., 2001, p. 95; Glaser and Fetter, op. cit., 2001, p. 90.

877   Glaser and Fetter, op. cit., 2001, p. 73.

878   Ibid., p. 73.

879   Ibid., p. 77.

880   "Once the radars, satellites, and command, control, and communications systems are deployed, integrated, and tested to provide an effective nationwide defense, the United States could quickly expand its NMD to handle larger attacks simply by adding interceptors, and possibly by integrating existing TMD interceptors into the NMD system." Glaser and Fetter, op. cit., 2001, p. 80.

881   Ibid., p. 74.

882   Ibid., p. 77.

883   Ibid., p. 76.

884   "The limited effectiveness of proliferation control measures to date should not discourage the international community; rather, perseverance in maintaining them, and in devising smarter and more effective control measures is mandatory until such time that the world's 'countries of concern' rid themselves of their radical regimes and join the family of respectable nations." UNIDIR and Wilton Park, op. cit., 2002.

885   Glaser and Fetter, op. cit., 2001, p. 86; Pullinger, op. cit., 2001, p. 10; J. Scheffran, "Raketenabwehr, Stabilität und präventive Rüstungskontrolle. Von SDI zu NMD", Wissenschaft und Frieden, January 2001, p. 23; J. Scheffran, "Moving Beyond Missile Defense: The Search for Alternatives to the Missile Race", INESAP Information Bulletin, no.18, September 2001, p. 9; Neuneck, op. cit., 2001, p. 52. In contrast, U. Rubin holds the view that, due to the novelty of the question a final assessment is not yet possible: "Passive and active defense against the missiles and WMD of States of Concern is a natural and understandable response of threatened nations, yet its impact on proliferation is controversial, especially that of missile defense. ... Critics of the US NMD program maintain that deploying a home front missile defense will not reduce the missile threat from States of Concern but rather prompt the deployment of more, better and deadlier missiles against the US ... Proponents of defense, on the other hand, argue that Defenses complicate the job of the aggressor, forcing him into costly improvements of his ... Due to the novelty of the issue, there is no evidence as yet either way." However, in the final result Rubin also pleads for the strengthening of the non-proliferation regime. UNIDIR and Wilton Park, op. cit., 2002, p. 9.

886   Glaser and Fetter, op. cit., 2001, p. 70.

887   See section 7.3 of this study.

888   *"Co-operative measures could reduce the risk of erroneous or unauthorised use far more effectively than limited NMD. For example, the United States could help Russia improve its attack warning systems or share uncensored data from U.S. sensors. Both countries also could agree to install systems that would allow leaders to destroy missiles launched in error or without authorisation.* The argument that limited NMD would reduce the risk of an erroneous or unauthorized Russian attack is deeply flawed. First, the size of such an attack could greatly exceed the capacity of a limited NMD system ... Second, Russia could respond to the deployment of limited NMD by equipping its missiles with sophisticated countermeasures ... Third, and most important, Russia would likely respond to the deployment of U.S. NMD in ways that would increase the possibility of an erroneous or unauthorised attack. If Russia believed that NMD heightened its vulnerability to attack, it could compensate by increasing the number of missiles at higher states of launch readiness" [emphasis added]. Glaser and Fetter, op. cit., 2001, p. 71; see also S. Frankel, "Aborting Unauthorized Launches of Nuclear-Armed Missiles through Postlaunch Destruction", *Science and Global Security*, vol. 2, 1990, p. 1.

889   CD/1569, 4 February 1999.

890   Scheffran, op. cit., September 2001, p. 52; Gottfried, op. cit., 1984, p. 132.

891   See section 2.5.1 of this study.

892   Jasani and Hafner, op. cit., 1991, p. 234; Jasani, op. cit., 1982, p. 435.

893   See also section 2.1.2 of this study.

894   "To prohibit the deployment of ASAT systems would, however, not be sufficient. If a weapon had been developed, tested and put into production it would be easy to deploy it rapidly and use it. Therefore, an ASAT ban would have to include a prohibition on the development , testing and production of such weapons." Danielsson, op. cit., 1984, p. 166.

895   Glaser and Fetter, op. cit., 2001, pp. 40 and 90; Korb and Tiersky, op. cit., 2001, p. 3; Mendelsohn, "America, Russia and the Future of Arms Control", *Current History*, no. 31, October 2001, p. 323; UNIDIR and Wilton Park, op. cit., 2002; Miller, op. cit., 2001, p. 107; Krepon, op. cit., 2001, p. 85; Garwin, op. cit., Summer 2000, p. 109; Garwin, op. cit., March/April 2000, p. 36; Postol, op.

cit., 1999/2000, p. 117; Bielefeld and Neuneck, op. cit., 2001, p. 95.

896   Glaser and Fetter, op. cit., 2001, p. 86.

897   "... early warning, communications and navigation satellites that are of critical importance to the strategic forces in wartime are all in GEO or other high orbits, and relatively secure against ASAT attacks." Gottfried, op. cit., 1984, p. 132.

898   Ibid., p. 133.

899   H. Gmelch, *Verifikation von multi- und internationalen Rüstungskontrollabkommen. Aufgaben, Probleme, Lösungsansätze*, Baden-Baden, 1993, p. 69.

900   See chapters 3 and 6.

901   Galloway, op. cit., 1983, p. 89; Galloway, op. cit., 1999, p. 251.

902   Fujita, op. cit., 1995, p. 81.

903   See section 7.3 of this study.

904   CD/PV.345, 6 March 1986, p. 12.

905   Including Egypt, Mexico, Peru, Venezuela, section 3.2.2.1 of this study; Gasparini Alves, op. cit., 1991.

906   Verdross and Simma, op. cit., 1984, p. 294.

907   "As the capabilities of civil and military satellites converge, it is possible that civil spacecraft could become targets for anti-satellite (ASAT) weapons." B. Jasani, "Security—A New Role for Civil Remote Sensing Satellites" in M. Benkö and Kröll (eds), *Luft- und Weltraumrecht im 21. Jahrhundert. Liber amicorum für Böckstiegel*, Cologne, 2001, p. 344.

908   DalBello, op. cit., 1986, p. 8.

909   Ibid.

910   CD/905, p. 10.

911   CD/375, 14 April 1983.

912   CD PV.279, 7 August 1984.

913   CD/708, 26 June 1986.

914   CD/PV.385, 3 February 1987.

915   CD/PV.402, April 1989.

916   Gasparini Alves, op. cit., 1991, p. 104.

917   CD/PV.374, 27 July 1976; ibid.

918   "... satellites contributing to the preservation of strategic stability which could be instrumental in monitoring arms limitations and disarmament agreements", CD/PV.374, 27 July, 1976; CD/PV.279.

919   Arms control literature: Gmelch, op. cit., 1993. Legal literature: Dekker, op. cit., 2001; Scheffran, op. cit., September 2001, p. 80;

Gasparini Alves, op. cit., 1991. For a good overview of the various methods of verification see F.R. Cleminson and P. Gasparini Alves, "Space Weapons Verification: A Brief Appraisal" in S. Sur (ed.), *Verification of Disarmament or Limitation of Armaments: Instruments, Negotiations, Proposals*, Geneva, 1992, p. 177; U. Ekblad and T. Orhaug, "Verification of Outer Space Treaties by an ISMA", Proceedings from the 31st Colloquium on the Law of Outer Space, 1989, p. 22; U. Ekblad, "Prospects of Verifying Space Weapons Treaties", Proceedings from the 35th Colloquium on the Law of Outer Space, 1993, p. 346; J. Ondrej, "Some Legal Aspects of Verification in and from Outer Space", Proceedings from the 33rd Colloquium on the Law of Outer Space, 1991, p. 338; W. von Kries, "Satellite Verification and European Arms Control", Proceedings from the 33rd Colloquium on the Law of Outer Space, 1991, p. 375.

920   Gasparini Alves, op. cit., 1991, p. 118.

921   An extensive definition is found in Gmelch, op. cit, 1993, p. 34.

922   Petermann, Socher and Wennrich, op. cit., 1997, p. 129.

923   UN Doc. A/48/305, 15 October 1993; Cleminson and Gasparini Alves, op. cit., 1992, p. 177.

924   "Ground- and space-based remote sensing technology for verification of a space-based weapon ban has meanwhile advanced since the mid-1980's Canadian PAXSAT studies [PAXSAT was the name of a proposal by Canada at the CD in 1986 for the establishment of a multilateral verification satellite, which concluded that such a ban would be verifiable even using then-available technology. Subsequent developments, including improved ground-based sensors, adaptive optics, laser atmospheric turbulence compensation and advanced processing techniques, can all contribute to the verification of a space-based weapon ban. Similar improvements in commercial remote sensing and national reconnaissance satellites' ability to image other satellites plus improved early warning systems which will be able to track space-based objects and ascending launch vehicles, will permit even fuller confidence. Such remote sensing techniques, supplemented where necessary with on-site inspections under managed access rules, could effectively and efficiently verify a space-based weapon ban." CD/1487, 31 March 2002, p. 6.

925   Cleminson and Gasparini Alves, op. cit., 1992, p. 187.

926   Baines, op. cit., 1998, p. 81; R. Biermann, *Verifikation durch Kooperation. Probleme und Perspektiven der Verifikation nuklearer Rüstungskontrollverträge*, Bonn, 1990; Dekker, op. cit., 2001, p. 117.

927   Biermann, op. cit., 1990 p. 1.

928   Biermann gives an overview of the provisions on inspection of the INF Treaty of 1987 according to the protocols on elimination and inspection. Ibid., p. 122.

929   Ibid., p. 38.

930   Dekker, op. cit., 2001.

931   Treaty on a Comprehensive Ban on Nuclear Weapons Tests, 24 September 1996 (as of this writing, 151 signatures).

932   Gasparini Alves, op. cit., 1991, p. 117; Cleminson and Gasparini Alves, op. cit., 1992, p. 188.

933   "The case for a regime to control and monitor space launches is greatly strengthened when considered in the context of preventing an arms race in outer space. Such a regime, in fact, could serve the function of verifying a ban on space weapons, in particular anti-satellite (ASAT) weapons. Since man-made objects in orbit would enter space through space rockets, a monitoring system at space launch facilities could not only search for indications of ballistic missile use, but also for the space-weapon usability of the payload. This would provide increased transparency concerning space activities in general, and would effectively exclude the deployment and testing of space weapons using ground-based space launchers. Other types of space weapons, in particular aircraft launch and ground-or air-based beam weapons, require different verification provisions. A combination of the available technologies would provide quite efficient means for verifying an ASAT ban, including a test ban, and the remaining risk would certainly be no higher than if the situation remained uncontrolled." Scheffran, op. cit., September 2001; M.B. Kalinowski, W. Liebert and J. Scheffran, "Beyond technical verification: Transparency, verification, and preventive control for the Nuclear Weapons Convention", *INESAP*, Breifing Paper No. 1, 1998.

934   Jasani, op. cit., 2001, p. 345; B. Jasani, "Arms Control Verification by Satellites", *International Defence Review*, vol. 23, no. 6, 1990, p. 643; and on the technical requirements see B. Jasani, "Satellites and Arms Verification", *Jane's Intelligence Review*, August 1992, p. 380.

935   Gasparini Alves, op. cit., 1991, p. 118.

936   "The difference between the capabilities of remote sensing and military reconnaissance is becoming so small that, to some extent, even the former could be used for military surveillance purposes." Jasani, op. cit., 2001, pp. 344 and 345; B. Jasani, "Commercial Observation Satellites and Verification" in M. Krepon, P.D. Zimmermann, L.S. Spector and M. Umberger (eds), *Commercial Observation Satellites and International Security*, London, 1990, pp. 142 and 144.

937   For a comprehensive analysis of the legal standards derived from the principle of the peaceful use of outer space see Wolter, op. cit., 2003, p. 327.

938   Gasparini Alves, op. cit., 1991, p. 7.

939   See section 3.2.2.1 of this study.

940   CD/1569, 4 February 1999. The proposal for a CSO Treaty is directed, like the Canadian proposal, at the adoption of a separate agreement on the implementation of the Outer Space Treaty.

941   Tomuschat, op. cit., 1988, p. 9.

942   See chapter 8 of this study.

943   *ICJ Reports 1984*, para. 111.

944   Tomuschat, op. cit., 1988, p. 28.

945   Ibid., p. 36.

946   *YbILC*, Art. 19, para. 3, vol. II, 1980; Paulus, op. cit., 2001, p. 387.

947   Tomuschat, op. cit., 1988, p. 37.

948   Paulus, op. cit., 2001, p. 423.

949   Tomuschat, op. cit., 1988, p. 37.

950   Pullinger, op. cit., 2001, p. 4.

951   Miller, op. cit., 2001, p. 107.

952   Glaser and Fetter, op. cit., 2001, p. 64.

953   J.F. Matlock, "Security: The Bottom Line", *Arms Control Today*, October 2000, p. 17.

954   A.W. Knauth, "Legal Problems of Outer Space in Relation to the United Nations" in Senate Committee on Aeronautical and Space Sciences, *Legal Problems in Space Exploration: A Symposium*, Washington DC, 1961, p. 13; M.S. McDougal and L. Lipson, "Perspectives for a Law of Outer Space", *AJIL*, vol. 52, 1958, p. 412; C.W. Jenks, "International Law and Activities in Space", *International and Comparative Law Quarterly*, vol. 5, 1956, pp. 99, 102-112; P. Sontag, op. cit., 1966, p. 172.

955 J. Kroell, "Einem Weltraum entgegen", *Zeitschrift für Luftrecht*, vol. 1, 1952, p. 254.

956 Jessup and Taubenfeld, 1959, p. 275.

957 Ibid., p. 278.

958 Ibid., p. 282.

959 Quoted in ibid., p. 275.

960 See section 1.1.1 of this study.

961 Guillaume, op. cit., 1985, p. 67.

962 Matte, op. cit., 1987, p. 327.

963 P.M. Haas, R.O. Keohane and M.A. Levy (eds), *Institutions for the Earth: Sources of Effective International Environmental Protection*, Cambridge MA, 1993, p. 409; Chayes, and Chayes, op. cit., 1995, p. 271.

964 M. Bourley et al., *Faut-il créer une organisation mondiale de l'espace?*, Centre d'études et de recherches sur le droit de l'espace, Rapport CNRS, Paris, 1992.

965 Young, op. cit., 1989, p. 297.

966 Matte, op. cit., 1998, p. 583.

967 A. Wiley, "Challenges Old and New in the Space Age: The Need for an International Space Organization", address prepared for Georgetown University, Washington DC, 24 February 1958 quoted in McDougal and Lipson, op. cit., 1958, p. 413.

968 Ibid., p. 413.

969 Jessup and Taubenfeld, op. cit., 1959, p. 254 refer to a "remarkable similarity between the Soviet program and proposals made by Senator Wiley on December 24, 1957".

970 See section 1.1.1 of this study.

971 Jenks, op. cit., 1969, p. 260.

972 I. Diederiks-Verschoor, "Observation on the International Civil Aviation Organization and an International Space Agency", Proceedings from the 20th Colloquium on the Law of Outer Space, 1978, p. 15.

973 A. Górbiel, *International Organizations and Outer Space Activities*, Lodz, 1984, p. 109.

974 Diederiks-Verschoor, op. cit., 1978, p. 15.

975 Horsford, op. cit., 1996, p. 203.

976 Ogunbanwo, op. cit., 1975, p. 205.

977 UN Doc. A/AC.105/C.2/L.15, 1966.

978 UN Doc. A/AC.105/C.1/SR.45, 1967; A.A. Gorounia and M. Bahrami, "Outer Space Treaty in 21st Century: A Change of

Concept", Proceedings from the 40th Colloquium on the Law of Outer Space, 1998, p. 307.

979 UNDoc. A/AC.105/C.2/SR.362.

980 See section 8.1.1.1 of this study.

981 Welck and Platzöder, op. cit., 1987, p. 134.

982 K. Gorove and E. Kamentskaya, "Tensions in the Development of the Law of Outer Space" in L.F. Damrosch, J.M. Danilenko and R. Müllerson (eds), Beyond Confrontation. International Law for the Post-Cold War Era, Boulder, 1995, p. 242.

983 Horsford, op. cit., 1996, p. 202.

984 The following is a mere sampling of the literature: S.E. Doyle, Civil Space Systems: Implications for International Security, Aldershot, 1993, p. 171; A.J. Emmanouel, "Space Policy Great Power's Business or Everyone's?", Proceedings from the 28th Colloquium on the Law of Outer Space, 1986, p. 13; A.L. Moore, "COMEUPS: Conditions Essential for the Maintenance of Outer Space for Peaceful Uses", Proceedings from the 27th Colloquium on the Law of Outer Space, 1985, p. 347; A. Yakovenko, "World Space Organization: pro et contra", Proceedings from the 3rd Colloquium on International Organisations and Space Law: Their Role and Contributions, Perugia, 6-7 May, 1999; Salin, op. cit., 2000, p. 443; S. Courteix, "Towards a World Space Organization?" in G. Lafferranderie and D. Crowther (eds), Outlook on Space Law over the Next 30 Years: Essays published for the Anniversary of the Outer Space Treaty, The Hague, 1997, p. 423; Galloway, op. cit., 1999, p. 249; DeSausssure, "The New Era in Outer Space", Akron Law Review, vol. 13, 1980, p. 600.

985 M. Filho, "About the Legal Definition of International Cooperation in the Exploration and Use of Outer Space", Proceedings from the 35th Colloquium on the Law of Outer Space, 1993, p. 358.

986 A.J. Emmanouel, "Space Policy: Great Power's Business or Everyone's?", Proceedings from the 28th Colloquium on the Law of Outer Space, 1986, p. 15.

987 O.M. Ribbelink and P.H. Tuinder, "State Sovereignty and Participation in Law-Making for Outer Space", Proceedings from the 33rd Colloquium on the Law of Outer Space, 1991, p. 341.

988 M. Williamson, "Protection of the Space Environment under the Outer Space Treaty", Proceedings from the 40th Colloquium on the Law of Outer Space, 1998, p. 296; D.E. Reibel, "Environmental Law Aspects of Maintaining Outer Space for Peaceful Purposes",

Proceedings from the 31st Colloquium on the Law of Outer Space, 1989, p. 67; D. Tan, "Towards a New Regime for the Protection of Outer Space as the 'Province of All Mankind'", *Yale Journal of International Law*, vol. 25, 2000, p. 145.

989   Riedel, op. cit., 1997, p. 91; Beyerlin, op. cit., 1996, p. 603.

990   Yakovenko, op. cit., 1999, p. 374.

991   Ibid., p. 372.

992   Salin, op. cit., 2000, p. 443.

993   Courteix, op. cit., 1997, p. 423.

994   Ibid., p. 423.

995   Galloway, op. cit., 1999, p. 249.

996   A.W. Dorn, "The Case for a United Nations Verification Agency: Disarmament under Effective International Control", Canadian Institute for International Peace and Security, Working Paper 26, 1990; Gmelch, op. cit., 1993.

997   M.S. McDougal, "Artificial Satellites: A Modest Proposal", *AJIL*, vol. 51, 1957, p. 77.

998   McDougal and Lipson, op. cit., 1958, p. 413.

999   M.E. Davies and B.C. "Murray, Space observations, disarmament and the United Nations", *Astronautics and Aeronautics*, September 1972.

1000   B. Jasani, "World Armaments and Disarmament", *SIPRI Yearbook 1973. World Armaments and Disarmament*, Oxford, 1973, p. 73.

1001   A. Chayes, W. Epstein and T.B. Taylor, "A Surveillance Satellite for all", *Bulletin of Atomic Scientists*, vol. 33, no. 1, 1977, p. 7.

1002   Ibid.

1003   UN Doc. A/S-10/AC.1/7, 1 June 1978; S. Courteix, "Les 'satellites Bleus' au service de la paix et du désarmement", *GYIL*, vol. 24, 1981; R. J. Dupuy, "Les structures et le rôle d'une agence internationale de satellites de contrôle", *AASL*, vol. 6, 1981. For an extensive arms control assessment of the French proposal see Gmelch, op. cit., 1993; H. Feigl, "Satellitenaufklärung als Mittel der Rüstungskontrolle. Entwicklungsstand und Einsatzmöglichkeiten", *EA*, vol. 34, 1979; H. Feigl, W. Heisenberg and J. Krause, "Arbeitspapier: Zum franzsischen Vorschlag der Errichtung einer Weltagentur für Kontrollsatelliten im Rahmen der Vereinten Nationen", *SWP*, 1979.

1004   UN Doc. A/S-10/AC.1/7, 1 June 1978.

1005   UN Doc. A/AC.296/14; UN Doc. A/RES/33/71/J, 12 December 1978 (vote: 121 in favour, 0 against, 18 abstentions) and UN Doc.

A/RES/34/83/E, 14 December 1979 (vote: 124 in favour, 0 against, 11 abstentions).

1006 UN Doc. A/34/374, 27 August 1979.

1007 C. Oudraat, International "Organizations and Verification" in Sur (ed.), op. cit., 1992, p. 234.

1008 Courteix, op. cit., 1981, p. 228.

1009 See section 8.1.1.1 of this study.

1010 Address by His Excellency Roland Dumas, Minister of Foreign Affairs, at the Fifteenth Special Session of the United Nations General Assembly, 2 June 1988.

1011 WEU Council of Ministers Communiqué, 27 June 1991.

1012 WEU Council of Ministers Communiqué, 18 November 1991.

1013 WEU Council of Ministers Communiqué, 13 May 1997.

1014 Y. Hashimoto, "Multilateral Verification Organizations—Case of WEU Satellite Centre", Proceedings from the 38th Colloquium on the Law of Outer Space, 1996, p. 264.

1015 Concrete plans are being discussed in relation to Latin America and Asia. Filho, op. cit., 1993, p. 358.

1016 "There is no doubt that to begin with it might be better to establish a number of RSMAs so that the international community could get used to the idea of being watched from space and that the resulting data could be shared with a number of countries." B. Jasani, "ISMA—will it ever happen?", Space Policy, vol. 8, 1992, p. 15.

1017 Hashimoto, op. cit., 1996, p. 264.

1018 Federal Republic of Germany, CD/PV.318, 4 July 1985; Poland, CD/PV.402; Sri Lanka CD/PV.404, 11; Pakistan, CD/PV.460; Australia, CD/PV.426, 3 July 1987; Sweden, CD/PV.516, 11 July 1989.

1019 CD/1271, 24 August 1994, p. 6.

1020 UN Doc. A/S-15/34.

1021 CD/385; CD/PV.428, 6 August 1987; and CD/817, 17 March 1988.

1022 CD/PV.428, 6 August 1987.

1023 CD/PV.817, 4 March 1999.

1024 CD/PV.367, 3 July 1986 and CD/PV.410, 30 April 1987.

1025 Department of External Affairs (Canada), "PAXSAT Concept: The Application of Space-Remote Sensing for Arms Control Verification", Verification Brochures No. 2, Ottawa, 1987, p. 41.

1026 Gasparini Alves, op. cit., 1991, p. 125.

1027 Ibid., p. 128.

1028   Printed in the "First Annual Report of the US Arms Control and Disarmament Agency", Washington DC, 1962, p. 32.

1029   Goldblat, op. cit., 1994, p. 323.

1030   International Law Association, *Report of the Sity-First Conference*, Paris, August 1984, p. 356.

1031   UN Doc. A/RES/41/65, 3 December 1986.

1032   Classen, op. cit., 1987, p. 81; T.A. Slink, *Satellitenfernerkundung zur Verifikation von Rüstungskontroll- und Abrüstungsverträgen*, Frankfurt, 1996, p. 182.

1033   R. Jakhu and R. Trecroce, International Satellite Monitoring for Disarmament and Development, *AASL*, vol. V, 1980, p. 524.

1034   While resort to appropriate international procedures does not exclude resort to an existing international organization - for instance, to the investigative powers of the UN Secretary General - it has of late tended to be interpreted more along the lines of the establishment of new mechanisms through which consultations on compliance issues can take place [emphasis in the original]. Oudraat, op. cit., 1992, p. 225.

1035   Courteix, op. cit., 1981, p. 224; Jakhu and Trecroce, op. cit., 1980, p. 524.

1036   In remote sensing the principle of access without discrimination for national military satellites is controversial. For contrasting views see Classen, op. cit., 1987, p. 208 and Slink, op. cit., 1996, p. 170.

1037   See section 2.1.3.1 of this study.

1038   Quizhi, Towards Legal Control of Space Arms, op. cit., 1985, p. 132.

1039   Jakhu and Trecroce, op. cit., 1980, p. 522.

1040   Classen, op. cit., 1987, p. 227; For a contrasting view see W. von Kries, "Towards a new remote sensing order?", *Space Policy*, vol. 16, 2000, p. 165. Kries is sceptical on the chances for a multilateralization of remote sensing: "Where military observation is concerned, sensing states will continue to be opposed to any common intelligence gathering rules."

1041   D. Deudney, "Krieg oder Frieden im Weltraum", *EA*, vol. 37, 1982, p. 556.

1042   Oudraat, op. cit., 1992, p. 207.

1043   Gasparini Alves, op. cit., 1991, p. 17.

1044   Friedmann, op. cit., 1964, p. 14.

1045   Tomuschat, op. cit., 1999, p. 89; Tomuschat, op. cit., 1993, pp. 216, 218, 222 and 227.

292

1046   Simma, op. cit., 1994, p. 248.
1047   Paulus, op. cit., 2001, p. 178.
1048   R. Ago, "Communauté internationale et organisation internationale" in R.-J. Dupuy (ed.), *Manuel sur les organisations internationales*, Dordrecht, 1998, p. 8.
1049   Bourley et al., op. cit., 1992. The report derives the need for a world space organization from the mankind clause and the CHOM principle in outer space law.
1050   S.E. Doyle, "Confidence Building Measures Using Space Resources", Proceedings from the 41st Colloquium on the Law of Outer Space, 1999; Fawcett, op. cit., 1984, p. 8; Ogunbanwo, op. cit., 1975, p. 75; Tan, op. cit., 2000, p. 190.
1051   Ago, op. cit., 1998, p. 9.
1052   Matte, op. cit., 1998, p. 583.
1053   Matte, op. cit., 1987, p. 327.
1054   Ibid., p. 335.
1055   Courteix, op. cit., 1997, p. 426.
1056   International Law Association, op. cit., 1988, p. 341.
1057   Courteix, op. cit., 1997, p. 427.
1058   Ibid.
1059   Oudraat, op. cit., 1992, p. 207.
1060   Courteix, op. cit., 1997, p. 427.
1061   Chayes and Chayes, op. cit., 1994, p. 102.
1062   Ibid., p. 103.
1063   Welck and Platzöder, op. cit., 1987, p. 631.
1064   See section 9.3.6 of this study.
1065   Dekker, op. cit., 2001, p. 318. For an assessment of the first four years of experience with the implementation of the CWC see P. Zanders et al., "Chemical and biological weapon developments and arms control" in *SIPRI Yearbook 2001. World Armaments and Disarmament*, p. 543 who states as a positive factor, that "all four declared possessor states—India, South Korea, Russia and the United States—are now in the process of destroying their CW".
1066   CD/1387; R. Johnson, "CTB Negotiation—Geneva Update No. 27", *Disarmament Policy*, March 1996, p. 18.
1067   Dekker, op. cit., 2001, p. 332.
1068   Resolution establishing the Preparatory Commission for the Comprehensive Nuclear Test Ban Treaty Organization, CTBT/MSS/RES 1, 19 November 1996.
1069   See section 7.3 of this study.

1070   Glaser and Fetter, op. cit., 2001, p. 40.

1071   See section 2.2.4 of this study.

1072   Baslar, op. cit., 1998, p. 375.

1073   Commission on Global Governance, "Our Global Neighbourhood", 1995, p. 251. See also the proposal of Malta, UN Doc. A/50/142, to charge the United Nations trusteeship council with the responsibility "to deal with the common heritage of mankind and issues such as the environment".

1074   Tan, op. cit., 2000, p. 180; Y. Hashimoto, "National Missile Defence and International Law: Environmental Perspectives", Proceedings from the 43rd Colloquium on the Law of Outer Space, 2001; C.C. Okolie, "Solar Energy Bank for Mankind in Contemporary International Space Law", Proceedings from the 22nd Colloquium on the Law of Outer Space, 1981, p. 11.

1075   Delbrück, op. cit., 1996, p. 348; Hobe, "Die Zukunft des Völkerrechts im Zeitalter der Globalisierung. Perspektiven der Völkerrechtsentwicklung im 21. Jahrhundert", AVR 37, 1999, p. 281.

1076   Commission on Global Governance, op. cit., 1995, p. 253.

1077   "Generally, the incoming warheads are armed with impact fuses so that they explode on landing. The KV [kill vehicle] interceptor is supposed to destroy the incoming warheads by colliding with them. Therefore, the chances are that the adversary's warheads will explode above the atmosphere, thereby spreading the highly toxic plutonium and, perhaps, other radioactive materials. These substances will quickly spread throughout the atmosphere and enter the human body by ingestion or via the food chain when they eventually settle on the earth's surface." Jasani, op. cit., 2001, p. 247.

1078   F.H. Knelman, "Solar Power Satellites—Technical, Social and Political Implications, in Earth-Oriented Space Activities and Their Legal Implications", Proceedings of the Symposium held on October 15-16 at the Centre for Air and Space Law, McGill University, 1981, p. 196; P.G. Dembling and D.D. Smith, "Solar Power Satellites and Security Considerations: The Case for Multilateral Agreements", JSL, vol. 11, 1983, p. 74; G.B. Dietrich and W.C. Goldstein, "Collective trusteeship for near space: the case for UNNESA", Space Policy, vol. 14, 1998, p. 12.; M. Williamson, "Protection of the Space Environment under the Outer Space Treaty", Proceedings from the 40th Colloquium on the

Law of Outer Space, 1998; Tan, op. cit., 2000, p. 151; Reibel, op. cit., 1989, p. 67.

1079 Similar arrangements of differentiated voting weight may be found in the Moon Treaty (Art. 11), the Governing Council of INTELSAT, the Inter-Governmental Maritime Consultative Organization, the International Monetary Fund and the World Bank.

1080 Cocca, op. cit., 1958, p. 36; Cocca, op. cit., 1992, p. 161; Cocca, op. cit., 1981 p. 15; Cocca, "Historical Precedents for Demilitarization" in N. Jasentuliyana (ed.), *Maintaining Outer Space for Peaceful Purposes*, The Hague, 1984, p. 29; Cocca, op. cit., 1998, p. 51.

1081 UN Doc. A/AC.105/C.2/SR.75, 12 August 1967.

1082 A. Schweitzer, *Out of My Life and Thought*, Baltimore, 1963.

1083 "There is nowadays a widely shared perception that if we are to succeed in building a new structure of international security, its foundations must be laid upon broadly shared values of development, disarmament and democratization of international relations. Their interrelationships may be either directly correlated or complexly permutable according to the conjuncture, but the trinomial equation remains constant." Fujita, op. cit., 1995, p. 89.

1084 B. Simma, "Völkerrecht in der Krise?", ÖZAP, vol. 20, 1980, p. 280.

1085 Filho, op. cit., 1998, p. 358.

1086 *ICJ Reports 1969*, para. 95, p. 262.

1087 Speech by George F. Kennan, quoted in Schell, op. cit., 1984, p. 162.

ACRONYMS

ABM	Anti-Ballistic Missile Treaty
ASAT	Anti-satellite weapons
BMD	Ballistic missile defence
BTWC	Biological and Toxin Weapons Convention
CD	Conference on Disarmament
CFE	Conventional Forces in Europe Treaty
CHOM	Common heritage of mankind
COPUOS	Committee on the Peaceful Uses of Outer Space
CSO	Common Security in Outer Space Treaty
CTBT	Comprehensive Test Ban Treaty
CTBTO	CTBT Organization
CTR	Cooperative Threat Reduction
CWC	Chemical Weapons Convention
ENMOD	Environmental Modification Convention
ESA	European Space Agency
FMCT	Fissile Material Cut-off Treaty
GPALS	Global Protection Against Limited Strikes
IAEA	International Atomic Energy Agency
ICBM	Intercontinental ballistic missile
ICJ	International Court of Justice
ICoC	International Code of Conduct against Ballistic Missile Proliferation
ILC	International Law Commission
INF	Intermediate-Range Nuclear Forces Treaty
ISMA	International Satellite Monitoring Agency
ITU	International Telecommunication Union
JDEC	Joint Data Exchange Center
MAD	Mutual assured destruction
MTCR	Missile Technology Control Regime
NASA	National Aeronautics and Space Administration
NATO	North Atlantic Treaty Organization
NMD	National missile defence
NPT	Nuclear Non-Proliferation Treaty
OCSO	Organization for Common Security in Outer Space
OPCW	Organization for the Prohibition of Chemical Weapons

PAROS	Prevention of an arms race in outer space
PTBT	Partial Test Ban Treaty
SALT	Strategic Arms Limitation Treaty
START	Strategic Arms Reduction Treaty
SDI	Strategic Defence Initiative
TMD	Theatre missile defence
UNISPACE	United Nations Conference on the Exploitation and Peaceful Uses of Outer Space
WEU	Western European Union
WMD	Weapons of mass destruction